Helena Barancová

SPECTRUM SLOVAKIA Series
Volume 5

Employment Conditions
of Business in Slovakia

VEDA
PUBLISHING HOUSE
OF THE SLOVAK ACADEMY OF SCIENCES

PETER LANG
INTERNATIONAL ACADEMIC PUBLISHERS

Bibliographic Information published by the Deutsche Nationalbibliothek
The Deutsche Nationalbibliothek lists this publication in the Deutsche Nationalbibliografie;
detailed bibliographic data is available in the internet at http://dnb.d-nb.de.

Author: prof. JUDr. Helena Barancová, DrSc.

Reviewers: prof. JUDr. Vojtech Tkáč, CSc.
                                                          doc. JUDr. Ján Matlák, CSc.

University of Trnava in Trnava
Faculty of Law
Slovak Republic
deprf@truni.sk

Translation: JUDr. Nataša Hrnčárová, PhD.
                                                         JUDr. Milan Jančo, PhD.

This publication was financially supported by the Agency to support research
and development in the project: Human dignity and fundamental human rights and
freedoms in labour law. no. APVV-0068-11.

Responsible coordinator: prof. JUDr. Helena Barancová, DrSc.

ISBN 978-3-631-65001-1   ISBN 978-80-224-1332-9
© Peter Lang GmbH   © VEDA, SAS Publishing House
International Academic Publishers   Slovak Academy of Sciences
Frankfurt am Main 2013   Bratislava 2013

www.peterlang.de   www.veda.sav.sk

Table of contents

Abbreviations

LC	Labour Code
ILO	International Labour Organization
EU	European Union
Coll.	Collection of Laws
R	Collection of Judgments and Opinions
EEA	European Economic Area
EC	European Community
EEC	European Economic Community
ECtHR	European Court of Human Rights
ECJ	European Court of Justice
TEC	Treaty establishing the European Community
TFEU	Treaty on the Functioning of the European Union

Preface

Cross-border movement of employees and services creates a very difficult environment for employers – entrepreneurs expanding to foreign markets. The same applies to foreign entrepreneurs expanding their business activities in the territory of the Slovak Republic. In this difficult process associated with international business and trade, the level and quality of labour-law relations in the "host" country of business in question is essential. This quality considerably affects the total production costs of the employer and, accordingly, also affects his competitiveness in European and global markets. The employer must accept the quality of working conditions of employees according to the national law of the state in which he pursues business, because of two reasons. Firstly, the employee themselves contribute considerably to these supranational economic processes. Secondly, they often affect the success of the entrepreneur, who employs them.

The Slovak Republic has been the Member State of the European Union since 2004. It is an open economy, relying to a great extent on foreign investments. Many foreign companies operate in the territory of the Slovak Republic and employ not a insignificant part of the economically active population. It must be said that acceptance of minimum labour-law standards in using dependent work is not the same in case of all foreign companies. Many companies do not find it difficult to respect elementary labour-law rules while employing their employees. However, there are also companies, which come from a highly cultivated legal environment of their home countries. They employ employees in a way that would not be possible in their own home countries. Some foreign companies comes to Slovakia from countries with a totally different legal system. They find it difficult to come to terms with elementary labour-law rules for the protection of employees. Research has shown various types of impermissible interferences with personal privacy of employees, often degrading their human dignity, as well as non-observance of minimum rest periods necessary for recovery of employees, an even an application of corporal punishments.

This book is addressed primarily to employers doing business in the territory of the Slovak Republic. It should, as a matter of precaution, protect them against significant mistakes in regard to using the labour potential of employees, which could be source of their various sanctions. On the other hand, it specifies the scope of legal space within which they can move safely in employing their employees.

Foreign businessmen in the Slovak Republic certainly take account of the fact , that in order to fulfil their tasks, they may employ not only the citizens of the Slovak Republic, but also the citizens of other EU Member States or third-country nationals. Besides citizens of other EU Member States, many third-country nationals also work in the territory of the Slovak Republic. With regard to their employment, the rules of conflict of laws shall be applied, which is the subject addressed in detail in one of the following chapters. Just like other Slovak employers, foreign companies employing employees expand, in particular, to European Economic Area countries and they shall observe legal rules concerning free movement of services in this area. Such companies often post their employees to another EU Member States or a European Economic Area country, as doing so, they shall comply with the Posted Workers Directive (96/71/EC). As it is well-known, the Directive contains many administrative obstacles fot the free formulation of employment contracts of posted employees that must be respected by the employer making the posting, observing the principle of employee's benefit.

Employment of employees in an employment relationship is a source of various types of discrepancies between employees and employers. This book should provide the guidance to the solution to these collisions. Simultaneosly, it should help foreign employers to get familiarised with the labour legislation and to observe it in practice.

Prof. JUDr. Helena Barancová, DrSc.
September 2013

Chapter 1

Flexibility of labour relations in the Slovak Republic in the light of European labour law

Introduction

The development of European labour law in recent years reflects the efforts of European Union bodies to substantially increase the flexibility of labour relations. Extensive economic competition at national and international levels necessarily requires a higher extent of flexibility in labour relations. On the other hand, flexibility of labour relations places demands on national systems of law in establishing equal initial conditions for such competition.

In historical retrospective of labour law in EU, this involves an apparent departure from the "soft", excessively social model of labour relations of the 1970s, considered the "golden era" of labour law development in scientific literature. On the other hand, legislative initiatives of the European legislator have quite unambiguously shown that at the European level, a hybrid social model should gradually be created as a symbiosis of new liberal content elements with those of job security. On the EU platform, this hybrid model has been termed flexicurity.[1] It would be too daring to claim that this model, which combines flexibility and security of labour relations, will hold up even in the situation of a world economic crisis. EU member states are obliged to establish their own national flexicurity programmes. Individual member states are confronted in varying ways with the new social model of labour relations initiated by the EU. The pessimists do not trust the model. They argue that like many other initiatives of EU bodies, it will fade to oblivion without tangible results. Supporters of flexicurity consider the symbiosis of flexibility and security of labour relations as a legitimate objective of increasing the influence of labour law on the economic development of states maintaining an acceptable measure of employee social security. Even in the current period of economic crisis, legislative initiatives of the European legislators directed at increasing the flexibility of labour law are not only topical but also capable of increasing the existing flexibility of labour relations and thereby positively influencing further economic development of the EU member countries.

Compared to the development of labour law provisions in the "old" EU member states, the "new" EU member states introduced a substantially more liberal model of labour relations in recent years. After the fall of communism, there was a lack of el-

---

[1] "Renewed social agenda: Opportunities, access and solidarity in 21st century Europe." COM(2008) of 2.7.2008

ementary economic conditions for a generous social model of labour law. On the other hand, the development in flexibility of labour relations was full of contradictions in these countries. On the one hand, the new member states could not venture into something other than a liberal model of labour relations. On the other hand, in their national labour legislation, there were numerous negative legal residues from the period before the fall of the political regime in 1989 and some of these residues are present in these countries' labour laws up to now.

Although on the European scale, numerous initiatives could be seen in recent years directed at improving the flexibility of labour relations, the implementation of these initiatives is not unlimited and has its legal limits. These initiatives are restricted by fundamental human rights laid down in international documents and in constitutions of individual EU member states. If, for example, the European labour law is faced with the requirement of a more substantial liberalisation of the provisions for employee working time, its legal limit is the right to life, to safety, to employee health protection and to the fundamental right of protection of personal dignity.

§ 1 Determining signs of increasing flexibility in labour relations in Slovak labour law

The current status of European labour law in relation to the pan-European requirement of flexibility in labour relations can be analysed in several directions.

The determining elements of flexibility in labour relations include flexible employment contract terms. Employment contract as a determining legal instrument establishes, often for a very long period of time, the level and quality of employee working conditions. In the course of employment, the central elements for increasing the flexibility in labour relations are the working time, non-standard employment, continued increase in employee qualifications, liberalisation of conditions for unilateral employment termination by the employer, corporate restructuring as an inevitable element for increasing the dynamics of production and new calls for European social dialogue.

Anti-discrimination law contributes to increased flexibility of labour relationships. Although on its own, it significantly increases the sense of certainty and security on the part of the employee. On the other hand, in some aspects, it significantly affects the flexibility of labour relations. The development of anti-discrimination law in recent years approaches discrimination relatively rather than absolutely. Even the prohibition of discrimination is understood relatively, with broadly defined exceptions having direct positive consequences for the labour market and a higher measure of liberalisation in employment termination (e.g., on the grounds of age).[2]

Current requirements for increasing the flexibility of labour relations are linked to the requirement of higher flexibility in access to the labour market which secondarily gives rise to natural pressures on expanding the contract types in access to the labour market.

---

[2] Burchell, B., Deakin, S., Honey, S.: The Employment Status of Individuals in Non-Standard Employment, UK Department of Trade and Industry, 1999, Green Paper – Modernising labour law to meet the challenges of the 21st century, Document of the Commission of the European Communities of 22 November 2006, COM (2006).

Within the complex of the determining instruments for increasing flexibility of the existing labour relations, non-standard employment appears to be a very effective legal instrument for the business practice to increase the existing level of labour relations flexibility. Working time can also be included in this category.

I. Non-standard employment contracts

The complex of non-standard employment contracts capable of increasing the existing flexibility of labour law is dominated by fixed-term employment contracts and by reduced weekly working time employment contracts (part-time jobs). In the field of work through agencies, there is an apparent need for more strict regulation to prevent its misuse at the expense of the employees.

Although it is highly probable that the expectations connected with the expansion of non-standard contracts will not be fulfilled in the practice of EU member states, the creation of legislative conditions for their expansion alone represents an important element in the effort towards higher flexibility of labour relations. As implied by the EC Implementation Report on Directive 1999/70/EC of 2007, a significant increase in the number of fixed-term employment contracts occurred in recent years on a pan-European scale. Although this increase is legally significant and was 13.7% for all of the EU, the share of these employment contracts in individual EU states varies. The lowest share of fixed-term employment contracts was found statistically in Slovakia, Malta, Great Britain, Ireland, Luxembourg, and Estonia. On the contrary, a high proportion of fixed-term employment contracts was found in Poland, Portugal, and Spain.[3] There are also major differences in the number of fixed-term employment contracts with respect to employee age and qualifications. The highest proportion of fixed-term employment contracts was found among young employees aged 15-24, primarily those with low qualifications. [4]

Experience gained with fixed-term employment contracts on a pan-European scale allows one to draw certain important legal conclusions. Business practice strongly pushes for substantial expansion of contract types that may significantly increase flexibility in the labour market but also flexibility in already existing labour relations.

How is this question responded to by the European legislator, by the practice of the ECJ, and by the national laws of the member countries?

On the part of the European legislator, there is a continued effort to administratively regulate fixed-term employment with the objective of protecting the employee from their misuse by the employer. Administrative obstacles created by the European legislator, and reflected in Directive 1999/70/EC, are intended to prevent fixed term contracts from displacing contracts of indefinite duration, which would significantly reduce an employees' sense of certainty and security. The extent of employee protection from the loss of employment under fixed term contracts is substantially lower than that under contracts of indefinite duration. On the other hand, there is quite an obvious effort on the part of the European legislator to expand this type of employment with the objective of increasing the flexibility of labour law. Is it fair to ask whether this objective can be met by the member

---

[3] EC Implementation Report on Directive 1999/70/EC of 11.08.2006, SEC(2006) 1074.
[4] Ibid.

states, not creating, at the same time, a situation for unjustified substitution of indefinite-term employment contracts with fixed-term employment contracts?

What needs to be changed in laws of EU member countries' to fulfil these apparently contradictory requirements?

The existing experience in application of Directive 1999/70/EC in the EU member states implies that for the time being, the member states still have considerable room for improvement in fulfilling the purpose of this important Directive. While one group of member states took a more liberal direction in their laws be disregarding the purpose of the Directive, particularly through the prohibition of discrimination, another group of member states failed to even use those possibilities that the Directive provides. This involves, above all, Clause 5 of the Directive that lays down conditions for regulation of fixed-term employment contracts in an alternative rather than cumulative way. Member States that designed the fixed-term employment limitations in a cumulative way apparently hindered broader application of fixed-term employment contracts. The Slovak legislator likewise failed to fully use the legal framework of the Directive for legislation that would be coherent with the Directive and, on the other hand, more accommodating for the employers.

It is interesting to watch how the issue of fixed-term employment contracts was approached for a certain period of time by the ECJ. Several cases from recent years tried by the ECJ point to the problem of exceeding the purpose of the Directive and, in their interpretations, rather drive at limiting fixed-term employment contracts, whether due to violation of the prohibition of discrimination or due to extensively approached substantive reason as a condition for chaining fixed-term employment contracts.[5]

In recent years, the European Union has implemented several initiatives supporting the work under non-standard labour relations as one of the possibilities of succeeding in the labour market.[6] The community law supports hiring natural persons for reduced weekly working time. On the other hand, however, it puts certain legal limits on member states' laws guaranteeing employee protection under social law. Likewise, further development of work under reduced weekly working time contracts is, in community law, subject to the principle of equal treatment of employees working part time versus employees working the specified weekly working time (full time).

Expanding the possibility of access to the labour market is connected with requirements for a minimum level of employee protection laid down in the directive on part-time work.

The main problem of part-time employment contracts is the compliance with the prohibition of discrimination of part-time employees versus full-time employees. For many employers, this requirement is difficult to comply with, particularly concerning compliance with equal legal conditions for employment termination. Since in several EU member states, there are residues of the previous regimes in the form of very strictly formulated conditions for unilateral full-time employment termination, one could suggest that it might

---

[5]   C-144/04 (Mangold) of 22.11.2005, C-196/02 (Nikolaudi) of 10.3.2005, C-180/04 (Vassallo) of 7.9.2006, C-212/04 (Adeneler) of 4.7.2006, C-53/04 (Marrosu Sardino) of 7.9.2006

[6]   See European Commission document Employment in Europe 2006.

be timely to make these conditions more flexible also for full-time employment. Only oc-casional work can be exempted from Directive 81; however, irregular work, even if of small scope, cannot be exempted, as provided for by Slovak labour law legislation.

Although the EC Treaty allows member states a certain discretion in transposing the Directive, in the Commission's opinion, the Slovak Republic, by reducing the legal pro-tection for employees employed for weekly working time shorter than 15 hours, acted in excess of such discretion.[7] By globally denying social protection to all employees employed with working times shorter than 15 hours (which protection is granted to full-time employ-ees), the Slovak legislation considerably exceeds the discretion, which is at variance with the principle of proportionality and with the invariable practice of the ECJ, according to which exemptions from the objective of non-discrimination must be construed and applied restrictively.

Another secondary legal consequence of the insufficient transposition of the Part-Time Work Directive is that it indirectly deepens the inequality between men and women, as women more frequently work in part-time jobs.[8]

Apparently, the transposition of the Working Time Directive (Part-Time Work Direc-tive) into Slovak legislation is not complete and needs to be optimised shortly. In the legis-lative amendment envisaged, it will be necessary to rely also on the current practice of the ECJ, which includes many significant legal statements concerning the correctness of the legislative solution for the reduced weekly working time.

II. Working time

The working time category is a determining factor in increasing the flexibility in labour relations. Working time legislation of EU member states is in the focus of European leg-islator's attention. Working time is governed by Directive 2003/88/EC concerning certain aspects of the organisation of working time. Working time is the most intriguing element for the employers at each current amendment to the existing labour law legislation.

At the level of the European legislator, the Directive does not explicitly provide for the issue of the maximum weekly working time for cases where the employee works in two or more jobs. The Directive 2003/88/EC has not expressed this explicitly, while the Protection of Young People Directive 94/33/EC explicitly states: "Where a young person is employed by more than one employer, working days and working time shall be cumulative". There are more supporters in the economic and legal practice who are in favour of not adding up the working time in several jobs when judging the compliance with the maximum weekly working time.

Although the ECJ legal practice in the field of working time has recently moved rather against flexibility and requirements of economic practice, several cases tried before the ECJ showed quite clearly that the working time category will give the European legislator a hard time in the years to come.

---

[7]   According to Article 249 of the EC Treaty, member states are obliged to guarantee the result that is required by the Community law.
[8]   C-170/84 (Bilka) of 13 May 1986 C-278/93 (Freers and Speckmann) of 7 March 1996, C-243/95 (Hill and Stapleton) of 17 June 1998, C-279/96, 280/96, 281/96 (Ansaldo Energia and Others) of 15 September 1998.

For example, previous practice of the ECJ implied a need to amend this Directive also with respect to the notion of standby duty that should have a special place in the contents of the Working Time Directive.[9]

On the basis of the previous development of the European legislation concerning working time, it can be expected with great probability that particularly in the amendment of the Working Time Directive 2003/88/EC under preparation, there will be a fierce struggle for a new social face of Europe between the "old" member states and the "new" member states. An especially important problem in the field of legal regulation of working time at the EU level is the optimisation of maximum weekly working time that would lead not only to fulfilment of the freedom of contract for the parties of labour relations but, at the same time, would not contravene fundamental human rights such as the right to protection of human dignity, the right to protection of life and health and the right to freedom of religious belief and faith and other freedoms.

Working time is and for the foreseeable future will continue to be the determining factor in increasing flexibility of labour relations. This is one of the reasons why the increase in flexibility of working time legislation is looked upon by business entities and employers with both trust and insistence. This problem is especially resonating at the time of the economic crisis. For working time to become the driver of increasing flexibility in labour relations, national legislators of member states must very carefully consider as to which individual aspects of working time may be liberalised and to what extent. At the same time, they must consider the limits for such liberalisation. Such limits undoubtedly include human rights such as personal rights and the right to protection of dignity. Limits of this kind, such as human life, human health and human dignity, should have precedence over any legal or economic instrument that further increases working time flexibility.

III. Equal treatment principle

The adoption of new Directive 2006/54/EC brought new definitions of direct and indirect discrimination, harassment and sexual harassment, as well as that of pay and the notion of occupational social security schemes.[10]

Of interest are the conclusions of the Commission Report on the application of Directive 2000/43/EC of 15 December 2006,[11] as well as the conclusions of the Commission Report on equality between women and men of 7 February 2007.

The understanding of the exemptions from the prohibition of discrimination, such as, on the grounds of age, will have far-reaching legal consequences. Eventually, they will enable the replacement of employees of retirement age that are eligible for old-age pension to be replaced with younger job seekers. In this respect, we should note the development of the ECJ practice that admits employment termination on the grounds of reaching retirement age, whether on the basis of a law or on that of collective agreements.[12] The introduc-

---

[9]   C-303/98 (Simap) of 3 October 2000, C-151/02 (Jaeger) of 9 September 2003, C-437/05 (Vorel) of 11 January 2007

[10]   See Article 2 and Article 9 of Directive 2006/54/EC.

[11]   http://www.eukn.org/binaries/eukn/news/2007/2/implementation-equal-treatment-directive.pdf

[12]   C-411/06 (Palacios de la Villa) of 16 October 2007, C-144/04 (Mangold) of 22 November 2005

tion of a general age limit for the purpose of employment is a legitimate objective of social policy, in which the member states have broad discretion over. However, if the social selection of employees at collective redundancies was limited exclusively to employee's age, such selection would have to be considered discriminating.

Broadly worded exemptions from the prohibition of discrimination on the grounds of age will shortly bring a substantial change in access to the labour market. This also brings about changes in increasing flexibility of labour relations of employment termination on the grounds of age.

IV. Corporate restructuring

At a time of world economic crisis, corporate restructuring is very current. Legal practice is confronted daily with companies ceasing to exist, with or without a successor. Employer insolvency occurs with similar frequency, as do collective redundancies due to the employer ceasing to exist without a successor.

During the so-called golden times of European labour law development in the 1970s, the European legislator created relatively good legal foundations for corporate restructuring with comparatively broad legal space to deal with labour consequences for the employees.[13]

A. Transfer of undertaking

As shown by the experience of our previous economic practice, it is especially necessary in the near future to optimise the European legislation governing the transfer of an undertaking or part thereof, so that in each case the joint responsibility of the transferor and transferee with respect to employees is guaranteed. Although outsourcing is one of the forms of transfer of a part of an undertaking connected with assignment of rights and obligations under labour relations, the experience from the previous economic practice quite clearly points at negative consequences of the "dispersion" of transferee's and transferor's responsibilities with respect to basic legal entitlements of the employee.[14] With regard to the transfer of an undertaking or its part, even the practice of ECJ involves (in comparison with other labour law issues) the largest number of cases. Even though ECJ has gone through an interesting doctrinal development in this area, it still does not provide a basis for the less ambiguous legal interpretation.

---

[13] Numerous decisions of the ECJ on Directive 77/187/EEC, later on Directive 01/23/EC

[14] According to case C-24/85 (Spijkers) of 18 March 1986, a situation is classified as a transfer of an undertaking only where the economic entity maintains its identity; case C-13/95 (Suezen) of 11 March 1997, in which the ECJ did not find attributes of a transfer of an undertaking as the legal grounds for the transfer of rights and obligations under labour relations; case C-209/1991 (Rask) of 12 November 1992, which involved the assumption of authorisation for distribution through a new distributor although there was no contractual relationship between Anto Motors SA and Novarobel SA. In case C-104/98 (Berg and Busschers) of 23 May 2000, the Court of Justice concluded that a transfer of an undertaking *ipso jure* causes the employer obligations under labour relations to be transferred from the seller to the buyer, however, with the proviso for the right of member states to stipulate liability of the seller and of the buyer

Despite numerous decisions of the ECJ and new Directive 2001/23/EC issued in the meantime, many problems remain unclear and disputable in practice.[15] This involves, for example, specific practical problems, particularly in relation to assessing whether a specific restructuring process may be classified as a "transfer of an undertaking or part thereof" and whether social consequences with respect to employees will have to be addressed in this respect.[16]

What makes this problem even more complicated is that, particularly through outsourcing, enormous deregulation of manufacturing structures occurs and an employer's responsibility towards the employee becomes even more anonymous. Yet labour law cannot declare only support to these processes, relying purely on economic reasoning about efficiency. Economic and organisational freedom of companies needs to be linked to the protection of employee interests.

It is inevitable to seek new legal models of shared responsibility systems divided between parent companies and subsidiaries concerning obligations connected with the work of the employees who work for a subcontractor and the equal treatment aspects applicable thereof. In the field of manufacturing decentralisation, community labour law and national labour law of member states show a number shortcomings. It is rather apparent that national labour law of a member state on its own is not sufficient to give an adequate answer to the question of economic decentralisation processes. The existing new economic and production structures require that a new, flexible notion of employer be defined at the community level in the immediate future. This need is also important with respect to the broader understanding and definition of the notion of employee. Considering the importance and influence of these basic legal categories on free economic competition, it would be desirable to consider laying down these notions in community law binding for all member states. The definition of the notion of "employee" in Article 39 of the EC Treaty is obviously insufficient for the above-mentioned purposes, as it is focused only on the purpose of free movement of employees.[17]

B. Insolvency of employer

Insolvency of employer is a frequent phenomenon in a country's economic life not only corresponding to times of economic crisis. The Slovak and also the Czech legislator approached the scope of employees' labour law entitlements linked to insolvency of employer very broadly, in excess of the purposes of Directive 77/187/EEC. However, such a scope of employees' labour law entitlements at employer insolvency laid down in such a "social" manner is pointless, as indicated by the experience, since in most cases, there are insufficient funds to cover even the wages of the employees when insolvency of employer occurs. A problem indicated

---

[15] Fuchs, M.: Marhold, F.: Europäisches Arbeitsrecht, 2, vollständig überarbeitete und erweiterte Auflage, Springer Wien New York, 2006.

[16] Zöllner, W.: Der EuGH und Widerspruchsrecht des Arbeitnehmers beim Betriebsinhaberwechsel nach § 613, BGB, Europäische Zeitschrift für Wirtschaftsrecht, 1993.
Fuchs, M., Marhold, F.: Note 5, pg. 19, and n.
Birk, R.: Note 4.

[17] Rebhahn, R.: Der Arbeitnehmerbegriff in vergleichender Perspektive, Recht der Arbeit, 2009, Heft 3, p. 154-175.

by the Slovak legal practice seems to be the determination of the guarantee institution in cases where the employee works in transnational companies or has worked for several employers not only in their own country but also abroad. This problem continues to be present in the economic practice despite the fact that the current ECJ practice has addressed the liability of guarantee institutions (guarantee funds) several times.[18] Along with the existing problems linked to the contents of the Directive, the legal practice in Slovakia also struggles with an additional problem, the relatively low enforceability of law. The economic practice sees new cases where employees cannot achieve the satisfaction of their elementary wage entitlements due to insolvency of their employer on a daily basis, even for several years after the insolvency of the employer occurred. This is also interesting due to the fact that since 1st January 2004, Act No 461/2003 Coll. on Social Insurance enacted special guarantee insolvency insurance of employers in the Slovak Republic.

C. Collective redundancies

Collective redundancies are linked not only to employers ceasing to exist without a legal successor but also to other economic problems on the part of the employer. The development of the ECJ's practice in recent years brought rather broad constructions of reasons for establishing of the legal grounds for collective redundancies. Such reasoning of ECJ exceeded the framework by adding of the "purely economic reasons"expressed through res gestae.[19] The applicability of the Collective Redundancy Directive in Slovakia's economic practice is controversial particularly in relation to major employers that disregard the definition of the notion "undertaking" in application of collective redundancies as defined by the ECJ in several decisions. Such state of law is contributed to by the *de lege lata* state of law which, in connection with the labour legislation governing collective redundancies, considers an employer with legal personality to be the entity involved in collective redundancies. Practical issues in this respect occur also in the cases of transnational undertakings.[20] In one of its decision adopted in September 2009, the ECJ concludes that "it is always for the subsidiary, as the employer, to undertake consultations with the representatives of the workers who may be affected by the collective redundancies contemplated and, if necessary, itself to bear the consequences of failure to fulfil the obligation to hold consultations." [21]

V. Fundamental human rights – limits for increases in labour relations flexibility for the future

If we identify the determining attributes of increase in the existing level of labour relations flexibility, we cannot ignore additional flexibility of labour relations with respect to fundamental human rights.

---

[18]   C-125/01 (Pflücke) of 18 September 2003
[19]   C-188/03 (Junk) of 27 January 2005, C-303/2002 (Commission/Portugal), C-44/08 (Keskusliitto AEK) of 1 September 2009.
[20]   C-449/93 (Rockfon) of 7 December 1995, C-270/05 (Chartopoiia) of 15 February 2005, C-44/08 (Keskusliitto AEK) of 10 September 2009.
[21]   C-44/08 (Keskusliitto AEK) of 10 September 2009, item 69.

Although most of the social rights as laid down by the Constitution of the Slovak Republic can hardly be considered fundamental human rights (and this is also supported by the practice of the Constitutional Court of the Czech Republic),[22] certain rights exercised within labour relations are of the nature of fundamental freedoms as first-generation human rights.[23] Fundamental freedoms – first-generation human rights, include, for example, the right to protection of human dignity, the right to freedom of religion and belief, the right to protection of personality, the right to protection of life, the right to prohibition of discrimination, and the right to equal treatment. These right were classified by the ECJ in several of its decisions to be fundamental human rights. The right to protection of employee's life as well as the right to protection of human dignity form a legal limit for further increases in flexibility of the existing labour legislation governing working time. Current efforts to further liberalise working time may collide with the employees' right to freedom of religion and its specific manifestations in their personal lives. For example, the labour legislation governing working time cannot be liberalised to the extent that it would threaten the life and health of the employees, as laid down by Article 15 of the Constitution of the Slovak Republic. It cannot be liberal to the extent that it would fail to create the necessary room for natural manifestations of faith and religion (for example, by permanent work on Sundays). Further liberalisation of the existing legislation governing working time (for example, by reducing the minimum daily rest period) may cast serious doubts upon the constitutional right to human dignity laid down in Article 19 of the Constitution of the Slovak Republic, to the special protection of family, as well as to special protection of children and juveniles. It is apparent that in these cases, we face values of two kinds, economic values and values representing fundamental human rights, and that we do not have to think too much as to which of them should be given preference by the national legislator.

The enlargement of the EU shows after a relatively short period of time that the accession of new member countries will sooner or later mean a substantial increase in the dynamics of change to the existing model of social development in the EU. It can therefore be expected that in the future, we will witness intense struggle at the EU level for not only a new economic face but also for a new social face of a unified Europe, in the formation

---

[22] See Finding of the Constitutional Court of the Czech Republic Pl. 13/94 of 23 November 1994 that did not include economic, social, and cultural rights among fundamental human rights. According to the Constitutional Court of the Czech Republic, fundamental rights in the field of labour law and social security include rights implied by the Universal Declaration of Human Rights, the International Covenant on Civil and Political Rights, the Convention on the Elimination of all Forms of Racial Discrimination, the Convention on the Elimination of all Forms of Discrimination Against Women, the Convention for the Protection of Human Rights and Fundamental Freedoms, and the European Social Charter. Yet the Constitutional Court of the Slovak Republic, in Finding of the Constitutional Court of the Slovak Republic Pl. 8/94 of 6 October 1994, says: "The content of the fundamental rights and freedoms in the Constitution is worded more abstractly than the specific rules of behaviour in its implementation in the law. This is without prejudice to the fact that fundamental rights and freedoms have the nature of an entitlement, as it is always the occurrence, existence, or exercise of possible behaviour of a specific entity that is involved (for example, it is a subjective right)."

[23] Together with numerous other Slovak authors, the present author considers such classification of rights obsolete. Such classification of rights cannot be found in the Community law. The theory in the Slovak Republic is dominated by opinions that the essence of individual generations of human rights is undifferentiated and that it would be desirable to eliminate the historic schism in formulation of human rights in municipal law as well as in international law

---

of which we should use all proven social and liberal approaches to further development of society. The new social face of Europe should not reflect the obsolete model of social state, but neither should it be a society development model that would fail to provide elementary prerequisites for human and dignified life of employees.

It becomes quite apparent that community law will not be able to avoid a certain degree of liberalisation and flexibility in labour law. At present, and in the forthcoming future, it will be desirable to find an acceptable compromise between extremely liberal views of the world and socially and economically sustainable social ideas of the arrangement of society.

Chapter 2

Reform of labour law in the Slovak Republic

§ 1 General legal framework of the current legal state

The development of labour law in the Slovak Republic in recent decades shows that the change of governments and their political orientation causes (often quite substantial) changes in labour law. As can be seen from the historical development in a European context, labour law affects broad masses of people who make their living from results of dependent work. Hence, any change in the area of labour law in a specific country creates a political problem.

Since 1965, labour law is codified in the Slovak Republic. The legislation in the area of labour law maintained codified form in Slovak Republic after the fall of the totalitarian regime. Even today, this considered an advantage in comparison with the fragmentation of the legislation. In 2001, a new LC was adopted, which in terms of content had already reflected requirements of the EU law. On the other hand, it is necessary to state that Labour Code is not the only legal source of labour law in the Slovak Republic. Collective labour-law relations are governed by individual act no. 2/1991 Coll. on collective bargaining and employment relationships are governed by act no. 5/2004 Coll. on employment services. This act was substantially amended as of 1ˢᵗ May 2013, whereas amendments adopted reflect on-going economic crisis and fundamentally change the whole complex of obligatory benefits into optional benefits.

More than 100 legislative changes in the LC create among professionals view of a major reform of employment relationships. Despite such large number of legislative changes, only a few of them represent a major legislative change in comparison with the previous legal regulation. One of the essential changes should consider a new definition of dependent work, which creates in recent years the most serious challenge for theory of labour law as it vitally affects individuals and their social protection in labour-law relationships and in their future legal entitlements, particularly in the area of sickness benefits or retirement or disability pension. Termination of employment relationship and regulation of working time had been changed by the Amended Labour Code in favour of employees. Other relevant changes in the LC, which deserve the greatest attention, are in a fundamental change in the systematic part of collective labour law where the competence of trade unions is significantly strengthened, in improvement of the status of employee's representatives and in amendments related to the nature of the agreements on work performed outside employment.

In 2012, after the fall of the right-wing government and winning of social democrats in elections, the Parliament of the Slovak Republic adopted labour law reform. This labour law reform entered into force as of 1st January 2013. It consists of more than 120 legislative changes in the text of LC. Although theamendment of the LC is extensive, fundamentals of basic labour-law institutes (for example working time, a very important element of flexibility of labour-law relations and other legal institutes, which should be compatible with EU law) remain unchanged. Previous text of the LC, before it had been amended by "social-democratic" reform, reflected the relatively liberal model of labour law. It was characterized by flexibility of labour-law relations especially in the area of working time, reduction of trade union rights, deteriorating of working conditions and wages of employees by collective agreements, and by removing of the extension of higher degree collective agreements and other specifics in favour of employers. In the area of working time, leftist reform of the LC only very slightly amended its liberal character. After the reform of the LC, employees can still have two or three full-time employment contracts. Hence, there are no legislative restrictions for concurrent full-time employment contracts even after the reform of labour law from 1st January 2013.

Before its reform, legislative development in the area of labour law in the Slovak Republic was characterized, for example, by the fact that there was no extension of collective agreements of higher degree. A few years ago, major change in the act no. 2/1991 Coll. on collective bargaining caused a situation in which an extension of collective agreements was directly dependent only on the will of an employer. When the employer didn't want extension of an agreement, such extension could not be invoked against his will. And as the will to extend collective agreements did not exist on the side of employers, even an extension of collective agreements of higher degree didn't exist. This situation of absence of extension of collective agreements still remains. Especially, currently employers intensively hinder the efforts of the Government of the Slovak Republic to reintroduce extension of collective agreements.

Prior to its reform by social-democratic Government of the Slovak Republic, the LC had been very liberal in relation to the scope of intervention from staff representatives. Weakening of the involvement of employee representatives formed the essential characteristics of the previous relatively liberal development of labour law in the Slovak Republic. In recent years, employers in the Slovak Republic became accustomed to a high degree of autonomy in decision-making regarding the activities of their own business and similarly, for the future, employers do not want involvement of employee representatives into the area of labour-law relations.

Reform of labour law that entered into force on 1st January 2003 returned to the involvement of employee representatives into the labour-law relations and significantly expanded and strengthened the quality of the legal status of employee representatives.

The following changes in Slovak Republic's labour law effective from 1st January 2013 should be considered as central:

- New definition of dependent work,
- New labour-law regulation of probationary period,
- Tightening of legal conditions for fixed term employment contracts,
- Changes relating to the termination of employment and severance allowance,
- Legislative changes in the area of working time,

- Qualitatively new status of agreements on work performed outside an employment relationship which by content are converging to employment relationship,
- Fundamental change in the legal status of employee representatives, not only regarding their involvement into labour-law relations, but also with regards to the increase of their legal protection and the quality of their legal status in labour-law relations.

I. New legal definition of dependent work

A new definition of "dependent" work should be considered as one of the fundamental legislative changes of the LC in the Slovak Republic. This concept has previously been defined on the basis of eight indicators, all of which had to be met cumulatively. This legal situation posed considerable problems for labour inspection while controlling for the fulfilment of labour-law regulations. Often the absence of a single indicator of dependent work really caused that dependent to not be not considered as dependent work (for example, if the work must be carried out by means of production of the employer). In business practice, the previous concept of dependent work had been abused by employers and instead of employment contracts, employers used performance of dependent work civil law or commercial law contract types. Performance of work under the civil or commercial law contract types is economically advantageous for the employer, as it doesn't burden the employer with paying of contributions to social funds. This way an employee's position with regards to their current and future claims in the area of health insurance or pension insurance had been deteriorated.

During the previous two years, employers had been changing large number of employment contracts to other types of agreements, which do not contain an obligation on the side of the employer to pay social security contributions. Also, employers had been forcing employees to change their employee status to that of a self-employed person. Under the new text of LC, the concept of dependent work is defined in Section 1 by narrowing of the current indicators of dependent work. Dependent work is hence defined in the LC as work carried out in a relation where the employer is superior and the employee is subordinate, for a wage or remuneration, according to the employer's instructions, in the employer's name and during working time set by the employer. We may assume that a reduction in the number of indicators of dependent work shall narrow legal space for legal coverage of performance of dependent work by civil and commercial law contact types. By concluding of employment contracts and thus by establishing the employment relationship, employees themselves will be provided with more legal security. New text of the LC expressly provides for command to exercise dependent work in employment relations and simultaneously prohibits the exercise of dependent work by contract types of civil or commercial law.

II. Establishment of employment

Pre-contractual relations are considered by the LC as part of employment relationships. One of the earlier amendments to the LC cancelled the ban of the employer to gain information from the prospective employee about his union affiliation. Pressure particularly from the side of trade unions during the preparation of last amendments to the LC caused this ban to be reintroduced again. Already during preparation of amendments to the LC, social partners of the Government of the Slovak Republic argued that the legalized opportunity of employers to gain information about the union affiliation of their future employee prior to the establishment of employment puts employees into a disadvantageous position, if it is non-unionized.

According to amended Section 41 of the LC, an employer may not request information on the prospective employee concerning his union membership.

III. Agencies for employment

The amendment to the LC, effective from 1st January 2013, commits temporary employment agencies to exercise temporary assignment solely in the form of employment relationship.

This is the only legal restriction, which was brought by the recent amendment to the LC in relation to agencies for temporary employment. From 1st May 2013, legally effective amendment to the act no. 5/2004 Coll. on employment services established an irrefutable presumption of employment for an indefinite period if the agency repeatedly concludes fixed term employment contracts more than 5 times. The sixth renewal of an employment contract for fixed term employment is considered as employment relationship of an employee to the user employer.

IV. Probationary period

In comparison with the previous legal situation, the amended LC leaves the length of the probationary period up to three months for ordinary employees and up to 6 months in the case of managers within two management levels (those who report directly to the statutory authority and those managers under their direct control levels). Compared with the previous legal situation until 31stDecember 2012, the LC no longer allows by collective agreements to exceed this period.

V. Fixed-term employment relationship

At the occasion of each legislative amendment of the text of the LC, employers are fighting for the most liberal regulation of fixed term employment relationship. However, this legal regulation in any EU Member State must be compatible with the Directive 99/70/EC concerning the framework agreement on fixed-term work. The main idea of this Directive is the principle of equal treatment. Previous regulation of the LC allowed the employer to conclude the first fixed term employment relationship without substantial reasons for up to three years with the possibility of extension or re-conclusion of employment up to three times. Such an extension or re-conclusion of the employment relationship had to be reasoned by the employer by substantial grounds. New legislation within the LC changes the existing situation for the advantage of the employee and allows the employer to conclude a first fixed term employment without substantive grounds for a maximum of two years and to extend such contract or renew it a maximum of two times. Over a time horizon of two years, the employer is required to have substantial reason for additional chaining of fixed term employment contracts. Chaining of contracts for fixed term employment is allowed under the LC on the basis of explicitly enumerated grounds. For example, this is allowed in representing employees during illness, during maternity or parental leave, in seasonal work and in cases where such is agreed upon in collective agreements. Such new legislative solutions are in accordance with Directive 99/70/EC, although it is less favourable for employers, compared to previous legal situation.

VI. Termination of employment relationship

With regards to termination of employment relationship, amendments to the LC provide for a number of legislative changes in favour of employees. Of these, the most significant should be considered the tightening of existing grounds for the termination of employment relationship, which are also in the historical context in the area of labour law in the Slovak Republic conceived as an exhaustive list of reasons. This can be seen in legal regulation of notice of termination of employment according to Section 63(1)(a), in cases of dissolution of the employer or his relocation, or if an employee doesn't want to perform work in another place of employment. In favour of the employee, the amendment of the LC also changes notice pursuant to Section 63(1)(d) point 4, which authorizes the employer to terminate employment for reasons of unsatisfactory work performance. This may be applied by employer only if the employer alerted the employee in the last six months in writing to correct the deficiencies and the employee failed to do so within a reasonable time. Hence, the amended LC extends the previously applicable statutory period for written warning to the employee by the employer from two months to six months. In practical application, it was often not possible or realistic for the employee to correct deficiencies in performance of work in very short time and thus should be provided with a another chance by the employer.

VII. Notice period

Since 2011, notice periods are distinguished by the LC depending on the total duration of the employee's labour-law relationship with a particular employer. Regulation of notice periods is of relatively cogent legal nature.

Recent amendment to the LC fundamentally changed the existing legal regulation of notice periods. The length of the notice periods is set as a minimum and thus allows an employer to agree with employees on longer notice period within employment or collective contract. Statutory regulation of the minimum duration of the notice period on the other hand protects the employee. In this way, the current text of the LC achieved a higher standard of harmonization with international commitments of the Slovak Republic, in particular with the European Social Charter, which requires Member States to ensure that employees receive reasonable duration of notice period. The Slovak Republic ratified the European Social Charter in 2008. As to the length of the duration of notice period, the basic period of notice is set for the employee and the employer for at least one month. An amployee whose employment lasted at least one year and less than five years is entitled to a minimum a two-month notice period. In case the employee worked for the employer on the day of the delivery of notice for more than five years, such employee is entitled to a minimum three-month notice period.

In cases when notice is given by the employee, he is entitled to at least a two-month notice period, if on the date of notification of notice, the employee worked for the employer for at least one year. In cases of an employment relationships shorter than one year, an employee has a legal right to a minimum one-month notice period.

As it is apparent from the above, the notice period depends only on the length of employment and not on the nature of notice, as it was under the previous legal regulation (for example, period of notice on the grounds of economic reasons).

A.Monetary compensation in case when employee does not continue to work for employer until the end of notice period

Monetary compensation for an employee who doesn't continue to work for employer until the end of notice period was first enshrined in the LC at the time of economic boom and low unemployment. Employers used this legal regulation to ensure that their employees didn't leave during the duration of notice period and before they were able to secure adequate replacement of the employee. The amount of this monetary compensation, if it was agreed in writing with the employee in the employment contract, represented the amount of one average monthly salary of the employee. The amendment to the LC allows an increase in the monetary compensation directly based on the law.

According to the new legal regulation, if the employee does not remain in an employment relationship during the whole time of notice period, the employer is entitled to a monetary compensation of the amount which is a multiple of the notice period.

VIII. Offer of another suitable work – substantive condition of notice

Throughout the past decades in the Slovak Republic the employer could give a valid notice to the employee if one of the reasons for notice provided by the LC had been met and the employer offered another suitable work to employee prior to notice. Still, employers didn't have this obligation in cases of all notice grounds (for example, in cases of termination or relocation of the employer, or in the case of professional misconduct of the employee).

Up until now, the LC allowed social partners to agree to be excluded from this obligation of the employer on the basis of the collective agreement. Hence, if the collective agreement excluded this obligation of the employer, he was allowed to give the employee a valid notice without offering the employee with another appropriate work. According to the new regulation of the LC, such possibility of exclusion had been cancelled. It was mainly based on economic reasons on the side of the employer (for example, redundancy), which in relation to employees pose an uncaused social risk. As of 1st January 2013, the LC again requires as a substantive requirement of notice to offer the employee with other appropriate work (assuming the employer has any suitable work available). The employer doesn't have to meet this obligation in cases of notice due to unsatisfactory performance of work duties of the employee, misconduct of work discipline and in cases of notice of reasons allowing the employer for immediate termination of the employment relationship.

Offer of another appropriate work doesn't have to correspond to the qualification of the employee and the work doesn't have to be of the same kind as parties had agreed upon in the employment contract. In cases of full-time employment, it is sufficient if an employer offers the employee part-time work. The work offered by the employer must, however, reflect his health condition.

IX. Collective redundancies

In addition to smaller legislative changes brought by recent amendment of the LC, one should consider a substantial legislative change to be the provision of Section 73.13, according to which for the purpose of collective redundancies, the organizational unit of the employer with no legal personality is considered as integral of a part of the employer. In this way, the LC allows for situations in which legal obligations of the employer with legal personality in the event of collective redundancies may be performed by the organizational units of employer (branches). Such newly regulated status particularly suits employers with a complex organizational structure, who used to have great difficulty in meeting their notification obligations on collective redundancies related to Labour Offices.

X. Participation of employee representatives in termination of employment relationship

The amendment to the LC re-embedded the participation of employee representatives at the unilateral termination of employment relationship from the side of the employer (for example, in situations of notice given by employer or of immediate termination of employment relationship by the employer). Participation by representatives of the employees is required in the form of a prior hearing of notice given by the employer or by the immediate termination of the employment relationship. Such prior hearing is set as a condition for the validity of notice or immediate termination of the employment relationship. However, the consent of the representative of employees with notice or immediate termination of employment relationship is not considered as a substantive requirement of notice or immediate termination of employment. The aim of the new legal regulation is to force the employer not to ignore employee representatives while giving notices or while giving immediate terminations of employment relationships.

However, if the social partner of the employer and the employee representatives fail to discuss the request for termination of employment by notice or by the means of immediate termination within the statutory period, the LC creates the fiction that the consultation with employee representatives took place. The Labour Code provides for a 7-day period for negotiation on notice and for a 2-day period on immediate termination of the employment relationship, which begins from the day of receipt of the request by the employer.

XI. Invalidity of termination of employment

The issue of invalidity of termination of employment is very important because it is a procedural guarantee of the rights of employees, enshrined not only in Section 79.2 of the LC, but also in Section 14 of the LC, which provides for the judicial review of rights of employees. Judicial review of the rights of employees is enshrined also in the Code of Civil Procedure and in the Constitution of the Slovak Republic. According to the current legal regulation, employees and also employers may defend against invalid termination of an employment relationship in a preclusive period of two months. The possibility of judicial review of invalid termination of employment relationship remains, but the amendment to the LC sets differently from previous regulation the question of financial demands of the employee in cases when employer invalidly terminated the employment relationship. According to the previous regulation, in cases of invalid termination of employment by the employer, the employee could claim from the employer to pay wage compensation for a maximum of nine months if total time for which remuneration should be provided exceeded nine months. If the total time for which an employee should get compensation had been longer than nine months, the employee could not get such compensation. This situation had been partially corrected by the mentioned amendment to the LC by allowing an employee to receive wage compensation for a maximum of 36 months, if the total time for which compensation should be provided exceeds 12 months.

XII. New legal regulation of severance allowance upon termination of employment relationship

Unlike previous regulation, the most significant legislative amendment should be considered in the case of severance allowance at termination of employment relationship, which requires the reintroduction of concurrence of the notice period and severance allowance. According to previous regulation such concurrence was not possible and the LC contained principle of "allowance or notice period".

Also, according to the new amendments to the LC, provision of severance allowance is possible in case of termination of employment relationship by the employer for organizational reasons or for health reasons, but also in case of agreement on termination of employment relationship. Sum of severance allowance differs depending on the number of years of work conducted for the employer.

The new legal model of allowance provided in relation to the number of years worked is less favourable for employees. Although previous regulation was based on the alternation of "severance allowance or notice period", the differentiation of amount of allowance according to number of years worked for employer was significantly more favourable for employees. New regulation addresses the provision of allowance independent of the duration of the notice period, and links it to the sum of the number of years worked for the employer.

If the employment relationship lasted less than two years, the employee is entitled to severance allowance corresponding to the amount of average monthly salary. Employees are eligible for severance allowance corresponding to the amount of double average monthly salary if they worked for the employer for at least five years. For example, an employee is entitled to allowance of four average monthly salaries if the duration of employment was at least ten years and less than twenty years. If employment lasted at least twenty years, the employee is entitled to allowance of five average monthly salaries.

XIII. Regulation of competing earning activities of employee

According to previous legal regulation, the employee was required to promptly notify the employer on his earning activity which may be of competitive nature to the activities of the employer. According to the new legal regulation the employee must ask the employer for prior approval to pursue such earning activity. At the same time, the amended LC establishes an irrefutable presumption in the sense that if the employer does not respond to the request of the employee within 15 days of its receipt, the employer's consent is considered to be provided. Unlike under previous legal regulation the employer is now entitled to withdraw consent for serious reasons in writing (Section 83.3). Such withdrawal is required to be justified.

XIV. Legislative changes of regulation of working time

LC of the Slovak Republic is based on the 48-hour maximum weekly working time enshrined in the Directive 2003/88/EC concerning certain aspects of the organization of working time. At the same time, as an EU Member State, the Slovak Republic must comply with the minimum rest period after the work is done.

Prior to its social democratic reform, one of the particularities of flexibility of employment relationships in the Slovak Republic was the particularly high range of overtime (at total of 400 hours per year, 150 hours of mandated overtime and other agreed 250 hours of overtime). The same extent of overtime remains even after the reform of labour law.

The problem of Slovak legislation in the area of working time is that for reduced daily and weekly rest after work is done, adequate rest periods in accordance with the current case law of the ECJ are not provided. The employer is not required to compensate employees for rest periods without undue delay, but the actual provisions of the LC allow for the long term, 30 days at daily rest periods and within eight months at weekly rest periods.

Another problem of Slovak legislation regulating working time is the constant pressure of businesses to expand the personal and material scope of the opt-out system. Until 31st December 2012, opt-out had been allowed by the LC not only to health workers but also to a broadly defined category of managers. Recent amendments to the LC narrowed the personal scope of the opt-out system and since 1st January 2013, the LC allows opt-out to be applied only to health workers.

Despite adopted legislative changes in the area of working time, the LC leaves for the future possibility to conclude full time employment contracts also in relation to several employers and maximum weekly working time of 48 hours is considered in relation to every employer separately. Section 50 of the LC states that rights and obligations of concurrent employments are to be considered quite separately with the exception of young employees less than 18 years of age.

Previous legislation application practice has proven the account of working time and flexiaccount as helpful tools used in order to avoid the reduction of employees in times when the employer is facing economic problems and its employees are not sufficiently used. This legal instrument of the organization of working time is left untouched by the LC. However, its implementation is bound exclusively on agreement with employee representatives or by collective agreement. Working time account shall not be introduced only on the unilateral decision of the employer without agreement with the employee representatives or without a collective agreement.

A special feature of introducing of a working time account is up to 30 month schedule period.

Reduced daily rest after work is possible even after the reform on the enumerated grounds. Legislative formulation of these enumerated grounds in Section 92 of LC is so wide that the application practice often leads to the reduction of the daily rest period up to 8 hours after the work is done. Granting of compensatory rest periods even after the reform is not in accordance with Directive 2003/88/EC on certain aspects of working time, and the current case law of the ECJ. Even after the reform of labour law legislation is allowing flexi-account for working time and a very liberal legislation on flexible working time remained in the text of LC.

XV. New legal regulation of paid holiday

Previous regulation of paid holiday according to LC left determination of the time of paid holiday at the discretion of the employer. In practice, there were frequently situations when the employer has not drawn paid holiday until the end of the following calendar year. Hence, the reform of the LC responds to these situations, as well as to the current case law of the ECJ, which confers the power to draw paid holidays into the hands of the employees themselves. According to the amended provisions of Section 113.2 of the LC, if the employer doesn't draw paid holiday to an employee until the 30th June of the following calendar year so that the employee can complete it until the end of calendar year, the employee can draw his[24] paid holiday. In this case, the employee is required to notify the employer in writing and at least 30 days in advance of the paid holiday. This period may be shortened with the consent of the employer.

XVI. Agreements on work performed outside of employment relationship

Agreements on work performed outside of the employment relationship, along with the employment contract, create freer labour-law relationships. Up until now, employers in Slovakia used to replace such agreements with employment contracts. As such, agreements did not constitute obligations for employers to contribute to social funds.

Such legal regulation is currently substantially amended. New legal regulation converges the content of labour-law relationship based on agreements on work performed outside employment with those labour-law relationships based on the employment contract. For labour-law relationships based on agreements on work performed outside employment (for example provisions of the LC concerning the employment relationship) particularly on working time (with certain exceptions such as regarding overtime or on-call duty and the performance of night work), are to be used. Section 119.1 of the LC on the minimum wage standard has to be applied with regards to agreements of work performed outside of the employment relationship. On the other hand, regulations of holiday do not apply. As of 1st September 2012, agreements on work performed outside of an employment relationship create insurance obligations for the employer with respect to the relevant social funds, even though certain advantageous rates of levies in case of employing of persons in the retirement age and of students are provided.

---

[24] in the entire publication „he, his, him and himself" includes marking „she, her, herself"

XVII. New legal regulation of collective labour law

Since 2001 the new LC introduced dualism in representing employee's rights, not only through trade bodies but also through employee's councils. Two years ago the dramatic reduction of trade union rights in favour of employee councils took place which in terms of the number until today didn't gain such level of representativeness as trade unions. Moreover, until the leftist labour law reform, the LC enabled a trade union to represent the interests of employees, hence to be in position of a social partner to employer, only if they represented at least 30% of employees. This problem some time ago raised great acclaim and controversy, and currently is to be resolved by the Constitutional Court of the Slovak Republic. The recent amendment to the LC has provided for substantial legislative changes in the system of collective labour law. Since 2001, Slovak labour law was already characterized by dualism in representing employee's rights. In addition to trade unions, the rights of employees are represented by employee councils, which can function alongsidethe trade union. In practice, it is rather the case that the employer either has an employee's council or a trade union. Exceptionally, there are cases when a trade union operates alongside with an employee's council. The number of employee's councils is still relatively low compared to the number of trade unions. Therefore, in the planning of the amendment of the LC, unionists demanded a wider range of competencies compared to those employee's councils possess. While according to previous labour-law legislation, employee's councils had crucial competence in the field of labour-law relationshipsandtradeunionswereentitledonlytotherightforinformation,controlovercompliance with safety and health at work and collective bargaining and participation. Consultation hadbeeninthecompetenceofemployeecouncils.TheLCamendmentfundamentallychanged this situation. Under the amendment of the LC, trade unions have the right to co-decide, and the right for consultation, information and collective bargaining. Employee councils have the right to information. Such division of powers between the employee's councils and trade unions shall apply only in cases, when employer has both a trade union and employee's council operating side by side. If only one of the social partners operates at an employer, this social partner performs all tasks regarding interference to labour-law relationships, which the LC grants to employee representatives (with the exception that the employee's council is not entitled to collective bargaining).

Unlike previous legal regulation, according to Section 230.2 of the LC, the trade union body is no longer required to prove to the employer that it represents at least 30% of all employees of the employer (representativeness) as a condition to enable it to operate under the LC in the legal position of the employees' representative.

The amendment to the LC in the area of collective labour law also changed the present range of the interference of employee representatives in the management of the employer. In many places it has changed the way that the interference from the form of the consultation to co-decision, whether in the form of prior approval, agreement or co-decision.

Until now, Act number 2/1991 Coll. on collective bargaining has not been amended. Therefore, inpractice, the application of higher level collective agreements don't operate and is almost non-existent. In the near future, amendment to the law on collective bargaining is envisaged, which will solve this problem.

XVIII. Entitlements of employee representatives to time off from work

Unlike previous legal regulation, extensive amendment of the LC establishes relatively high standards of employee representatives for paid time off from work. Both trade union officials and members of the employee's council are entitled to paid time off from work. According to Section 240 of the LC, the extent of such paid time off from work is 15 minutes per one employee. For example, if the employer employs 100 employees he is required to provide 25 hours of paid time off from work to representatives of employees. The allocation of paid time off from work is left to employee representatives. This part of the LC is particularly subject to criticism from the side of employers.

Conclusion

Labour law reform, which entered into force on 1st January 2013, harmonizes Slovak labour law more with EU law (for example, in the area of regulation of employment for a specified period of time or with regards to regulation of collective redundancies). The most positive effect of labour law reform is considered to be the repeal of the existing possibilities to worsen working and wage conditions of employees through collective agreements in comparison to conditions set directly by law. Such legal situation has often been subject of justified criticism because it contradicted the basic function of collective agreements. On the other hand, the extent to which the LC grants paid time off from work to employee representatives is currently under criticism as it disproportionately favours representatives and interferes with the legitimate interests of employers. Amendment of the LC significantly increased involvement of employee representatives into employer's decision making, which should be positively evaluated because the prior trend was gradually eliminating employee representatives from employer's decision-making processes.

Amendment to the LC did not comprehensively change the nature of other systematic parts of the LC. As approaching a higher degree of compatibility of Slovak labour law with EU law, the most recent reform of labour law in the Slovak Republic somehow remained halfway. The LC still allows for liberal regulation of working time and mostly liberal regulation of agencies for temporary employment. Through regulation of the annual maximum permissible overtime, as well as through concurrent full-time employment or liberal labour-law regulation of work on Sundays and on public holidays, it allows employees to work until their "self-destruction", which cannot be considered in the third millennium as dignified work.

Chapter 3

Fundamental principles of slovak labour law

Fundamental principles of labour law are contained in specific labour-law rules. They reflect the main characteristics not only of labour law, but of the entire legal system. They are based on the Constitution of the Slovak Republic, which is the fundamental law of the state. This relationship is important mainly because in labour-law relationships, fundamental freedoms and social rights of citizens enshrined in the Constitution of the Slovak Republic apply. They differ from other labour-law rules due to a higher degree of abstraction and a different mechanism of functioning. The practical importance of fundamental principles of labour law consist in their interpretation and application functions. They help in legal interpretation and application of labour-law rules.

Fundamental principles of labour law are contained in Articles 1 to 11 of the Fundamental Principles of the LC.

Article 1 and Article 2 of the LC Fundamental Principles reflect and guarantee equality and freedom in labour-law relationships. Article 1 of the LC Fundamental Principles guarantees equality before the law by means of prohibition of discrimination. The constitutional freedom is enshrined in Article 2 of the LC Fundamental Principles as the contract principle in labour-law relationships. The freedom of coalition enshrined the Constitution of the Slovak Republic is partially expressed in Article 10 of the LC Fundamental Principles. Other fundamental principles of the LC expressed in Articles 3 to 8 contain constitutional social rights implemented in labour-law relationships. Article 11 enshrines the principle of protection of the employee's personal privacy. The LC as the fundamental source of labour law also guarantees other constitutional freedoms, even though this guarantee is not reflected explicitly in the LC Fundamental Principles.

The crucial part of provisions of the LC consists of fundamental constitutional social rights of natural persons implemented in labour-law relationships. However, there is no doubt that in these relationships, fundamental freedoms are also implemented and in this field, the legal position of the state is, unlike social rights, of different quality.

During the employment relationship, a considerable part of fundamental freedoms are also implemented, with such freedoms having, in comparison with social rights, a different legal/dogmatic structure. Not all freedoms of natural persons that are legally relevant for labour law are explicitly enshrined in the LC. Apart from equality and freedom to choose profession and the right to coalition freedom, all other fundamental freedoms may be inferred only indirectly from the legal construction of individual labour-law institutions.

§ 1 Protection of human dignity

Human dignity as the foundation of rule of law, as the value of values, should be the foundation of law in every civilized country. The guarantee of human dignity in objective law, and also in practice, is even more important because human dignity is the essence of human existence. Values contained in the system of the law should take into account the value of man and his freedom. The law should reflect the respect for personal dignity of other people. Labour law, as part of the legal system, should guarantee, above all, appropriate working conditions of employees consistent with human dignity. Examples known until now in the application practice of the Slovak Republic on the verge of the third millennium do not suggest that the legal system of the Slovak Republic fully complies with these functions, which also applies to the field of labour law. In contrast, given the current social practice in Slovakia, it seems as if law cannot be coupled with morals.

Just like in other countries, economic values have become the priority in society.

Physical and mental integrity of people is, nowadays, on the verge of the 21st century, threatened and harmed in various ways. Many of these threats and harms are disguised under the veil of freedom of business.

How can we define the content of common legal situations where human dignity is infringed? These situations include pressures on conscience, slavery, exploitation, humiliation and, in the recent decade, the more and more common mobbing and bossing in the workplace (bullying). This is an open list of cases of possible infringements of human dignity. Infringements of human dignity in the field of labour-law relationship leads to a loss of self-confidence and trust in the world as the basis of dignity. Precisely this basis of the right to human dignity is the reason why human dignity is considered as the „axiom" of law in the 21st century.

Constant pressure of many employers on increasing work performance of employees are reflected, in case of certain employers, not only in requirements of all-year work on Sundays and illegal increases of overtime work, but also in absurd restrictions on the number of visits to the toilet during working time. This is also the form of labour-law relationships in the 21st century that humilitates people in the human essence. Only recently, the competent authorities of the Slovak Republic dealt with cases of female employees of a company in Eastern Slovakia where the security service of the employer checked such employees before and after visiting the toilet in order to avoid theft of pantyhose manufactured there.

These cases from the application practice are very distant from the majestic and respectable character of the topic of human dignity, but they are based on real life situations and they show the humiliation that may be experienced by employees in an employment relationship in the 21st century.

Another example of What is the dignity of an employee who does not receive any wage from their employer in several consecutive months? What is the dignity of an employee who does not receive any wage from the employer in several consecutive months? What is he supposed to do in such a situation when he does not have funds for elementary subsistence? (example of an Italian employer in Vranov nad Topľou, Eastern Slovakia). How does the legal system of the state work in practice if it allows the employer a long-term non-payment of contributions to social funds, of taxes and wages? In this case, it is not only a failure of the employer, but of the existing legal system, and especially of observance of law in practice by all competent authorities in the Slovak Republic tolerating the non-payment of contributions to social funds and of taxes and wages by the employer. The employer, assisted by a well-paid legal service, threatened them, intimidated them and discouraged them with illegal means from strike, invoking the strikes dealt with by the ECJ in *Viking and Laval*, where the ECJ preferred freedom of business over the fundamental human right to freedom of coalition and its manifestations.

I. Legal foundations of protection of human dignity

Human dignity, together with freedom and equality, constitute the fundamental structure of legal principles of rule of law. They may be regarded as constitutional principles.

The right to human dignity, as declared several times by the ECJ, is part of the foundations of EU law. Human dignity and its inviolability has a foremost place also in the European Convention on Human Rights and Fundamental Freedoms.

The LC of the Slovak Republic as such or a different labour-law regulation does not enshrine the right to protection of human dignity. The right to protection of human dignity is enshrined in the constitution. Article 39 of the Constitution of the Slovak Republic also enshrines the right to a minimum extent of material assets and for appropriate subsistence of a person in the form of elementary life needs if he is not able to procure them himself. This minimum extent is still not sufficiently specified by law in order to avoid in practice numerous cases of threatening and harming human dignity.

An optimum scope for protection of human dignity is provided by the Charter of Fundamental Rights of the EU.

The right to protection of human dignity and its inviolability has become important, particularly after the conclusion of the Lisbon Treaty. The Charter of Fundamental Rights of the European Union, which has become part of the TFEU, enshrines human dignity and its protection in Article 1, which provides that human dignity is inviolable. By putting human dignity in the first place in the list of all other human rights, the European legislator has shown, for the first time in the history of the EU, explicitly that human dignity is a crucial value in the constitutional and social order of the EU. It is a value, a fundamental principle and a fundamental right equipped with a legal claim enforceable in court.

Therefore, the term human dignity as such must be, after conclusion of the Lisbon Treaty, regarded not only as a fundamental value and fundamental principle, but also as a fundamental right equipped with a legal claim.

An equally important problem is the relationship between the right to protection of human dignity and other fundamental rights. In particular, those enshrined in the systematic part Solidarity, some of which are, according to the Lisbon Treaty, legal principles. Human dignity, which is at the top of the hierarchy of human rights in the Charter is given its primary position, which is crucial for the interpretation of other fundamental rights and legal principles of the Charter. Human dignity is formulated in Article 1 of the Charter of Fundamental Rights of the EU as a fundamental subjective right of the highest rank and it is not sufficient to understand it only as a right guiding the exercise of all other rights. As a fundamental right, it is not subject to any restrictions, even though dignity of one person is limited by the dignity of another person.

The exercise of other classic fundamental rights and freedoms as rights of the first generation is covered by Article 1 of the Charter, which enshrines the right to human dignity. None of the rights enshrined in the Charter may be exercised in a way threatening or infringing human dignity. According to the Charter, the right to human dignity and its inviolability and protection is the supreme value of the entire EU. And, at the same time, it is a fundamental legal principle, as well as a fundamental right equipped with a legal claim.

When examining the issue of human dignity, the relationship between fundamental human rights and private law with respect to direct horizontal application of fundamental human rights in private-law relationships. Quite a new focus of fundamental human rights is the protection of individuals in horizontal, formally equal private-law relationships. It is the horizontal effect of fundamental human rights, not only a vertical relationship between the individual and the state.

The normative dimension of human dignity, the right to protection of human dignity, includes the protection of physical and mental integrity of individuals, protection and guarantee of elementary equality and guarantee of elementary foundations of life.

It is obvious that in the content of the Charter of Fundamental Rights of the EU, not all rights are full-fledged subjective rights with an actionable legal claim. If these fundamental rights are not sufficiently specified in the Charter so that an individualized legal claim may be derived from their content, they are regarded as principles addressed to the authorities of the EU or Member States, which should not only specify, but also guarantee such rights. However, if non-observance of these principles contained in the Charter also concerns fundamental rights (the right to human dignity), a subjective right with an actionable legal claim may be derived from the content of principles, as well.

The text of the Charter is surprising for the legal theory and practice, not only due to differentiated legal understanding of fundamental freedoms as subjective rights, but also due to the differentiated legal understanding of rights and principles. According to previous case law of the ECJ, in connection with the provisions of the Charter, fundamental freedoms include, in particular, economic freedoms on which the EEC was based. Fundamental human rights enshrined in international instruments as rights of the first generation are, in part, included in the Charter and the Lisbon Treaty, which directly refers to the European Convention of Human Rights, which the EU regards as legally binding. According to previous case law of the ECJ, some fundamental rights may be derived from primary law and the ECJ considers certain rights as fundamental principles that are common to the legal orders of all Member States, which was explicitly declared in *Stauder* (C-29/69), which is of significant legal importance for the development of the theory of fundamental rights.

Right to protection of human dignity must be applied in the application practice also in case of infringement of social rights, which infringement threatens or infringes the right to human dignity. In the application practice, there are numerous cases where the employee in a labour-law relationship is enslaved to such extent that he is not interested in invoking his legitimate claims and he only fulfils the employer's will, concentrating on mere survival, because he is aware of all risks connected with the loss of employment at current high unemployment lebels in the Slovak Republic.

§ 2 Prohibition of forced or compulsory labour

Prohibition of forced labour is enshrined not only in international labour law, but also in the law of the Council of Europe.

The term forced labour does not cover a certain group of exhaustively listed cases, such as military service, civil service and work resulting from common civic duties.

According to Article 2 of the ILO Convention No. 29 concerning forced or compulsory labour, for the purposes of this Convention, the term forced or compulsory labour means all work or service which is exacted from any person under the menace of any penalty and for which the said person has not offered himself voluntarily.

By the ILO Convention No. 105 concerning abolition of forced labour, the ILO defined five forms of forced labour, including labour:

- as a means of political coercion or as a punishment for holding or expressing political views;
- as a method of mobilising and using labour for purposes of economic development;
- as a means of labour discipline;
- as a punishment for having participated in strikes;
- and as a means of racial, social, national or religious discrimination.

In his subsequent case law, the ECtHR declared that forced labour requires two cumulative conditions to be met: performance of work must be involuntary and unfair or under coercion, or the work or service itself constitutes suffering that may be avoided if its performance is unnecessarily severe.

According to the case law of the ECtHR, forced labour is not work to be performed by an unemployed person as a condition of further payment of unemployment benefit, even if this work does not correspond with his qualification, (application no. 7402/76, Reports of Judgments and Decisions, no. 7, p. 161).

According to Article 4 of the European Convention on Human Rights, forced or compulsory labour does not include:

- any work required to be done in the ordinary course of detention imposed according to the provisions of Article5 of this Convention or during conditional release from such detention;
- any service of a military character or, in case of conscientious objectors in countries where they are recognised, service exacted instead of compulsory military service;
- any service exacted in case of an emergency or calamity threatening the life or well-being of the community;
- any work or service which forms part of normal civic obligations.

§ 3 Freedom of association

The content of the freedom of association includes not only the right to establish various coalitions on an independent basis, but also the right of autonomy of collective agreements, the right to establish intercompany associations as well as free activity in such associations. According to the European Convention on Human Rights, this fundamental right has the legal quality not only of a positive, but also negative coalition freedom.

Freedom of association means not only the right to establish associations, but also the right of their members to protection of their interests by these associations.

The right to freedom of association is enshrined not only in the law of the Council of Europe in Article 11 of the European Convention on Human Rights, but also in the European Social Charter, the Revised European Social Charter and ILO conventions.

For the area of labour-law relationships, the trade union freedom is of particular importance.

The ECtHR confirmed the will to apply the Convention also in the area of labour relationships, including pure private-law relationships, by means of control over national legislation pertaining to trade union freedom. According to the ECtHR, the trade union freedom is a right derived from the freedom of association, and it refuses to recognize the trade union right as a special and separate right. Article 11 concerning freedom of coalition does not specify the method of exercise of this right and "does not guarantee a certain treatment to trade unions and their members by the state". According to the ECtHR, there is no reason to recognize "necessary elements proper to a trade union right", *a fortiori* because the relevant provisions of the European Social Charter are too general. The ECtHR excludes the possibility of deriving, from Article 11 of the European Convention on Human Rights, the right of trade unions to consultation, the right to collective negotiation, the right to benefits resulting from collective agreements and the right to strike. In his opinion, these rights are not irreplaceable for an efficient exercise of the trade union freedom. The concrete exercise of a trade union right is defined by the state. The right to strike should be exercised within the limits of the law of the state in question and the state may limit its exercise. According to Article 8 of the Covenant on Economic, Social and Cultural Rights, the right to strike should be exercised in conformity with the laws of the particular country. However, the Covenant clearly requires from the States Parties to the Covenant that national legislation must allow trade unions to fight for protection of interests of their members. For this purpose, trade unions should have the right to be heard and to submit their requirements.

The Covenant guarantees the trade unions the right to establish trade union organizations, which includes the right to adopt their own rules, the right to manage their own affairs and the right to join trade unions (*Johanssen v Sweden*). On the other hand, the ECtHR deals very strictly with the so-called "closed shop" (agreement between an employer or an organization of employers with one or more trade union organizations, which is a condition of employment). "The said practice cannot exert unbearable pressure on the individual (for example under the threat of dismissal), a real freedom of choice of trade unions must be preserved and the freedom of thought, conscience and religion must be respected and the very substance of the freedom of association may not be impaired" (*Sibson*).

The ECtHR recognized that the content of Article 11 represents not only positive, but also negative freedom of coalition (*Sigurdur A. Sirgurjonsson*).

§ 4 Protection of employee's privacy

According to Article 11 of the Fundamental Principles of the LC, employers may collect personal data on employees only where these relate to the qualifications and professional experience of employees and data that may be significant for the work that employees are expected to carry out, are currently carrying out, or have carried out. The employer may not, without serious reasons consisting in specific nature of the employer's activity, infringe the employee's privacy in the workplace and in common premises of the employer by monitoring him, recording telephone calls carried out by means of the employer's technical equipment and check e-mail sent from the office e-mail address or delivered to this address without informing the employee. If the employer implements a control mechanism, he must consult the scope of control, method of performance of control and its duration with employee representatives and inform the employees of the scope of control, method of performance of control and its duration.

The right to protection of personal data falls within the category of employee's rights to protection of personality. The importance of protection of personal data has increased due to dissemination of automated personal data processing systems. Certain elements of this right are reflected in Section 73 of the LC, which forbids employers from providing personal data to other employers where the employee has applied for work. If the employer infringes the Personal Data Protection Act, the employee is entitled to apply in court for a prohibition of unlawful interventions into the right to protection of personality and an injunction to eliminate the consequences of these interventions and for award of monetary compensation of immaterial loss.

The employee's personality rights with respect to his legitimate interests of protection of personal data are most commonly infringed in the pre-contractual relationships. The employer often requires the future employee to provide more detailed personal data concerning not only himself, but also about his family, parents, spouse and children. The LC forbids employers to require information that might harm the personality of the applicant for employment from natural persons applying for work. The employer's questions that might interfere with personal rights of employees include those concerning their health condition, family situation, and membership in political parties or trade union organizations. Under Section 17 of the Act No. 125/2006 Coll. on Labour Inspection, the National Labour Inspectorate and labour inspectorates process data necessary for the activity of state administration authorities in the field of labour inspection without the consent of persons concerned. For the purposes of labour inspection, the employer must provide the inspectorate with the employee's personal data, including: name, surname, title, date of birth, and address of permanent residence or temporary residence. For the purposes of demonstrating observance of working conditions and conditions of employment imposed, in particular health capability, pregnancy, care for a person younger than 15 years of age, loneness, wage and qualification, the employer must also provide other data to the labour inspectorate that are necessary for proving the above facts. The employer has certain duties with respect to the labour inspectorate concerning personal data also as far as other natural persons, not situated in the legal position of employee, but present at his workplace at the moment of labour inspection being performed, are concerned. The employer must provide personal data of these natural persons to the work inspectorate, including: name, surname, title, date of birth, and address of permanent residence or temporary residence. This information concerning personal data of natural persons present at the workplace at the moment of a labour inspection is being performed should be related to information concerning the occurrence of occupational accidents, imminent threat of serious industrial accidents and occupational diseases.

The right to respect for private life consists in particular in the right to confidentiality with respect to private life, which implies in particular a guarantee of intimacy in places where private life takes place.

The ECtHR defines the right to protection of private life quite extensively.

In this respect, the right to respect of the individual's home is very important. The home means, according to the case law of the ECtHR, the place where a person lives or exercises his usual profession. The premises used for exercise of profession are, under Article 8 of the Convention and the case law of the ECtHR, protected against home searches and visits from public authorities (*Niemetz*). The ECJ has a partially different opinion on this point with respect to premises used for business, which are, for example, not protected against home searches (*Hoechst*, C-46/87).

The content of protection of private life includes protection against recording of telephone calls or interferences with the respect for protection of written correspondence. In the field of labour-law relationships, this legal protection must be understood through the prism of separation of professional tasks and private interests. For example, monitoring of telephone calls is often performed by the employer in order to verify whether employees do not use this form of communication for personal purposes during working time. The ECtHR has declared in one of its rulings, illegality of interference with private life also when recording of telephone calls concerned business affairs (*Huvig v France*). Extension of the term right to privacy within the meaning of the case law of the ECtHR concerning Article 8 of the Convention to professional activities and business activity has been confirmed by several subsequent rulings of this court.

Interferences with personal rights of employees may take form not only of recording telephone calls, but also other secret recordings. However, secret recording is not a sound record from an employee's public speech.

According to the case law of the Strasbourg authorities for protection of law, not every recording of telephone calls constitutes an interference with the right to privacy. Secret monitoring of telephone calls may be imposed only for reasons of national security.

In developed countries, other forms of interference by the employer are known (for example, constant surveillance of employees by TV cameras primarily aimed at preventing theft).

State interferences with the right to privacy must be governed by the principles of:
- legality,
- legitimacy and
- proportionality.

§ 5 Freedom of contract in labour law

The contract principle in labour-law is based on the Constitution of the Slovak Republic itself. Personal freedom, enshrined in Article 17 of the Constitution of the Slovak Republic, is founded on private individual autonomy, which is, however, a wider legal category when compared with the contracting principle.

In the context of the constitutional principle of freedom, the contract principle in labour law is one of its important manifestations.

The contract principle in labour-law relationships has the real form of freedom of contract of parties pertaining not only to the stage of conclusion of an employment contract or a different contract, but also to the content of the legal relationship established by the contract and the conditions of contract termination.

The basic content of freedom of contract in individual labour law consists, in particular, in the freedom of:

- selection of contracting partner,
- conclusion of contract,
- determination of its content,
- its dissolution,
- selection of contractual form.

I. Freedom of selection of contracting partner

The freedom of selection of contracting partner when concluding an employment contract is partially limited by the legislator by means of the so-called quota system based on the Act No. 5/2004 Coll. on Employment Services, amending certain acts, as amended. The quota system (3.2 % of persons with health disability out of the total number of employees) interferes with the freedom of selection of contracting partner by the employer, even though it does not eliminate this freedom completely.

The freedom of selection of contracting partner is, to a certain extent, limited by the labour law of the Slovak Republic with respect to nationals of third parties who need a work permit for performance of work in labour-law relationships.

II. Freedom of conclusion of contract

The freedom of conclusion of an employment contract or a different contract includes freedom of selection of adequate contractual forms, although the legislator attributes different legal consequences to each of them. In contrast, it forbids employers to regulate dependent work by means of contractual forms of civil law or commercial law and, in Section 1 of the LC, it provides that employers must regulate performance of dependent work exclusively by means of labour-law relationships.

III. Freedom of determination of content of contract

The freedom of determination of content of, in particular, employment contracts is, to a great extent, still determined by the prevailing mandatory nature of provisions of the LC. Even though the extent of default nature of its provisions has recently been increased considerably it still does not provide such a wide scope for application of freedom of contract of parties to employment relationships as in civil law or commercial law.

Freedom of contract of parties to employment relationships is, under legislation in force, is also limited by the legislator by means of limitation of performance of a competing activity by the employee under Sections 83 and 83a of the LC.

IV. Freedom of dissolution (termination) of contract

Contractual autonomy also consists in a free decision of the contracting parties to terminate a contract already concluded. When concluding an employment contract or a different contract, the limitation of freedom of a contract in case of termination of a contract substantially interferes with the freedom of parties, in particular with the exercise of ownership right. Under legislation in force, this applies, in particular, to the fact that reasons for notice given by the employer are listed exhaustively. Non-observance of this prohibition may lead not only to nullity of notice, but also to a duty to employ again the employee dismissed by means of a void notice, or the employer's duty to pay wage compensation in case of void termination of employment relationship.

Freedom of termination of employment contract by the parties to the employment relationship is, under legislation in force, limited also by previous consent of employee representatives in cases of notice given by the employer to an employee representative under Section 240 LC, or by previous consent of the competent district office for work, social affairs and family, in case of notice or immediate termination of employment relationship with respect to persons with health disability.

V. Freedom of choice of contractual form

Freedom of choice of contractual form as an immediate manifestation of the contract principle in individual labour law may be understood in two basic levels, as a free choice of contractual form and also as a free choice of written or oral form. Free choice of contractual form, with respect to choice of type of contract, is directly connected with freedom to conclude a contract. Under Section 18 of the LC, only those types of contracts may be used in labour law that are governed by labour-law regulations.

Under legislation in force, the LC, under pain of nullity of legal act, requires observance of written form in case of those contracts that, with respect to the employee's legal status, establish serious legal consequences. This is fully consistent with the protection function of labour law, which has a dominant position in labour law. Therefore, it must be presumed that in the future, observance of written form under pain of nullity will be necessary, which will beyond doubt, contribute to preserving social and legal certainty of both contractual partners (the employee and the employer).

VI. Contract principle in collective labour law

Collective labour law serves, in relation to individual labour law, as an important control mechanism of application of contractual autonomy of parties. In this relationship, it serves as a legal guarantee against possible abuse of freedom of contract of parties to employment relationships. This legal construction between contractual autonomy of parties in labour law and collective labour law is, under current legislation, reflected in the LC. Under Section 236 of the LC, the part of an employment contract containing a lower level of labour-law claims of employees than the collective agreement is void.

Collective labour law with respect to the contract principle in individual labour law is also a prerequisite of application of freedom of contract of parties. Collective agreements allow, in particular, to achieve a certain real balance between the contracting parties, the employer and the employee.

§ 6 Principle of equal treatment

I. General characteristics

The application practice in the Slovak Republic provides many examples of infringement of the principle of equal treatment, not only with respect to men and women, but also infringement of prohibition of discrimination based on age, health disability or other reasons. On 14th September 2012, the Minister of Work, Social Affairs and Family of the Slovak Republic stated in the report of the National Council of the Slovak Republic that horizontal and vertical segregation of women in Slovak society due to serious reason exists. Representation of woman in Slovak political life is so low that women have almost no possibility of influencing strategic decisions concerning the present and the future of our society. Feminization of poverty is increasing dynamically because women with considerably lower income that men have considerably lower old-age pensions, which does not ensure life in dignity.

If we examined the observance of the principle of equal treatment in social life of Slovak society, we would find many shortcomings, not only with respect to legally standardized forms of infringement of the principle of equal treatment (for example, between men and women), but also between the old and the young, and the healthy and the sick. The rate of social exclusion, in particular of long-term unemployed persons, is so high that it does not allow them to live their life in dignity. On a daily basis we are confronted, with a total lack of intergenerational solidarity, and also with many other situations involving discrimination of the poor as opposed to the rich, of the weaker as opposed to the stronger, and of the sick as opposed to the healthy.

Despite the numerous cases of breach of prohibition of discrimination in Slovak judicial case law, judicial disputes in this field are lacking. One may ask what is the cause of this situation. There is no case law. Why? This is because there is no judge without an applicant. At first sight, it may seem that observance of the prohibition of discrimination in the Slovak Republic causes no problems. In reality, this is not the case.

II. Legal basis of prohibition of discrimination in Slovak labour law

Understanding of prohibition of discrimination, not only as the principle of principles of the EU law, but also as an independent right is consistent with its legal understanding also according to the law of the Council of Europe, which, after adoption of the Supplementary Protocol No. 12 to the European Convention on Human Rights, understands the prohibition of discrimination, not only as a criterion for exercise of human rights, but understands equality as a fundamental human right.

The right to equal treatment is applied most frequently in connection with a breach of some of the rights enshrined in the European Convention on Human Rights.

The principle of equal treatment does not mean only equal treatment of individuals in the same situation, but the application of this fundamental human right also reflects the requirements for public authorities to treat beneficiaries of human rights differently in different situations. According to the judgment of the ECtHR in *Chapman, Costr, Beard, Le and Jane Smith v United Kingdom* (applications no. 27238/95, 2876/94, 25154/94), discrimination may arise where States without an objective and a reasonable justification fail to treat differently persons whose situations are significantly different. Different treatment without an objective and reasonable justification, contrary to Article 14 of the European Convention on Human Rights, arises if there is no legitimate aim and proportionate relationship between the means used and the aim pursued.

Not every different treatment is considered by the ECtHR as discrimination (for example, judgment in *Abdulazis, Cabales and Bankandaliv United Kingdom*).

According to the ECtHR, different treatment is defined as discrimination if there is no objective and proportionate reason for differentiation, (for example, if it does not allow pursuing a legitimate aim or if there is no relationship of proportionality between the means used and the aim pursued).

The ECJ considers the prohibition of discrimination as a fundamental human right.

III. General prohibition of discrimination in labour-law relationships

General prohibition of discrimination in labour-law relationships follows from Article 1 of the Fundamental Principles of the LC and from Section 13 of the LC. In general terms, prohibition of discrimination is imposed for labour-law relationships by the Act No. 365/2004 Coll. on Equal Treatment in Certain Sectors and Protection against Discrimination, amending certain acts ("Anti-Discrimination Act"), which is the common legal basis for observance of the principle of equal treatment in the entire legal order of the Slovak Republic including labour law.

General part of this act define the basic terms associated with the issue of discrimination in a uniform basis for the entire legal order of the Slovak Republic.

A. Concept of direct discrimination

Section 2 of the Anti-Discrimination Act defines the terms direct discrimination and indirect discrimination for the entire legal order including labour law.

Beyond the content of these two central terms, the Act also defines the terms harassment, instruction to discriminate, encouragement of discrimination and unlawful sanction. In Section 2(1), the Act also defines the content of observance of the principle of equal treatment.

The Anti-Discrimination Act defines direct discrimination as an action or omission where where one person is treated less favourably than another is, has been or would be treated in a comparable situation.

B. Concept of indirect discrimination

The Act states that indirect discrimination occurs where an apparently neutral provision, decision, instruction or practice puts one person at a disadvantage compared with another person (for example, the term indirect discrimination is defined in the Anti-Discrimination Act in the singular [person] and not plural [persons]). Section 3 of the Anti-Discrimination Act is based on the principle that legal identification of discrimination is determined by objective situation and it does not take account whether considerations or reasons for such discrimination were based on reality or a wrong presumption.

According to Article 2 of the Framework Directive (2000/78/EC), indirect discrimination shall be deemed to occur where an apparently neutral provision, criterion, or practice would put persons having a particular religion or belief, a particular disability, a particular age, or a particular sexual orientation at a particular disadvantage compared with other persons unless that provision, criterion or practice is objectively justified by a legitimate aim and the means of achieving that aim are appropriate and necessary.

IV. Application of principle of equal treatment in labour-law relationships

The principle of equal treatment as a general principle is also applied in labour-law relationships. It should be reflected in all measures, decisions and instructions of the employer. It imposes a duty on the employer to establish, in his internal regulations, common and equal working conditions for all employees or to establish these conditions according to certain material criteria. The principle of equal treatment does not apply only in individual labour-law relationships, but also in collective labour-law relationships.

The principle of equal treatment in labour-law relationships may occur not only in case of mandatory performance provided by the employer, but also in case of optional performance provided by the employer, e.g. in connection with the companies' social policy. The rights of employees may result from a collective agreement, an employment contract, or from work rules, wage rules, or a different internal regulation of the employer.

The EU law and the ECJ consider the principle of equal treatment as a fundamental principle of EU law and a fundamental right of EU citizens.[25]

Current case law of the ECJ defines the terms occupation and employment quite extensively.[26] These terms are not limited to performance of dependent activity according to an employment contract, but they also cover self-employment and professional training. The scope of the Framework Directive applies not only to private-law employment relationships, but also to public-law employment (service, public service) relationships. This suggests that the terms occupation and employment enshrined in the Framework Directive must be interpreted extensively.

During previous years, the ECJ has created its own dogmatic model of prohibition of discrimination in labour-law relationships.

The widely formulated exceptions to the principle of equal treatment show a brand new approach of the EU to discrimination, which is, as mentioned above, not defined by the Framework Directive as absolute discrimination, but as relative discrimination.

V. Grounds of discrimination

European labour law differentiates prohibition of discrimination of employees according to individual discrimination characteristics as specific features of personality of natural persons, as well as according to the nature of the labour-law relationship. The features characterizing the employee's personality include: sex, age, religion or belief, health disability or sexual orientation. Prohibition of discrimination due to the nature of the labour-law relationship applies

---

[25] *Age Concern England* (C-388/07), paragraph 40, cf. *Werner Mangold* (C-144/04), paragraph 75.
[26] *Werner Mangold* (C-144/04).

in EU law (for example, in case of fixed-term employment relationships or employment relationships for reduced weekly working time).

The grounds of prohibition of discrimination exhaustively listed in Article 1 of the LC Fundamental Principles and in the Anti-Discrimination Act are formulated above the standard, with respect to EU requirements. The list of grounds of discrimination in the LC of the Slovak Republic and in the Anti-Discrimination Act is implicit.

A. Sex and gender

Although the Anti-Discrimination Act does not distinguish between the terms sex and gender, Article 1 of the LC Fundamental Principles differentiates discrimination based on sex and discrimination based on gender. If discrimination based on gender occurs in practice, it is often covered by discrimination based on sex. According to Section 2a(11)(a) of the Anti-Discrimination Act, discrimination based on sex includes discrimination based on pregnancy or maternity and discrimination based on sexual or gender identification. Material scope of protection with respect to sex and gender, according to the Anti-Discrimination Act, applies to employment and occupation.

B. Religion and belief

Directive No. 2000/78/EC establishes only the term religion as a ground of discrimination. Article 24 of the Constitution of the Slovak Republic establishes the term "religious confession and belief". Article 1 of the LC Fundamental Principles uses religion and belief separately as a ground of discrimination and it prohibits discrimination for this reason in a way similar to Section 13 of the LC.

C. Racial and ethnic origin

The terms racial origin and ethnic origin are not defined by Directive No. 2000/43/ES or the Anti-Discrimination Act. Prohibition of discrimination on this ground is include in Article 1 of the LC Fundamental Principles and Section 13 of the LC.

D. Age

Age as a ground of discrimination differs from other grounds of discrimination. Directive No. 2000/78/EC does not define the term age and uses it in a neutral sense, protecting also younger persons from being disadvantaged compared with older persons. At the time of high unemployment rate in the Slovak Republic, age is envisaged as a reason for notice on the employer's part. Determination of general minimum or maximum age limits for exercise of profession is also a problem in the practice.

E. Sexual orientation

Sexual orientation denotes preference in sexual choice, which can be heterosexual, homosexual or bisexual. The Anti-Discrimination Act does not define the term sexual orientation. It is necessary to distinguish the term identity of sex from the term sexual orientation, which denotes the feeling of being a man, a woman or a hermaphrodite. If the identity of sex does not correspond with anatomical sex, it is called transsexuality.

F. Health disability

With respect to health disability, positive discrimination should be applied. It is applied partially in Slovak labour law, although the last significant amendment to the Act No. 5/2004 Coll. on Employment Services was a "heavy blow" to persons with health disability. A whole range of mandatory statutory benefits for employees with a health disability or their employers turned into optional benefits. Nowadays, these optional benefits are determined by special commissions at competent district work offices.

Section 40 of the Labour Code uses the term employee with health disability, which is defined as an employee recognized as invalid under special regulation, who submits a decision on invalidity pension to his employer. This special regulation is the Act No. 461/2003 Coll. on Social Insurance, as amended, which establishes conditions of invalidity. According to Sections 70 to 72 of this act, these conditions include: 40 % loss of working capacity, acquisition of the necessary number of years of insurance and duration of decreased ability to perform paid activity of more than a year.

In order to implement the principle of equal treatment with respect to persons with health disability, the employer must carry out appropriate adjustments and other appropriate measures to allow a person with a health disability to become employed. This also includes allowing the individual to take part in professional training, unless such measures are an excessive burden for the employer. Such burden is not considered excessive if it is sufficiently compensated by measures existing on the labour market as part of policy concerning persons with health disability in the EU Member State concerned. Discrimination based on health disability is, according to the Anti-Discrimination Act, also discrimination based on prior health disability or discrimination of a person, in case of whom it may be presumed, on the basis of external signs, that he suffers from health disability.

VI. Concept of harassment

Besides the terms direct discrimination and indirect discrimination, the Anti-Discrimination Act also defines the term harassment as a general term that should be used only with respect to harassment based on sex, but also on other grounds. As far as legal meaning is concerned, the most important circumstance in defining the term harassment is that the Anti-Discrimination Act, just like EU law, defines harassment as discrimination.

Under Section 2 of the Anti-Discrimination Act, harassment is such treatment of a person that may be reasonably considered by this person as unpleasant, inappropriate or offensive and the purpose of effect of which is or may be to violate the dignity of this person, in particular to create a hostile, humiliating,degrading or offensive environment.

VII. Concept of sexual harassment

Harassment, which was established for the first time in the Directive No. 2002/73/EC (now Directive 2006/54/EC), must be distinguished from the term sexual harassment because harassment is a more general term than sexual harassment and because sexual harassment can be, accordingly, considered as a special type of harassment.

Sexual harassment is a situation where the unwanted verbal, non-verbal or physical conduct of a sexual nature occurs, with the purpose or effect of violating the dignity of a person, in particular, when creating an intimidating, hostile, degrading, humiliating or offensive environment.

VIII. Exceptions from prohibition of discrimination

Article 1 of the LC Fundamental Principles, as well as the Anti-Discrimination Act, create quite a broad legal basis for different treatment, not only due to racial or ethnical origin, but also due to age, health condition, belief and religious confession, and other reasons. According to the EU law and previous case law of the ECJ, it is very important to distinguish exceptions from prohibition of discrimination on the basis of direct or indirect discrimination. In case of direct discrimination, different treatment may only be based on an exception provided directly in legislation (and in case of indirect discrimination, under certain circumstances, the EU law allows, exceptions based on legitimate reasons, which are, according to previous case law, often economic reasons). Under EU law, the aim pursued by providing exceptions must be legitimate, the means used for achieving the aim must be proportionate and, if possible, the aim should interfere with the principle of equal treatment only to the necessary extent. The burden of assessing the legitimacy of the aim and the proportionality of means used for achieving it (essential legal terms of assessment of legitimacy of exceptions to the principle of equal treatment) is a matter for national courts of EU Member States to determine. Exceptions from the principle of equal treatment, as such, must meet certain legal characteristics, not only with respect to their nature and content, but also their number. This also applies to cases of "positive discrimination", which may also be regarded as an exception from the principle of equal treatment. Exceptions from the principle of equal treatment must pursue a legitimate (justified) aim.

It follows from previous case law of the ECJ, and of national courts of Member States, that exceptions from the principle of equal treatment based on sex, consisting in economic reasons, are generally accepte, because it is presumed that economic development constitutes, in the absolute majority of cases, a legitimate aim. Assessment and verification of admissibility of an exception from the principle of equal treatment is a matter for national courts to determine. However, if, in case of a judicial dispute, the employer fails to convince the court that the aim (objective) is legitimate, the court needs not to admit the exception in question.

When verifying the admissibility of exceptions from the principle of equal treatment, national courts verify whether the aim pursued by the employer is consistent with the means of different treatment applied. Existence of a causal link between the reason for exception applied and its aim is required. Examination of causal link between the reason for the exception applied and its aim should lead the judge to a conclusion as to whether the aim in question would not be achieved by other means that do not affect fundamental rights.

§ 7 Prohibition of abuse of rights

The prohibition of abuse of rights is contained in Article 2 of the LC Fundamental Principles. The prohibition of abuse of rights in labour-law relationships complements the statutory requirement to exercise rights and duties resulting from labour-law relationships in accordance with good morals. Compared with the statutory requirement to exercise rights and duties in accordance with good morals, which is a "positive limit of exercise of right", the prohibition of abuse of rights constitutes a "negative limit" of exercise of rights and duties resulting from labour-law relationships.

These statutory requirements, established in Article 2 of the LC Fundamental Principles, expressed both in positive and negative terms, have, apart from their peculiarities, a common legal basis, as they regulate the way of exercising subjective rights in labour-law relationships. Not every misuse of rights contrary to good morals (Article 2 of the LC Fundamental Principles) is also an abuse of right. However, not every abuse of rights is an action contrary to good morals.

Bullying is directly connected with the abuse of rights. Just like the abuse of rights is a special type of illegal action, bullying may also be understood as a special type of abuse of rights. It differs from other cases of abuse of rights in the sense that one of its essential characteristics is material loss and the qualified intention of a person aimed at causing loss. Prohibition of bullying is not established in the LC. Even though it is a qualified "exercise of right", it is beyond doubt, an exercise of right contrary to good morals.

I. Requirement to exercise rights in accordance with good morals

The term "good morals" is closely intertwined with the terms morals and morality. Legal development in Europe and in current academics building on that development usually distinguish between the terms "good morals", and "morals", a "morality", whit the term „fairness" being considered as a term that is, in essence, identical with the term „good morals".[27] Unlike abuse of right, the *contra bonos mores* principle may be understood in more objective terms. In principle, it is not required that the person acting be aware of the fact that he is acting in a way contrary to good morals. Unlike action contrary to good morals, the abuse of rights relies more on the subjective element (fault) most frequently as intention. Not every conduct of an entitled person that is contrary to good morals is an abuse of rights. On the other hand, every abuse of right is a conduct contrary to good morals. It follows from the above that the statutory requirement to exercise subjective rights and legal duties has legal meaning besides the general prohibition of abuse of right.

---

[27] Herzog, H.: Zum Begriffe der „gutten Sitten" im bürgerlichen Gesetzbuche, 33. Breslau, 1910, p. 2

The application practice has, in particular, shown that not all cases of conduct of the entitled person when exercising a subjective right in a way contrary to morals can be regarded as conduct contrary to good morals. The term "good morals" was originally used as a legal and not moral concept. Good morals, in the legal sense, were to serve as a positive limit of exercise of subjective rights. Legal literature started, in this respect, to use the concept legal morals. The term "good morals" was defined by Fischer as morals adapted to the law, which, unlike morals, sets certain "minimum moral thresholds" for the exercise of subjective rights, is guaranteed by the law and the requirements it establishes are, unlike morality, considerably diminished.[28] The basic purpose of the requirement to act in accordance with good morals is to exclude gross violations of morals in exercising rights, to ensure elementary fairness in exercising subjective rights and to observe a certain ethical minimum in exercising subjective rights.

Conduct contrary to good morals must include elements setting a bad example
Conduct contrary to good morals and abuse of right are, according to provisions concerning nullity of legal acts, sanctioned by absolute nullity of legal acts in labour law.

---

[28] Fischer, H. A.: Die Rechtswidrigkeit. München, 1911, p. 77. Orzechowski, W.: Der Verstoss gegen die guten Sitten. Wroclaw, pp. 41–43.

Chapter 4

Terms employee and employer

§ 1 General legal characteristics of the term employee

In labour-law theory, the term employee is not defined, although the legal definition of this term is, under labour legislation in force, is contained in Section 11 of the LC, which states that an employee is a natural person who in labour-law relations and, if stipulated by special regulation, also in similar labour relations, performs dependent work for the employer.

The ECJ has repeatedly dealt with the definition of the term employee in its case law, in particular for the purposes of free movement of employees.[29] In *Lawrie-Blum* (66/85), it was ruled that an employee (worker) is a person who "performs services for and under the direction of another person in return for which he receives remuneration". Individual sources of EU law do not insist on a uniform definition of the term employee in the entire EU. For example, under EU law, Member States may, for the purposes of temporary posting of employees abroad, define the term employee differently (for example with respect to legal position of an employee working for a reduced weekly working time according to the Part-Time Work Directive).

If follows from Section 11 of the LC itself that the essential criterion of defining the term employee is performance of dependent work, which is the object of labour-law relations.

As far as its material scope of application is concerned, under Section 1, the LC regulates only dependent work of employees in labour-law relations or other similar labour relations.

If the work meets the criteria of dependent work and it is performed by a natural person within the meaning of Section 11(1) of the LC, this natural person should always have the legal status of an employee, rather than a trader or an entrepreneur.

The personal dependence of the employee from the employer, his subordination, is not a typical administrative-law dependence because it is established on a contractual basis of an employment contract. Its content is, in principle, determined by the employer's margin of discretion, which depends on the scope of the type of work and the place of performance of work agreed in the employment contract. The degree of dependence of work is determined by the level of the employee's work position.

It follows from the general characteristics of an employment relationship, which include the exclusively personal character of performance of work, that an employee may only be

---

[29] R 53/81, R 13/76, R C-415/93, R 53/81, R 66/85, R 75/63.

a natural person who engages, on the basis of an employment contract, to perform dependent work in person for the employer. In his work in the employment relationship, the employee as a person may not be substituted.

A natural person in the legal position of an employee performs dependent activity in subordination to the employee, on his behalf, and the risk of performance of work is borne by the employer.

The term employee is used in a wider sense and a stricter sense. The wider definition of the term employee includes, not only a natural person as a party to the employment relationship, but also natural persons working in a public service relationship and natural persons working on the basis of agreements on work performed outside of an employment relationship.

In the stricter sense, the term employee denotes only a natural person who, on a contractual basis, performs dependent work in an employment relationship.

From the perspective of previous legislative practice, the labour-law legislation in the Slovak Republic uses, in generally binding legal regulations, the term employee in the wider sense.

The employee's obligation to perform work for another is based on a private-law employment contract, unlike the obligation of a public servant performing work for the State on the basis of an administrative-law decision, even though the Public Service Act uses the term employee also in case of a natural person being in a public-service relationship with the State.

Although they may be included in the general term employee, public servants do not have the necessary legal characteristics of the term employee in labour-law relationships. A public-service relationship is, unlike labour-law relationships, a public-law relationship and not a private-law relationship, in which the State has the legal position of an employer.

It follows from the above that Slovak legislation uses the term employee in the wider sense, which goes beyond the framework of labour-law relations. The wider definition of the term employee is also reflected in Section 11(1) of the LC, which provides that an employee is a natural person who, not only in labour-law relations, but, if stipulated by special regulation, also in similar labour relations performs dependent work for the employer according to his instructions in return for wage or remuneration. Natural persons in the legal position of the employee work under direct control or in accordance with guidelines and instructions issued by the employer himself or by persons employed by the employer. Employees are usually remunerated by means of wages and fixed salaries, although they may also be paid on the basis of profit from sales in monetary form or in kind.

If the performance of dependent work is not covered by the employer with a labour-law relationship, but with a commercial-law relationship, the employee proceeds in contradiction to the LC. If the employee performs working activity having all characteristics of a dependent activity for the employer, he must cover this relationship with an employment relationship and not a commercial-law relationship or a civil-law relationship.

According to current labour-law theory, the employee is also a natural person being in a void labour-law relationship. (for example, in a *de facto* employment relationship)

I. Trader – entrepreneur

A trader is, according to the Trade Act, an entrepreneur, not an employee.

The entrepreneur is often in the legal position of an employer, although not every entrepreneur must be an employer. He is employer only if he employs at least one employee.

According to Section 2 of the Trade Act, a trade is a continuous activity carried out independently, in one's own name, at one's own responsibility and with a view to achieving profit. This type of business is a trade business activity according to the Trade Act.

According to Section 2 of the Commercial Code, business activity is a continuous activity carried out independently by the entrepreneur in his own name, at his own responsibility and with a view to achieving profit. According to the Commercial Code, an entrepreneur is a natural person carrying out a continuous activity in his own name, at his own responsibility, with a view to achieving profit.

According to the judgment of the Constitutional Court of the Czech Republic (case no. III ÚS 140/1999), an entrepreneur is any natural or legal person lawfully performing a business activity (for example, carrying out, independently and continuously, a business activity in his own name, at his own responsibility and with a view to achieving profit). The Commercial Code regulates relations between entrepreneurs (for example, relations connected with business activity [Section 1 of the Commercial Code]). Other legal relations entered into by entrepreneurs as individuals are governed by other regulations, depending on the character of social relations concerned.

The legal position of a bankruptcy administrator or liquidator does not correspond with the legal characteristics of an employee. Natural persons in both work positions perform part of powers of the statutory body, although, in case of a liquidator, this power is limited by the purpose of liquidation.

II. Employee working from home and teleworker

According to Section 52 of the LC, the employment relationship of an employee who performs work for an employer at home or at another agreed place, pursuant to conditions agreed in the employment contract (hereinafter referred to as "home work") or who performs work for an employer at home or at another agreed place, pursuant to conditions agreed in the employment contract, using information technology (hereinafter referred to as "telework") within the working time arranged by himself, is governed by the LC, with the following derogations:
a) provisions on the arrangement of determined weekly working time, continuous daily rest, continuous weekly rest and on stoppage do not apply to such an employee,
b) in cases of important personal obstacles to work, the employee is not entitled to wage compensation from the employer, except in case of death of a family member,
c) such an employee is not entitled to wage for overtime work, to wage surcharge for a period of work on a public holiday, to wage surcharge for the period of night work and to wage compensation for work in difficult working conditions, unless the employee agrees otherwise with the employer.

The employer must adopt measures to facilitate telework, in particular:

a) he shall provide, install and perform regular maintenance of hardware and software necessary for the performance of telework, except in cases where an employee performing telework uses his own equipment,

b) he will ensure, especially with regard to the software, protection of data processed and used in telework,

c) he will inform the employee of all restrictions on the use of hardware and software and also on the penalties for any breach of these restrictions.

The employer must adopt measures to prevent employees that are performing home work or telework from becoming isolated from other employees and give them an opportunity to meet with other employees.

Working conditions for employees who work from home or telework may not disadvantage such employees in comparison with comparable employees who work in the employer's workplace.

An employee is not considered to perform home work or telework if he works at home or at another agreed workplace than usual occasionally or in exceptional circumstances with the consent of the employer or under an agreement with him, provided that the type of work that the employee performs under the employment contract allows this. The employer's duty to adopt measures preventing isolation of an employee performing home work or telework, is not specified by the LC. However, this category of employees should be subject to the employer's social policy in order to avoid their discrimination compared with other employees. This aim is pursued by the employer's duty in Section 152(6) of the LC, which states that the employer must provide the employee performing home work or telework with catering or a financial contribution for catering if no catering in kind is provided or providing catering would be contrary to the nature of the home work or telework performed.

In accordance with the ILO Convention No. 177, the LC defines when an employee is not considered as an employee working from home, although he has certain characteristics of an employee working from home. It is an employee who, with the consent of the employer or after agreement with him, works at home or at another agreed workplace than usual only occasionally (not regularly) or in exceptional circumstances. Apart from the employer's consent or an agreement with him, it is required that the type of work that the employee performs under the employment contract allows this.

With respect to the above mentioned issue, the LC creates quite a wide legal scope for application of freedom of contract of parties to the employment relationship. It is a situation when the place of performance of work is agreed in the employment contract for example in the employer's seat and the parties agree that the employee will work occasionally at home.

III. Professional sportsmen

Sport as fun or game is not work. It becomes work if a professional sportsman is part of a specific sport club, receives remuneration on a regular basis for performance of his work, or he is integrated in the collective of other sportsmen colleagues. Such a professional activity of a sportsman has all the characteristics of a dependent activity, such as an employment relationship, and the sportsman himself has all the characteristics of an employee. Just like in an employment relationship of other human working activities, it is a personal, free performance of work in personal and economic subordination to the beneficiary (sport club in question). Such work is dependent work, even though it is not a typical private-law relationship.

Under legislation in force, subsidiary application of the LC covers professional sportsmen. This also results from the case law of the ECJ, which ruled in *Bosman*[30], that a professional sportsman has, for the purposes of free movement of employees, the legal characteristics of an employee in an employment relationship.

IV. Managers and statutory body members

The LC of the Slovak Republic does not use the term manager. In various places, it only regulates the legal position of an executive employee. Those managers who are not members of the statutory body of the legal person usually have the status of an employee and is in an employment relationship with the legal person. In fact, these managers constitute a category of executive employees of the employer in question that concludes an employment contract or a manager's contract with the employer. If this manager's contract contains essential elements of an employment contract, it must be, with respect to its content, regarded as an employment contract. However, this does not apply to members of statutory bodies of legal persons who do not have the characteristics of an employee in an employment relationship. A manager's contract concluded with members of statutory bodies of legal persons could only be regarded as a contract within the meaning of the Commercial Code (for example, a designation contract or an atypical contract under Section 269(2) of the Commercial Code).

From the perspective of his personal position in the company in question, the term company manager is a considerably broader term than a member of statutory body of a legal person. A manager may, but need not be a member of the statutory body. Members of statutory bodies of legal persons can be characterized as first-rank managers constituting top management.

Besides the members of statutory bodies, there is a wide group of managers (executive employees) at a lower level. In accordance with the terminology of the LC, it is a category of executive employees that performs a certain extent of the employer's functions, but according to labour law, they clearly have the legal position of employees.

Executive employees have a special legal position in labour law. Since he performs not only the employee's, but also the employer's functions, his legal position is at an intermediate level between the legal status of an employer and the legal status of an employee. Executive employees in an employment relationship have, according to the LC, not only more rights, but also more working duties than ordinary employees. Not all working duties applicable to all employees without distinction apply to them, but they are also bound by a whole range of work duties, which only apply to their legal status of executive employee.

---

[30] C-415/93.

The function of a statutory body member should not be carried out in an employment relationship because the position of members of statutory bodies of legal persons does not correspond with all legal characteristics of an employment relationship. They do not perform work in subordination to the employer and they do not comply with his instructions; however, they issue instruction for the entire staff of the employer.[31]

If a manager's contract with respect to managers who are not members of statutory bodies of legal persons does not contain the necessary elements of an employment contract, it cannot be considered as a legal basis of establishing an employment relationship. However, it could have a practical meaning if it existed beside an employment contract if the manager in question carried out, for the employer, not only dependent work, but also work according to a type of contract under the Commercial Code.

§ 2 Term employer

According to labour-law theory, an employer is a person, entitled on the basis of the employment contract, to exact performance of work from the employee. There is still no legal definition of the term employer in Slovak labour law. Unlike the employee, an employer may be not only a natural person, but also a legal person. A natural person or a legal person acquires the legal status of an employer if he employs at least one employee.

Under Section 7(1) of the LC, an employer is a legal person or natural person employing at least one natural person in a labour-law relation and, if stipulated by special regulation, also in similar labour relations.

From the perspective of the employment relationship as a bilateral obligation relationship, the employer may be characterized as an entitled person who, in a labour-law relationship, is not only in the legal position of an entitled person, but also in the legal position of an obliged person. With respect to the legal nature of the employment relationship, the employer has, in particular, a right to exact performance of work from the employee. The employer is, at the same time, in a debtor's position in the labour-law relationship, particularly with respect to his duty to pay wages to the employee for the work carried out.

An employer is a person who, in the labour-law relationship, has a workforce at his disposal and is entitled to give instructions to the employee.[32] The right to give instructions as such does not characterize the term employer. These instructions should be aimed at the employee and they should guide the employee as to the way to perform of work in the employment relationship.

The employer usually owns the company. However, the employer's legal status does not depend on whether he owns the means of production. Often, he will only hire the means of production from another entity

---

[31] Grüll, F., Janert, W. R.: Der Anstellungsvertrag leitenden. Angestellten und Führungskräfte. Wien, 1996.
[32] Handlexikon Arbeitsrecht, Sonderausgabe. Verlag C. H. Beck 1991.

I. Categories of employers

Employers may be classified into categories according to various criteria. The primary criterion of classification of employers is the distinction between employers as legal persons and as natural persons. Another differentiation criterion is the distinction between employers performing business activity and non-business activity. Another important classification criterion results from Section 20 of the Civil Code, which concerns distinction between employers as private-law legal persons and public-law legal persons. Private-law legal persons are established by legal acts of parties to private-law relationships. Public-law legal persons are established either by statute or on the basis of a public-law act adopted on the basis of statute. However, classification of employers on the basis of their legal position in labour-law relationships does not affect their legal position in labour-law relationships because the LC is based on equality of employers.

A. Employer – legal person

Labour law attributes the employer's legal status to every legal person if this person has this legal status according to the Civil Code and provided that the person in question employs at least one employee.

It follows from the above that the status of a legal person is not sufficient for the employer's status, but that the legal person must meet a substantive condition consisting of employing at least one employee. Entities that do not meet this substantive condition may not be in the legal position of an employer.

According to the Civil Code, legal persons are:
- associations of natural or legal persons,
- purpose-based associations of property,
- territorial self-governing units,
- other entities stipulated by statute.

The Civil Code is based on the principle that a legal person has legal capacity (including labour-law capacity), even though it does not define the term legal person. It only establishes its basic identification characteristics, which include name, seat and object of activity of a legal person.

1. Acting on behalf of an employer – legal person

A legal person in the employer's position cannot act on its own, but natural persons must act on their own behalf. The statutory body has full powers to act on behalf of the legal person in all matters. Within the limits set by the employer's internal regulations, other executive employees or other employees empowered in writing may accomplish legal acts on behalf of the legal person.

A legal person may also act by means of a representative, who can either be a legal person or a natural person.

a) Statutory bodies

Legal acts of an employer (legal person) are accomplished in all matters by statutory bodies (for example, by those entitled to do so by a contract establishing the legal person, by a deed of establishment or by statute). Acts of a statutory agent are regarded as personal acts of the legal person. Therefore, acts of a statutory body of a legal person are not acts performed by a representative, but they are acts of the legal person itself. If a legal act of the statutory representative comes into effect, the employer is directly bound by this act.

Statutory bodies are entitled to perform legal acts on behalf of the legal person in all matters. A legal person can have only one statutory body. The statutory body of a legal person is determined by the statute, by a contract establishing the legal person or by a deed of establishment.

The statutory body of a legal person can be individual or collective. State undertakings, budgets or contribution organizations have individual statutory bodies. Business companies, cooperatives, foundations, professional chambers, financial institution, etc. have collective statutory bodies.

Only in certain cases does the statute allow a legal person to have either an individual or a collective statutory body (for example in case of a limited liability company), which can have a statutory body consisting of one or several agents.

The legal position of the statutory body is important not only with respect to its external powers to act on behalf a legal person externally (agent's authorization), but in particular with respect to its internal powers to decide not only issues concerning property (business management), internal administration and organization of a legal person, but also with respect to employees in labour-law matters.

b) Labour-law capacity of an employer – legal person

According to the Civil Code, legal persons are granted full legal capacity. A legal person has capacity for rights and duties, capacity for legal acts, as well as procedural capacity and delictual capacity. Under Section 7(2) of the LC, employers act in labour-law relations in their own name and they have responsibilities resulting from these relations. Legal persons come into being on the date of their registration in the Commercial Register or other register stipulated by statute unless provided otherwise in special regulation.

Regulation of labour-law capacity of an employer (legal person) according to the LC is based on the fact that the employer has the legal status of a legal person, which is granted by civil-law rules. If the employer has the legal status of a legal person according to civil law, the LC also grants labour-law capacity to such an employer provided that the employer employs at least one employee.

c) Labour-law capacity of an organizational unit

Unlike in civil law, a special trait of labour law is that an organizational unit of a legal person can also have legal capacity in labour law, although such unit does not have the status of a legal person according to civil-law rules. Only the legal person as a whole, including the organizational unit, has this capacity under civil law.

The position of organizational units of employers (legal persons) in labour-law relationships results from legislation on the basis of which they were established or from by-laws of citizen association under special legislation.

If an employer (legal person) is party to a labour-law relationship, their organizational unit cannot be party to such a relationship and *vice versa*. An organizational unit that was granted legal capacity under special regulation, has the same position as a legal person, in labour law relationships including the organizational unit.

This peculiarity in assessing labour-law capacity of organizational units collides with the understanding of legal capacity of legal persons under the Civil Code, which grants full legal capacity only to legal persons. Qualification of organizational units as legal entities results explicitly from Section 7 of the LC and it applies exclusively to labour-law relations.

The position of a subsidiary business is different because it is registered in the Commercial Register; however, it is not a separate legal person, but rather, its organizational unit. Legal acts concerning this organizational unit are to be carried out by the manager of the organizational unit of the business registered in the Commercial Register. However, the manager of the organizational unit (subsidiary business) does not act on behalf of the organizational unit, but on behalf of the legal person.

Unlike the employee's legal position during an employment relationship, the employer may be changed, in principle, without any negative effect on the existence of the employment relationship and the employee's legal position. Such a change of employer is, in principle, associated with a general succession of rights and duties resulting from labour-law relations. The new employer enters into all rights, duties and responsibilities of the previous employer. General succession of rights and duties resulting from labour-law relations covers the rights and duties resulting from the normative part of the collective agreement. Transfer of rights and duties resulting from labour-law relations takes place also in case of a transfer of a part of the employer. It is a transfer of rights and duties concerning the part of the employer being transferred. With respect to the transfer of rights and duties resulting from labour-law relations, in case of the transfer of a part of the employer, the principle states that the corresponding personal element must be transferred with the part of material element. For example, if only one business is transferred as part of the undertaking, all employees working in that business are transferred to the new employer and the transfer of undertaking or part of it as such cannot be a reason for notice given by the employer.

B. Employer – natural person

An employer (natural person), unlike an employee (natural person), does not acquire labour-law capacity simultaneously, but similarly (not in the same way) to civil law. Capacity for rights is acquired by a natural person (employer) upon his birth. A conceived child, provided that it is born alive, has this capacity as well. Capacity for legal acts is acquired upon majority. The LC does not regulate explicitly termination of capacity of natural persons for rights and duties. Therefore, also in this case, it is necessary, by analogy of law, to apply civil-law rules according to which capacity for being a legal entity in the position of an employer terminates upon death.

Legal capacity of a natural person (employer) ends upon his death.

According to the LC, the rights and duties of an employer (natural person) resulting from labour-law relations pass, upon his death, to his heirs. If the heir is a minor, he cannot exercise active legal capacity consisting of acquiring rights and duties by his own legal acts. Capacity for legal acts (for example, capacity to assume rights and duties resulting from labour-law relationships by one's own acts) will be exercised until the minor attains 18 years of age, by his statutory representative on his behalf.

Under Section 31 of the Family Act, the statutory representatives of a minor are his parents. A child may be represented by any of his parents that have the capacity for legal acts and the parental rights. A statutory representative is not entitled to perform all legal acts on behalf of a minor. He cannot represent the minor in legal acts that may lead to a collision of interests between parents and children (Section 37 of the Family Act). In contrast, under the Civil Procedure Code, a statutory representative cannot act on behalf of the person represented in a situation where a collision between the interests of the representative and the person represented already exists. In this legal situation, the Family Act should prevail, which is a special act with respect to the Civil Procedure Code.

According to the LC, upon death of an employer (natural person), there is a general succession of heirs concerning the rights and duties resulting from labour-law relations. The heir of the deceased employer enters into all rights, duties and responsibilities. However, until the heritage is settled, the legal position of employees is often difficult. It is not regulated in a way that at least partially protects the interests of employees.

That status of a natural person with labour-law capacity is not sufficient for the employer's status, but the natural person must meet a substantive condition consisting in employing at least one employee in a labour-law relationship. Persons that do not meet this substantive condition may not be in the legal position of an employer. This may be, for example, self-employed traders under the Trade Act. They may be self-employed persons but they are not employers if they do not employ at least one employee.

Legal capacity of a natural person for being an employer does not depend on a trade authorization. A natural person without any authorization for business activity or other activity may be an employer, as well.

Unlike the employee's legal position during an employment relationship, the employer (natural person) may be changed, in principle, without any negative effect on the existence of the employment relationship and the employee's legal position.

§ 3 Employer's legal position

The employer is, in a labour-law relationship, the subject of rights and duties. His main legal duty is to assign work to the employee and pay him for the work carried out.

The employee's legal position is not determined by the agent's authorization of the employer (for example, the authorization to act on his behalf and at his responsibility externally with respect to other entities), but, in particular, the employer's authorization inside the employing entity, by means of which the employer performs his rights and duties also with respect to his employees.

The employer's primary rights include the right to exact performance of work from the employee based on the employee's contractual obligation and the right to exact observance of work discipline from the employee. The employer's legal status constitutes not only a complex of duties, but also a complex of rights. In special provisions of the LC, a whole list of rights of employees linked with the employer's legal duties is contained. In particular, the employer's rights are not listed exhaustively in the LC and may be derived mainly from the statutory list of the employee duties as a counterpart of the employer's rights, which are regulated not only in the LC, but also in other labour-law regulations.

In general, fundamental duties of the employer may be derived from Section 47 of the LC, which characterizes the employee's work obligation.

More specifically, they are regulated in other provisions of the LC and also in other labour-law regulations.

In foreign labour-law literature, besides the main right of the employer to exact performance of work from the employee based on the employee's contractual obligation and to pay him for the work carried out, the right to require loyalty of employees to their employer is mentioned. This is reflected, in particular, in the principle that an employee must refrain from any action liable to harm legitimate interests of his employer and his reputation. On the other hand, unlike in Slovak labour-law rules, the employer's main duties, besides the duty to assign work to the employee and pay him for the work carried out, also include the duty of social care for the employee as a certain compensation for observance of the employee's duty of loyalty with respect to his employer. Previous legislative practice shows that in the LC itself, it will be necessary to find a more suitable and appropriate legal scope for formulation of the employer's rights and duties. Also, it will be necessary for stricter sanctions imposed for non-observance of the employer's main working duties, in particular with respect to his duty to assign work to the employee (to employ him) and to pay him wage for the work carried out. The legal guarantee of observance of these elementary duties by the employer is, in practice, still not satisfactory.

Chapter 5

Employment of foreigners in the Slovak Republic

§ 1 General characteristics – sources of law

Employment of foreigners is one of the problems that is, in every country, in the centre of attention not only with regards to the legislation of the country in question, but also of the entire society. Opinions on employment of foreigners do not always correspond with moral requirements of a civilized society on the verge of the 21st century. The problems associated with employment of foreigners are often used by politicians to increase their political prestige. As well, their attitude to employment of foreigners is often a good basis for increasing nationalism. On the other hand, the fact remains that the EU is growing older and it cannot function without foreigners in the next decades. Due to a long-term adverse demographic development in Europe and in the EU, it is generally presumed that the EU Member States will need in every year in the near future, such a high number of foreign employees that it may lead to a change in Europe's identity.

Slovak labour law establishes, as regards to employment of foreigners in a functioning labour-law relationship, the principle of equal treatment, which is enshrined in Article 1 of the LC Fundamental Principles and Section 13 of the LC. Pursuant to Section 21 of the Act No. 5/2004 Coll. on Employment Services, a foreigner being a party to labour-law relationships has the same legal position as a citizen of the Slovak Republic.

This principle applies to full extent to labour-law relations already established by an employment contract.

By contrast, Slovak legislation contains different rules with respect to access to the labour market of the Slovak Republic, depending on whether the person in question is an EU citizen (who is not regarded as a foreigner) or a foreigner (third country national). Third country nationals are subject to different rules of access to the labour market of the Slovak Republic. With regard to EU citizens, pursuant to Article 45 of the TFEU, no restrictions concerning access to the labour market may apply. On the other hand, for a third country national to be employed in the territory of the Slovak Republic, he needs a work permit and a residence permit. The work permit may be granted to a foreigner by the competent authority if the free post cannot be occupied by a work applicant registered in the register of work applicants.

Just like in other EU Member States, a special regime of the EU blue card applies to highqualifed professions of third country nationals, whose access and presence in the EU labour markets is regulated by the Directive 2009/50//EU. The possibility of employing third country nationals in the territory of the Slovak Republic also applies to asylum seekers that may access the labour market under special regulation.

§ 2 Conflict-of-law rules

With regards to the employment of foreigners in the territory of the Slovak Republic, Section 5 of the LC establishes subsidiary application of the LC, unless legal regulations on international private law provide otherwise.

Under Section 5 of the LC the labour law relations of employees performing work in the territory of the Slovak Republic and of a foreign employers are governed by the LC, unless legal regulations on international private law provide otherwise. Similarly, labour law relationships between foreigners and stateless persons working in the territory of the Slovak Republic and employers with a place of business in the territory of the Slovak Republic are governed by the LC, unless legal regulations on international private law provide otherwise.

The application of international private law comes into consideration in the cases of an employment relationship where one party is a foreigner. This includes labour relationships in which either the employee is an foreigner or a Slovak citizens is employed by an employer who has status of a foreigner.

Of fundamental significance for the determination of the concrete applicable law are:
- The Convention on the Law Applicable to Contractual Obligations, the so-called Rome Convention of 19 June 1980 is binding for the Slovak Republic from 01.08.2006 (Notice published in the Coll. under no. 414/2006 Coll.),
- Regulation (EC) No 593/2008 of the European Parliament and of the Council of 17 June 2008 on the law applicable to contractual obligations ("Rome I Regulation"),
- Act No. 97/1963 Coll. on International Private and Procedural Law, as amended.

I. Rome I Regulation

Current EU Member States and EEA countries are bound, in regard to contractual obligations, by the Rome I Regulation, which regulates the actions of parties to an employment relationship in detail. According to the principle of subsidiarity, the Rome I Regulation prevails over the LC. In matters regulated by the Rome I Regulation, the Act No. 97/1963 Coll. on International Private and Procedural Law currently applies only to a very limited extent.

In particular, the parties to the labour-law relationship may choose the applicable law. If the parties to the employment relationship do not make full or partial choice of foreign law, their labour-law relations will be governed by the LC and other labour-law regulations of the Slovak Republic (the law of performance of work by the employee).

A. Choice of law

Choice of law is a special type of conflict-of-law contract. An employment contract may be, with regard to conflict-of-law rules, governed by several legal orders. In this case, the labour-law relationship may be governed by several subjective statuses of employment contract. Rome I Regulation allows changing a choice of law made before or during the labour-law relationship by agreement.

In this respect, however, it must be observed that choice of law according to conflict of laws under Rome I Regulation applies only to individual labour law and not collective labour law.

Under Rome I Regulation, choice of law with regard to employment contracts should not cause employees to be deprived of the protection afforded to them by mandatory provisions of the legal order that would apply if there had been no choice of law.

B. Principle of employee's benefit.

How does one assess the employee's benefit, comprehensively or individually, according to the employee's specific legal claims? The problem of the application practice of international private law is a certain degree of doubt and uncertainty as to how such comparison, with a view to determining the employee's benefit, should be carried out. It must be assessed whether the employee's benefit should apply to every aspect of his legal status specifically, or if the quality of the employee's legal status under the law chosen is to be determined globally on the one hand, and on the other hand, it must be compared with the quality of his legal status under the law that would have been applied if there had been no choice of law. Rules of conflict of labour laws do not regulate this problem specifically.

In regard to protection of the employee, competing legal orders should be assessed more comprehensively than individually. Comparison of competing legal orders should be focused only on that part of these legal orders that regulates protection of the employee and that the parties cannot derogate from by agreement.

The employee's benefit could be determined by a global comparison between competing regulations, by an individual comparison or by a comparison of legally and substantively related working conditions. According to academic literature, the best option is to carry out a comparison according to legally and substantively related working conditions.

When the contracting parties do not make any choice of law, the contract will be governed:
a) by the law of the country in which the employee habitually carries out his work, even if he carries out this work temporarily also in another country,
b) by the law of the country in which the employer's seat is situated, if the employee does not habitually carry out work in one country, provided that the employment contract or employment relationship does not have a closer relationship with another country, where the law of the country of this country and not the law of the employer's seat would have been applied.

As follows from the above, the objective contract status is defined by two alternatives. In the first place, the place of habitual performance of work is decisive. This does not change if the employee is temporarily posted in another country. If such a habitual place does not exist, it is necessary to determine the objective contract status according to the law of the employer's seat.

The so-called "escape clause" prefers a close link with another country, which results from an assessment of all circumstances of the case at hand. The factors legally relevant for assessing a closer link with another country include, in particular, nationality, language of contract or place of conclusion of contract. This so-called "escape clause" is aimed at preserving justice in labour-law relationships in particularly extreme situations (for example, in labour-law relations in maritime law, which are connected with the country in question solely by its flag).

1. Examples of subjective status of employment contract and objective status

Fundamental rights and freedoms

Choice of law cannot be applied by the parties to the employment relationship if its application is contrary to fundamental rights and freedoms in the country where the work is carried out (e.g. coalition freedom).

Establishment, modification and termination of employment relationship

These essential legal aspects of employment relationship are assessed according to the status of employment contract, which also applies to the complex of rights and duties resulting from establishment, modification and termination of the employment relationship. Pre-contractual relations are also assessed according to the subjective status of the employment contract even if the parties have not yet signed an employment contract.

Problem of agency employment

Irrespective of which law governs the employment contract or where and which place the employment contract was signed, the contracting parties must submit to public-law regulations of the Slovak Republic on agency work. Since these regulations affect the employer's legal status, this status must be governed by legal regulations on agency employment of the country where the work is carried out.

Legal regulation of work permit

Legal regulation of work permits for foreigners would be applied even in cases where the contracting parties submitted the employment contract to foreign law, which also applies in case of work carried out in a country different than an EU Member State or a EEA Member State.

Interferences with the principle of equal treatment

Given the mandatory nature of the principle of equal treatment according to the legal order, if there are any problems concerning its application, possible interferences with the principle of equal treatment would be governed by the legal order of the country in which work is carried out, even if the parties to the employment relationship applied a choice of a different legal order. The legal order of the host country would not have to be applied and the contracting parties could abide by the law chosen in cases where the extent of protection of the employee in regulation of this problem would be, in case of application of choice of law, more favourable in comparison to mandatory rules of the host state.

Restrictions of performance of work for specific groups of employees

Given the public-law character of rules governing the objective status of persons with health disability, the objective legal status of the employment contract would have to be applied irrespective of the application of choice of foreign law, except for cases where the law chosen by the parties would be more favourable for the employee compared to the law of the Slovak Republic.

Admissibility of complementary forms of employment

This applies, in particular, to fixed-term employment relationships, partial employment obligation, and employee lending. Although the EU law is aimed at harmonizing the legal regulations of these so-called temporary employment relationships, this problem is very significant in regards to employees of third countries that are not EU Member States.

The admissibility of a fixed-term employment relationship is regulated by the subjective status of employment contract (for example, by the law chosen by the parties to the employment relationship and the maximum admissible duration of the fixed-term employment relationship) must be governed by the objective contract status. For example, if the legal order chosen by the parties does not contain any legal restrictions on the duration of a fixed-term employment contract, the foreign law chosen would be contrary to the principle of public order of the host country.

Work in an employment relationship for reduced weekly working time (partial-obligation employment relationship) does not cause any problems when the subjective and the objective contract statuses of the employment contract are not different from each other. Irrespective of the subjective status of the employment contract, it would be necessary to apply the objective status with regards to the principle of equal treatment, if, due to its non-application, the social-law protection of the employee would be less favourable than the legal regulation of the country where the employee habitually carries out his work.

Conditions of temporary posting of employees for performance of work with another employer are governed by the subjective status of employment contract that applied to the employee at the time before being posted for work with another employer. A different procedure would have to be applied in case of "pseudolending", where the agency needs approval from state authorities for this activity. In some countries, lent employees need a special permit. Therefore, in these cases, it is the public-law regulation of the state where employees carry out the work being the subject of lending that prevails. In these cases, the law of the place where the workforce is to be used for the performance of work is decisive. It follows from the above that a foreign undertaking would need an authorization from the country in question if it were to lend employees for temporary work in this country. Legal relations between the using employer and the lender are governed by general rules of conflict of laws, except for cases where the object of lending is a prohibited activity.

Employee's duties

In principle, the employee's duties are governed by the chosen law (for example, by the subjective status of employment contract). The subjective status of the employment contract also determines the specification of the employee's working conditions by means of the employer's right to give instructions to employees. The same applies to liability relations arising as a legal consequence of infringing these duties of employees.

Working time

In conflict of laws, the question of working time has particular importance. Since almost all aspects of working time are mandatory, the parties to an employment relationship must abide by the law of the place of performance of work (for example, maximum working time, night work, overtime work) if they are formulated in the law of performance of work legally formulated as requirements or prohibitions. This does not allow the application of subjective status of employment contract, but the law of real performance of work. Even if the question of maximum working time were not part of the "hard core" of working conditions, even then (irrespective of choice of law), from the perspective of conflict of laws, the question of maximum and minimum working time, public holidays and overtime work would be governed by the law of the country in which the work is carried out.

Work on public holidays

Since typical legal regulations of public law of mandatory nature are involved, parties to an employment relationship must abide by the law of the host country. This applies, in particular, to legal regulations concerning occupational safety and health, issues of working time, rest time, child work, working conditions of adolescent employees, special protection of mothers and protection of persons with health disability. Whether a specific day is a public holiday and whether it is a working day is a very important question for the application of conflict-of-law rules. This issue is not governed by the subjective status of the employment contract (for example, by the law chosen) but by the law of the place of performance of work. The employer must, on the day in question, not only respect the right of the employee to time-off from work, but he must also provide him with a wage or with wage compensation for a public holiday if the law of the country where work is carried out stipulates so. This conclusion also applies in cases where the subjective status of an employment contract explicitly excludes this (for example, with reference to the fact that the public holiday in question is not a public holiday according to the law chosen or most frequently according to the law of the habitual place of performance of work).

With regard to this problem, in practice, a situation may arise where, according to the law chosen (subjective status of employment contract), public holidays include such days that are not, in the place of performance of work, considered as public holidays and the number of public holidays according to the law chosen and the law of habitual performance of work are different. In these situations the employer should provide wage or wage compensation only for those public holidays that prevent the employee from working due to mandatory rules.

Annual paid holiday

Annual paid holiday is governed by the status of the employment contract, depending on the law chosen. This applies to the application of conflict of law rules to employment relationships except for the temporary posting of employees in EU Member States, in which case, paid holiday, just like working time, must be governed by the law of the host country according to Directive No. 96/71/EC.

Unlike this type of holiday, special complementary paid holidays (for example, for employees with serious health disability and for protection of adolescent employees) are, in several countries, legally formulated as strict public-law regulations that must prevail over the law chosen if this law does not guarantee such a level of social-law protection as the rules of the country in which work is carried out. The same applies to protection of employees on maternal or paternal leave.

Given the fact that these elements of the labour-law relationship also constitute the content of "hard core" of working conditions of employees under Directive No. 96/71/EC, the parties to the labour-law relationship must abide by the law of the host country.

Problem of stoppage and other causes of interruption of work due to *force majeure*

The issue of wage compensation provided by the employer is governed by the applicable law chosen according to the law of the subjective status of the employment contract.

Occupational safety and health

The issue of occupational safety and health, as the typical public-law part of employment relationships, is always governed by the law of place of performance of work, irrespective of the law chosen. Conflict of laws in this field within the EU is, in fact, losing importance given the relatively high degree of harmonization of rules on occupational safety and health in EU Member States.

C. Mandatory rules

Mandatory rules are such rules that are established primarily in public interest, due to aspects concerning public policy (employment, healthcare, social policy). They need not be public-law rules, although there is a clear superior interest that must prevail over the ordinary labour-law protection of employees. Mandatory rules apply, under Rome I Regulation, not only to the subjective status of the employment contract, but also to the objective status of the employment contract.

It is for the national legislator to define the category of mandatory rules. Beyond doubt, such rules should include rules concerning occupational safety, working time and working rest, and the protection of minors and adolescent employees, mothers and persons with health disability. It is dubious in legal literature if these rules include rules concerning the general protection of an employee against notice.

§ 3 Right to free movement of employees

The right to free movement of employees, just like the right to free movement of services, is one of the fundamental economic freedoms constituting the basis of the EU. Besides other economic freedoms, there economic freedoms are fundamental principles. It results not only from the founding treaties, but also from current case-law of the ECJ. Fundamental economic freedoms may be invoked by EU citizens directly against the State. According to case-law, fundamental economic freedoms are applicable also in the relationships between private parties. In *Laval* (C-341/05) and *Viking Line* (C-438/05), the ECJ recognized free movement of services and/or the freedom of establishment as a "fundamental principle".[33]

In the early history of the European Communities, fundamental freedoms did not have such a strong position as they do nowadays. In the 1970s, the ECJ derived a directly applicable right from the determination of objectives that were to be implemented by secondary law according to the founding treaties. This understanding of fundamental economic freedoms advocated by the ECJ led to an unexpected liberalization of the EU market.

The right to free movement of employees is enshrined in Article 45 of the TFEU. According to previous case-law of the ECJ, the right to the free movement of employees is the core of free movement of persons in the EU.

The right to free movement of employees covers all phases of occupation, including job seeking, performance of work and the residence of an employee in a Member State with a view to searching for a new job. The right to free movement of employees concerns not only labour-law issues, but it also concerns social security law. It also reflects elements of administrative law.

For labour-law relations implemented in the territory of the Slovak Republic, it is very important that, in free movement of employees, the term worker according to EU law must be applied. It is an autonomous concept of EU law, which cannot be freely modified by Member States. It is established in Article 45 of the TFEU and specified in abundant case-law of the ECJ.

The core of the right to free movement of employees under Article 45 of the TFEU is the prohibition of discrimination of employees from another EU Member State. The Directive 2004/38/EC codifies the rules on free movement of employees and is based on the principle of EU citizenship.

I. Prohibition of discrimination of employees in free movement of employees

A. Access to employment

There is a prohibition of discrimination in access to employment, as well as a prohibition of discrimination in performance of employment due to the employee's nationality.

The right to equal treatment irrespective of nationality is a legal claim that may be applied against Member States, which must guarantee equality in treatment, in particular

---

[33] Zwanziger, B.: Nationale Koalitionsfreiheit vs. Europäische Grundfreiheiten aus deutscher Sicht, Recht der Arbeit, 2009, Sonderbeilage Heft 5, pp. 110-111.

in regard to access to employment, directly binding the employers of the Member State. Besides equal access to employment, the prohibition of discrimination on the grounds of nationality also includes prohibition of discrimination in performance of employment with regard to working conditions and remuneration and conditions of notice, as well as the right to remain in the Member State after having been employed for the purposes of job seeking.

B. Right to free pursuit of employment and prohibition of discrimination

Every national of an EU Member State, irrespective of his permanent residence, is entitled to perform a work activity for remuneration in a different Member State, in accordance with the legal regulations of that State. Prohibition of discrimination applies to the pursuit of employment.

The legal basis of prohibition of discrimination in employment is described in Article 45 of the TFEU.

Prohibition of discrimination applies to the establishment, content and the termination of the employment relationship, the remuneration for work and requalification measures, as well as other social and tax benefits.

Prohibition of discrimination means that the employee's nationality may not be a differentiation factor of working conditions in the widest sense.

Indirect discrimination occurs frequently, mainly in regard to the employee's residence.

Prohibition of discrimination in pursuit of employment applies not only to remuneration for work and work reintegration after temporary incapacity for work of the employee, but also to other tax and social benefits and qualification and requalification measures. In recent years, the ECJ has paid increased attention to the definition of the term "social benefit". According to several rulings of the ECJ, the term "social benefit" includes all measures and benefits, irrespective of their direct link with the employment relationship, that may be deemed to be suitable for supporting mobility of employees within the EU.

§ 4 Temporary posting of employees

The temporary posting of employees in a different EU Member State or EEA Member State is governed by Directive 1996/71/EC.

One of the main purposes of this directive is to eliminate differences in basic conditions for free competition of entities doing business in the free movement for services. This purpose is achieved by the fact that, as a matter of administrative coercion, they require that, in the "hard core", in case of temporary posting of employees, the law of the host country applies, irrespective of conflict-of-law rules. Application of the law of the host country is not required only if the law of the country from which the employee is posted is more favourable to the temporarily posted employee. In this way, the European legislator protects the national labour market of EU Member States and EEA Member States. According to the directive, the term worker of the country where the worker is posted is decisive. This shows that, unlike conflict-of-law rules, the directive clearly goes beyond the individual level.

In case of the temporary posting of employees from an EU or EEA State in the Slovak Republic, the term employee in the host country is decisive as defined by Section 11 of the LC. In case of the temporary posting of employees from the Slovak Republic, the term employee as defined by the country of the temporary posting of employees, as well as the entire content of the hard core as defined by Directive 1996/71/EC and Section 5(2) of the LC, must be respected.

The Directive does not limit the temporary posting of employees with respect to time, although it entitles Member States to establish such time limits in regard to the temporary posting of employees. For the purposes of the temporary posting of employees to the territory of the Slovak Republic, the Slovak Republic does not establish a maximum duration for the temporary posting of employees.

Article 1(3) of the Posted Workers Directive defines three cases of the temporary posting of workers:

- posting in the stricter sense under a contract on provision of services (for example, in particular a work contract or supplier contract),
- posting within an undertaking or a group of undertakings (for example, in particular a concern),
- cross-border provision of the workforce.

In all three cases, cross-border activity of employees is involved. There must always be an employment contract with the undertaking making the posting situated in a different country. The temporary posting of employees should not apply to daily cross-border commuters, although it is not explicitly stipulated by the LC of the Slovak Republic. Likewise, the legal model of the temporary posting of employees should not apply to employees having no relation with the country from which the posting is made and having entered into their employment contract individually with a partner abroad. However, specific rules in this respect are not contained in the LC of the Slovak Republic.

Protection of employees also applies to those employed only with a view to posting. This protection is guaranteed even in case of short-term posting.

I. Guarantee of hard core of working conditions

The hard core is defined exhaustively in Article 3 of the Posted Workers Directive and it ranges from working time and protection applied, through to minimum pay and minimum paid annual holidays and through to non-discrimination. By contrast, the hard core does not include, in particular, rules concerning obstacles to work or the termination of the employment relationship, including various forms of protection against notice and dismissal. The Posted Workers Directive (1996/71/EC) has been transposed into the LC of the Slovak Republic under Section 5.

Provisions of Section 5 of the LC fully transpose the legal requirements under Directive No. 96/71/EC concerning the posting of workers to perform work in Member States of the EEA.

Section 5(2) of the LC states that the employment relationship of workers who are posted by their employers to perform work to another employer from a European Union

Member State to the territory of the Slovak Republic shall be governed by this Act, special regulations or the relevant collective agreement, which regulate:
a) the length of the working time and rest periods,
b) the length of holidays,
c) minimum wage, minimum wage claims and overtime wage rates,
d) occupational health and safety,
e) working conditions for women, adolescents and employees caring for a child younger than three years of age,
f) equal treatment for men and women and a prohibition of discrimination,
g) working conditions in the case of employment by a temporary employment agency.

It follows from the above that, in case of the temporary posting of employees to another EU or EEA State, legal orders of at least two countries apply. In particular, in case of the temporary posting of third country employees by their employer situated in the territory of a Member State to the territory of another Member State, the labour-law relationship is governed by several legal orders. This circumstance does not increase legal certainty of parties to the employment relationship, although it is beyond doubt, a sign and consequence of application of their contract autonomy.

In case of the temporary posting of employees within the supranational movement of services, very complicated legal situations may arise, which results from the necessity to apply several legal orders at the same time. It is, on the one hand, the law of the Member State from which the posting is made and, on the other hand, the law of the host State. However, this legal model is the simplest. In fact, considerably more difficult legal situations may arise in practice.

If an employer wants to avoid mistakes in numerous cases of the temporary posting of employees, he must, even before the temporary posting of his employees, know which legal order of which State and to what extent he must prefer, irrespective of what law governs the employment contract itself. Determination of the extent of necessity of application of applicable law according to Rome I Regulation, besides the duty to abide by the law of the host country with regard to the hard core of working conditions, is one of the fundamental legal problems concerning the temporary posting of employees. Determination of the necessary extent of the application of the law of the State in which work is carried out, beyond the hard core, depends on the specific labour-law problem of the labour-law relation. Each problem of a wide range of labour-law institutions is governed either by the subjective status of the employment contract chosen by the contracting parties or by the objective status of the host country that must be respected by the parties, irrespective of the law chosen. With regard to the temporary posting of employees in question, mandatory rules prevail over both statuses.

The application of these provisions is relatively difficult, in particular with respect to employers. Prior to the conclusion of contracts with their business partners, employers do not possess all the legal information necessary to fully comply with the cited "core" working conditions required by the Directive. Act No. 125/2006 Coll. on Labour Inspection transferred the competence to collect and provide this information to the National Labour Inspectorate headquartered in Košice. As confirmed by experience of employers, this headquarters does not perform this competence to the full extent.

With regards to the previous practice concerning the temporary posting of employees under Section 5 of the LC, Slovak employees are mostly posted to EU or EEA countries. Under the legal model of temporary posting of the employees, as regulated by Directive 1996/71/EC, it is better for Slovak employees, from the perspective of quality of legal position, to be working in the "old" EU Member States. Employees are posted to the territory of the Slovak Republic only from countries that are economically less developed than the Slovak Republic. This applies to the "new" EU Member States in which labour is even cheaper than in the Slovak Republic. The employees posted temporarily to the territory of the Slovak Republic come mostly from Romania, Bulgaria and Latvia.

Chapter 6

Establisment of employment relationship

The LC imposes certain duties on future parties to the employment relationship even before conclusion of the employment contract (for example, before establishment of the employment relationship).

Pre-contractual relations precede the conclusion of the employment contract, but they must be considered as labour-law relations under Section 1 of the LC.

The LC in force, within the pre-contractual relations, regulates pre-contractual relations in the form of a complex of information duties of the future employer and of a natural person seeking the establishment of an employment relationship.

§ 1 Employer's information duties

The duty of the future employer, before establishment of employment contract, to inform the natural person of his rights and duties resulting from the employment contract is formulated quite broadly and it includes, in part, the employer's duty to inform the natural person of working and wage conditions. At the same time, the employer must inform the future employee of the legal rules for securing occupational safety and health, which must be observed by the employee at work, and of the provisions regulating the prohibition of discrimination.

Under Section 41(2) and (3) of the LC, if the health capacity to work or the mental capacity to work pursuant to special law is required for the performance of work, the employer may only conclude an employment contract with a natural person having the health capacity or the mental capacity to perform such work. A similar legal restriction applies to the employer if he intends to conclude an employment contract with an adolescent employee.

In case of work for which health capacity to work or mental capacity to work pursuant to special law is not required or if such a special law does not exist, the employer is not entitled to require information concerning the health condition of the natural person applying for employment. Conclusion of employment contract irrespective of the employee's health capacity must be regarded as a breach of mandatory provisions of the law by the employer with a possibility of sanctions imposed, in particular, by the labour inspection.

The employer has duties also with respect to statutory representatives of adolescent employees. Before the conclusion of the employment contract, he must ask the statutory representative of the adolescent employee for his opinion. The opinion of the statutory representative before conclusion of an employment contract with an adolescent employee under the LC is important from the perspective of the interest of the adolescent employee himself. However, their lack of opinion does not affect the validity of the legal act of conclusion of the employment contract.

Under Section 41(6) of the LC, the employer may require only information concerning the work to be carried out from a natural person applying for employment. The LC or a different labour-law regulation does not define the scope of information concerning the employee's work because the scope of this information depends on the specific type of work to be agreed by the contracting parties in the employment contract.

Apart from the general legal definition of the employer's right to information within precontractual relations, the LC establishes an exhaustive list of information that may not be required by the employer from the employee in pre-contractual relations.

Under Section 41(6) of the LC, the employer may not require, from natural persons, information concerning:

a) pregnancy,
b) family relationships,
c) integrity, except for work requiring integrity as laid down by a special regulation, or
d) political affiliation, trade union membership and religious affiliation.

The Act No. 5/2004 Coll. on Employment Services, amending certain laws, as amended, extends the prohibition imposed on the employer in pre-contractual relations. Under Section 62(3) of the Act, the employer may not require, when choosing an employee, information concerning not only the sexual orientation of the applicant, but also any other information contrary to good morals.

This act also forbids employers to publish job offers containing any restriction and discrimination.

In this way, the legislator wanted to emphasize, in pre-contractual relations, the protection of rights of natural persons applying for establishment of a labour-law relationship.

The prohibition to require information concerning the employee's integrity does not apply in cases of work requiring integrity as laid down by a special regulation, or if the integrity requirement is demanded by the nature of work which the natural person is to perform in an employment relationship. The employee is demonstrated by an excerpt from the criminal record, for certain work categories, a copy of the criminal record.

The prohibition to require a specific type of information applies also to information concerning political affiliation, trade union membership and religious affiliation.

§ 2 Information duties of a natural person – future employee

The employee's answers should be true. A false answer given by the future employee could establish a ground for termination of the employment contract by the employer. The requirement concerning veracity of the employee's answers applies only to questions concerning information that may be required by the employer from the employee.

One part of the information duties relates to information concerning facts impeding the performance of work. The other part of the information duties concerns information that may cause harm to the employer.

The information impeding the performance of work should have been described by the legislator, with respect to a future employment relationship, in the conditional (for example, it should have been information that would impede the performance of work such as health-related reasons). Therefore, such information may include, in particular, information concerning the employee's health condition (for example, when the employer hires an employee for risky work).

The information that may cause harm to the employer is not specified in the LC. Such information includes information concerning the future employee with respect to performance of a competing activity for another employer.

The LC also imposes on an adolescent natural person (potential employee) a duty to inform his future employer of the length of working time carried out for another employer. This legal duty is very important in regard to Section 85 of the LC, which establishes a maximum weekly working time of 30 hours for an adolescent employee, if he is younger than 16 years of age, and a amximum 37,5 hours if he is over 16 years of age. This legal limit of maximum weekly working time applies also if the adolescent employee works for several employers. An employer who hires an adolescent natural person in an employment relationship must know, before the conclusion of the employment contract, the existing scope of work obligation of a potential employee with another employer. Once the adolescent applicant for work complies with his information duty concerning the length of working time with another employer, the employer is, in fact, able to decide, with full knowledge of the case, whether to establish an employment relationship with the adolescent applicant for work despite the fact that this applicant has an employment relationship with another employer. Such a pre-contractual information duty with respect to the future employer does not apply to an employee having attained 18 years of age. Under legislation in force, the employer cannot make the right decision, with knowledge of the case, whether to hire in an employment relationship, a natural person that will work only for him or that, when applying for an employment relationship, already has a different employment relationship with another employer.

If the employer infringes his legal information duties, under Section 41(9) of the LC, he may be sued by the applicant for employment in the competent court. Provided that he proves that the information beyond Section 41(5), (6) and (8) of the LC has been required, he is entitled, under paragraph (9) of that Section, to appropriate financial compensation. It would be a labour dispute resulting from labour-law relations, even though an employment contract has not yet been concluded.

§ 3 Establishment of employment relationship by employment contract

Establishment of employment relationship by means of an employment contract in labourlaw relations specifies the constitutional right of free choice of profession and other paid activity.

Establishment of the employment relationship by an employment contract is the only way of establishing an employment relationship. Designation as the legal basis of establishment of a public service labour relationship applies, according to legislation in force, only to labour relations governed by the Public Service Act.

In case of labour relations governed by the Act on Performance of Work in Public Interest, designation is legally formulated as a prerequisite of the establishment of the employment relationship by an employment contract if a special regulation stipulates so and does not establish an employment relationship.

The employer is not always fully aware of the fact that the process of the conclusion of an employment contract is very important. It can often, for a very long time, affect the quality of his legal status in a positive or negative way. This applies, in particular, to the scope of the discretion of the employer with respect to his employee. The employer should, in particular, pay attention to the extent of necessary elements of the employment contract, because these elements determine his discretion with respect to his employee.

Under legislation in force, an employment relationship may be established by an employment contract. Even though all employment contracts, with respect to legal effects, establish employment relationships, the content of the employment relationship is, with respect to its quality, different depending on whether it is a full-time or a part-time employment contract. Differences in legal position of the employer and the employee also arise depending on if it is an employment contract for indefinite period or for a fixed-term.

I. Form of employment contract

Section 43 requires a written form of employment contract. Non-observance of a written form of employment contract does not cause nullity of the employment contract as a bilateral legal act, although the employer infringes labour-law regulations by this, for which he can be sanctioned for by the labour inspection authorities. If a written employment contract does not contain the necessary elements according to Section 43 the LC, the employer must, within a month of the establishment of the employment relationship, issue a document confirming that the employee has been hired. Such document must contain elements established by the LC for the content of employment contract in Section 43 of the LC.

II. Content of employment contract

An employment contract establishes an employment relationship as an obligation-law relationship with a complex legal structure. It creates quite an extensive complex of rights and duties of parties, which, with respect to number and scope, cannot be reflected in the content of an employment contract. A great part of the rights and duties of parties to an employment relationship results from the mandatory provisions of the LC and other labour-law regulations, from which the parties cannot derogate from when formulating the content of an employment contract.

Given the importance of employment contract as a legal fact establishing an employment relationship, the legislator requires a certain minimum content of employment contract. Employment contract should be a bilateral legal act agreed upon by the contracting parties. It is important not only in regard to assessing validity of employment contract as a legal act, but also due to the fact that the content of employment contract agreed often, for a very long duration of employment relationship, directly determines the quality of legal status of both parties to the employment relationship.

Section 43 of the LC defines the following necessary elements of an employment contract:

a) type of work for which the employee was accepted, and its brief description,
b) place of work performance (municipality, part of municipality, or place otherwise determined),
c) date of commencement of work, and
d) wage conditions, unless agreed in collective agreement.

Apart from the above elements, an employment contract can contain other elements, in particular, further material benefits may be agreed in the employment contract.

Where the place of work performance is abroad, the employer shall also stipulate in the employment contract

a) duration of work performance abroad,
b) currency in which wages or part thereof shall be paid,
c) further settlements in cash or in kind relating to performance of work abroad, and
d) possible conditions of the employee's return from abroad.

This information contained shall only be provided to the employee only in the case that his time of employment abroad exceeds one month

A. Type of work

The LC or a different labour-law regulation does not specify what the type of work is and how it is to be agreed to by the parties. Although the LC does not specify how widely the type of work should be defined in the employment contract, it cannot be so wide as to cause nullity of the employment contract (in the part that is uncertain) as a legal act due to uncertainty. The type of work should not be agreed to by the parties so as to allow any work to be assigned.

The type of work is mostly the work position (function), for which the employee is hired in an employment relationship. With respect to the requirement of certainty of legal acts, the type of work agreed should correspond with the type of definition of work.

Correct definition of the type of work in the employment contract directly determines the scope of the employer's discretion with respect to the employee. The employer's discretion is as wide as the type of work is defined in the employment contract. By contrast, if the type of work is defined in the employment contract too strictly, the employer's discretion with respect to the employee will be very limited.

Besides the type of work, Section 43 of the LC requires that a brief description of the type of work should be included in the employment contract. This means that certain characteristic or typical working activities of the employee must be listed, which will be carried out by the employee within the type of work agreed more generally.

B. *Place of performance of work*

The place of performance of work, as the next essential element of an employment contract, is very important because it directly determines the scope of the employer's discretion with respect to the employee. The employer may not change the place of the performance of work agreed in the employment contract unilaterally and assign, on a temporary or permanent basis, the employee to a place of the performance of work other than that stipulated in the employment contract.

The LC does not specify the form and scope of the agreement on the place of performance of work in the employment contract. It is only based on the presumption that the place of the performance of work in the employment contract will be a municipality or a part of a municipality. It does not exclude a place defined differently.

Although one place of the performance of work is most frequently stipulated by the parties in the employment contract, the parties may also stipulate several places of the performance of work in the employment contract. If several places of the performance of work are stipulated, the parties should determine which of these places of the performance of work will be the principal place of the performance of work (regular workplace) This is necessary during the employment relationship, in particular with respect to providing travel reimbursement to the employee.

The place of the performance of work may also be the employee's home (home employee) or a different place, when the employee has the status of a home employee. Parties to an employment relationship should define the place of performance of work in the employment contract in form of a valid legal act.

The definition of the place of performance of work depends, in particular, on the employer's organizational structure. The nature of work performed is also a relevant factor in determining the place of performance of work. The place of performance of work must be distinguished from the workplace. The place of performance of work is usually a broader term. The workplace is a certain area where the employee should carry out his work within the organizational unit. It is an office, construction site or workshop. In rare cases, in case of a very narrow definition the place of performance of work, it cannot be ruled out that the premises of the employee's workplace will correspond with the premises constituting the place of performance of work stipulated in the employment contract.

The usual place of the performance of work is the seat of the employer or his organizational unit, although the contracting parties may agree in the employment contract that the employee will carry out the type of work agreed at home. In other words, the place of performance of work will be his own home.

The place of performance of work agreed is very important because it directly determines the scope of the employer's discretion with respect to the employee. In fact, under legislation in force, the employer may not change the employee's place of performance of work unilaterally. The place of performance of work agreed is also essential to legal qualification of business trips, although the Travel Reimbursement Act allows for an agreement on the regular workplace, which is useful , particularly in case of a more broadly defined place of performance of work.

If the work is to be carried out in various workplaces, which cannot be specifically defined at the time of concluding the employment contract, the place of performance of work must be defined in the employment contract differently, according to conditions under which work is to be carried out (for example, by defining a certain territorial unit or borders of a territorial unit).

C. Date of commencement of work

The date of commencement of work is also an essential element of the employment contract. The employment relationship is established from the date stipulated as the date of commencement of work. The date of commencement of work cannot fall on a date preceding the termination of compulsory school attendance. The date of commencement of work is usually determined in the employment contract as a specific calendar day. However, the date of commencement of work may also be determined in a different way raising no doubts as to the time of establishment of employment relationship (for example, as to what the parties to the employment relationship wanted to stipulate). The date of commencement of work can be conditioned, by agreement of the parties, by a specific event. However, it must always be certain that such an event will occur. A rest day may also be agreed to by the contracting parties as the date of commencement of work.

D. Wage conditions

Besides the type of work, the place of performance of work and the date of commencement of work, according to the LC, wage conditions are also an essential element of the employment contract, unless they are stipulated in the collective agreement.

The agreement of parties concerning working conditions should have the legal characteristics of a certain legal act and the parties should respect the definition of this term in Section 119(3) of the LC. According to this provision, in the wage conditions, the employer agrees, in particular, to the form of employee remuneration, the basic rate of wage and other types of compensation for work and to the conditions for their provision. The employer may also regulate the wage conditions in his internal wage regulation. However, such regulation does not release him from his duty to stipulate wage conditions in the employment contract, unless they are stipulated in the collective agreement.

1. Wage conditions after expiration of collective agreement

In the application practice, it is common that wage conditions are not stipulated in the employment contract because they have been stipulated by social partners in the collective agreement. If the collective agreement has, in the meantime, expired, the LC establishes an irrefutable legal presumption that these wage conditions are stipulated in the employment contract until they are stipulated again in a collective agreement. This guarantee of the employee's wage claims, which is formulated by the legislator as an irrefutable legal presumption, is, according to new legislation, provided for not more than 12 months. This period lasts until social partners conclude a new collective agreement. If they do not conclude such an agreement within 12 months, the presumption no longer applies.

This rule does not apply if the wage conditions were stipulated not only in the collective agreement, but also in the employment contract. If the wage conditions stipulated by the parties in the collective agreement were more favourable than those contained in the employment contract, this part of the employment contract would be void by operation of law.

By the irrefutable legal presumption, the legislator guarantees the level of wage conditions agreed in the collective agreement only for 12 months and not longer. Only until then is it presumed that wage conditions of the employee have been stipulated in the employment contract. It is presumed that, by then, this problem will have been resolved by agreement of parties in the employment contract or by agreement of social partners in the collective agreement.

E. Agreement on probationary period

Agreement on the probationary period is one of the regular elements of employment contracts. Agreement on the probationary period must be made, under pain of nullity, in written form and in the employment contract. Agreement on probationary period in an oral employment contract is void. Agreement on the probationary period in a written employment contract made during the employment relationship is also void because the employment contract is, under such circumstances, considered as orally or tacitly concluded.

If the probationary period expires and the employment relationship is not terminated during the probationary period, the employment relationship continues.

The maximum length of the probationary period is three months. The maximum the length of the probationary period for executive employees directly subordinated to the statutory body or a member of the statutory body and executive employees in direct managing power of these executive employees is six months.

In comparison to the previous legal situation, the amended LC leaves length of the probationary period up to three months for ordinary employees and in the case of managers within two management levels (those who report directly to the statutory authority and those managers under their direct control levels) up to 6 months. Compared with the previous legal situation until 31st December 2012, the LC now no longer allows exceeding of this period by collective agreements.

III. Types of employment contracts

Depending on whether the employment contract establishes an employment relationship for an indefinite period or a fixed-term employment relationship or whether the employment contract establishes an employment relationship for established weekly working time or an employment relationship for reduced working time, employment contracts are divided into:
- employment contracts for indefinite period,
- fixed-term employment contracts,
- employment contracts for established weekly working time,
- employment contracts for reduced weekly working time.

A common legal feature of all those employment contracts is that they establish an employment relationship as a legal relationship of dependent work. Nonetheless, as indicated above, various types of employment contracts have certain peculiarities. For example, a fixed-term employment contract not concluded in writing is, under Section 48 (1) of the LC, considered as an employment contract for an indefinite period. Similarly, a fixed-term employment contract is regarded as an employment contract for an indefinite period if the statutory conditions of the establishment of the fixed-term employment relationship were not observed when it was concluded.

A. Fixed-term employment relationship

At the occasion of each legislative amendment of the text of the LC, employers are fighting for the most liberal regulation of fixed term employment relationships, although this legal regulation in any EU Member State must be compatible with Directive 99/70/EC concerning the framework agreement on fixed-term work. The main idea of this Directive is the principle of equal treatment. Previous regulation of the LC allowed the employer to conclude the first fixed term employment relationship without substantial reasons for up to three years, with the possibility of extension or re-conclusion of the employment relationship up to three times. Following concatenating of contacts for fixed term employment, the employer had to have substantial reason. New legislation within the LC changes the existing situation for the advantage of the employee and allows the employer to conclude a first fixed term employment without substantive grounds within a maximum of two years and to extend such contract or renew it for a maximum of two times. Over a time horizon of two years, the employer is required to have substantial reason for additional chaining of fixed term employment contracts. Chaining of contracts for fixed term employment is allowed by the LC on the basis of explicitly enumerated grounds (for example in representing employees during illness, during maternity or parental leave, in seasonal work and in cases where such is agreed upon in collective agreement). Such new legislative solution is in accordance with Directive 99/70/EC, although it is less favourable for employers compared to the previous legal situation. An employment relationship shall be agreed to for an indefinite period if the duration of employment is not defined explicitly in the employment contract or if the agreement was amended and the conditions for fixed term employment to enter into force were not met. An employment relationship shall also have indefinite duration if a fixed term employment relationship was not agreed in writing. A fixed term employment relationship may be agreed to for at most two years. A fixedterm employment relationship may be extended or renewed at most twice within a two-year period. A renewed fixed term employment relationship is an employment relationship beginning less than six months after the end of the previous fixed term employment relationship between the same parties.

This legal model enables the employer, without any material ground, to conclude a fixed term employment contract for not more than 2 years. The maximum two-year period applies also in case of a fixed-term employment relationship established by one employment contract, (for example, if the fixed-term employment relationship is not extended or renewed within two years). Establishment of such a fixed-term employment relationship need not be justified by any material ground on the employer's part. This is also consistent with current case-law of the ECJ, according to which the first fixed-term employment contract should not be conditioned by the existence of a material ground.

1. Reestablishment or extension of fixed-term employment relationship

The reestablishment or extension of a fixed-term employment relationship is limited by the legislation, on the one hand, by the number of extended or renewed fixed term employment contracts and, on the other hand, by a total maximum duration.

The reestablishment of a fixed-term employment relationship is allowed by the LC only due to exhaustively listed reasons.

A further extension or renewal of the fixed term employment relationship to two years or more can be agreed only in the following reasons:

a) substitution of an employee during maternity leave, parental leave, leave immediately linked to maternity leave or parental leave, temporary incapacity for work or an employee who has been given long term leave to perform a public function or trade union function,

b) the performance of work in which it is necessary to increase employee numbers significantly for a temporary period not exceeding eight months of the calendar year,

c) the performance of work that is linked to the seasonal cycle, which repeats every year and does not exceed eight months in the calendar year (seasonal work),

d) the performance of work agreed in a collective agreement.

University teachers and scientists

A further extension or renewal of an employment relationship for a fixed term of up to two years or more can be agreed to with a teacher in higher education or a creative employee in science, research or development if there are objective reasons relating to the character of the activities, as stipulated in special regulation.

2. Principle of equal treatment

An employee in a fixed term employment relationship may not be given either more or less favourable treatment in comparison to a comparable employee with regard to working conditions and terms of employment under this act and working conditions relating to safety and health at work under special regulation.

The labour-law rules in force give the employer several options, not only with regard to the first conclusion of fixed-term employment contract, but also with respect to the extension of an existing fixed-term employment contract or its reestablishment.

For example, an employer may conclude the first fixed-term employment contract without a material ground for up to two years and, beyond two years, he cannot extend this employment contract without a material ground. In this way, the employer has exhausted the statutory maximum in concluding fixed-term employment contracts without a material ground. The second option offered by the LC to the employee is that the employer concludes the first fixed-term employment contract for a period shorter than two years and he can extend or re-establish this employment contract without a material ground within two years not more than twice.

A material ground is necessary when the employer extends or re-establishes a fixed-term employment contract more than twice, even if two years of duration of the fixed-term employment relationship have not been exceeded or if the extends or re-establishes a fixed-term employment contract beyond the two-year limit, whether this employment relationship was established only once, or re-established or extended not more than twice.

3. Written form of employment contract

When establishing a fixed-term employment relationship, the employer must make sure that the fixed-term employment contract is put into writing. Otherwise, this employment relationship would be regarded as an employment relationship for an indefinite period. After or before two years pass, the reestablishment or extension of the fixed-term employment relationship, if the employer has already extended or re-established such an employment relationship, is conditioned by the existence of a material ground.

4. Requalification to employment relationship for indefinite period

According to the LC, the ground for the extension or reestablishment of a fixed-term employment relationship must be indicated in the employment contract. This statutory requirement is not addressed directly to the employer, but it is, in particular, up to him to make sure that the labour-law regulations are observed in labour-law relationships. If no material ground for extension or reestablishment of the fixed-term employment relationship were contained in the employment contract, such an employment relationship would have to be regarded as an employment relationship for an indefinite period due to the non-observance of statutory conditions for the establishment of the fixed-term employment relationship.

B. Part-time employment relationship

Employment relationships with reduced working time as an atypical form of employment is not used in the Slovak application practice as much as it is in other more developed countries. Since part-time employment is not a legal form creating the minimum standard for the employee's existence, he does not choose part-time employment voluntarily. Employees in the Slovak Republic mostly choose part-time employment when they are not able to find a full-time job. It is very rare for employees to work at the same time in two or three part-time employments for various employers, although it is allowed by the LC. Part-time employment relationship are an employment relationship with a scope which is narrower than the scope of full-time employment for stipulated weekly working time. A part-time employment relationship may, with respect to the scope of weekly working time, be often similar to full-time employment. In other cases, parttime employment for a half weekly working time are most common.

An essential aspect of part-time employment relationship according to Section 49 of the LC is the principle of equal treatment of employees. This principle must apply to all part-time employment relationships, irrespective of the extent of weekly working time. Under Section 49 of the LC, an employee in an employment relationship with reduced working time may not be advantaged or limited in comparison to a comparable employee. Reduced working time need not be distributed over all working days.

An employee in an employment relationship with reduced working time is entitled to wages corresponding to the agreed reduced working time. An employer informs employees and employee representatives in an understandable manner of the possibility of vacancies with reduced working time and of the established weekly working time.

C. Job sharing

The LC defines job sharing as a special type of part-time employment. This special type of part-time employment has been introduced in the LC only recently. Therefore, there is no sufficient information as to whether it has been accepted in practice. Many employers point out that this legal model (job sharing) is very demanding as to its administration, and therefore they opt for two parallel part-time employment relationships established individually with every employee with no mutual link.

Job sharing is a job in which employees in an employment relationship with reduced working time themselves distribute amongst themselves the working time and the job description appertaining to the job. Before concluding an agreement on the assignment of an employee in an employment relationship with reduced working time to a job sharing, the employer shall inform the employee in writing of the working conditions that apply to the job sharing agreement. An agreement on the assignment of an employee to a job sharing arrangement concluded between an employer and an employee must be done in writing, otherwise it shall be invalid. It must include written notification accordingly. If there is an obstacle to work on the side of an employee in a job sharing arrangement, the employees with whom the employee shares the job must substitute for the employee unless there are serious reasons preventing this on their side. The employer is obliged to inform an employee without unnecessary delay, should the need arise for them to substitute, pursuant to the first sentence. An agreement on the assignment of an employee to a job sharing arrangement can be terminated by notice in writing by the employer or employee. An agreement on the assignment of an employee to a job sharing arrangement shall dissolve by lapse one month from the date of notification if the employer does not agree otherwise with the employee.

If a job sharing arrangement ceases to exist but the job description appertaining to the job continues to exist, the employee shall have the right to be assigned work equivalent to the full working time in the job description that was assigned to the employee in the job sharing arrangement. If the job sharing was shared between multiple employees, each shall be entitled to their proportionate share of the equivalent working time and job description.

IV. Concurrence of employment relationships

The LC does not allow employers over 18 years of age to work in several concurring employment relationships. Many employees have two full-time employment relationships and their employers do not know about it. An employee need not inform his future employer, when applying for full-time work, of the fact they are already working in a full-time employment with another employer. This practice is allowed by Section 50 of the LC.

Under Section 50 of the LC, an employer may agree on several employment relationships with the same employee only for activities consisting of work of a different type. The rights and obligations arising from these employment relationships are considered separately. However, this does not apply to adolescent employees, in which case, concurring employment relationships are accumulated and their total extent cannot exceed 48 hours per week.

An employee may have, also with the same employer, two full-time employment relationships in the case of work of the same type (for example, combination of work as a secretary and cleaner, which is quite common in practice). It is up to the employer to arrange his contract relations with his employee so that the employee, in the time determined in the employment relationship for stipulated weekly working time, does not perform work subject to another employment relationship. The legislator's requirement that "the rights and obligations arising from these employment relationships shall be considered separately" means that separate labour-law claims (for example, working time, paid holiday, obstacles to work) result for the employee from every employment relationship.

Chapter 7

Atypical employment contracts

§ 1 Manager's contract

In practice, manager's contracts are often concluded, even though the LC does not regulat them as a specific form of contract and does not allow an employment relationship to be established by a manager's contract. Such contracts cover, in particular, labour relationships between the company and its higher managers. Since the LC allows an employment relationship to be established only by an employment contract, the manager's contracts concluded in practice are, in fact, often employment contracts. If the manager's contract covers performance of dependent work and contains the elements under Section 43 of the LC, it is an employment contract establishing an employment relationship. If the manager's contract does not contain the elements of an employment contract under Section 43 of the LC and if performance of work, with respect to its content, corresponds with an autonomous business activity, a manager's contract is, within the meaning of Section 269 of the Commercial Code, an atypical contract (in most cases, a contract on performance of function, mandate contract or agency contract). Many managers of companies prefer a labour-law relationship, which protects them more than a commercial-law relationship. They also prefer this because the issue of material responsibility is also important, as it is formulated very generously for the employee in an employment relationship. In a majority of cases, he does not pay real damages, but, in case of damage caused by negligence, he must pay only the damages not exceeding 4 times average monthly earnings. Being in an employment relationship is also more favourable for managers with respect to duties concerning payments in social funds. If they are in a commercial-law relationship, such payments are covered by themselves. In case of an employment relationship, approximately two thirds of such payments are covered by their employer.

Therefore, a contract designated by the parties as a manager's contract is the legal basis of an employment relationship only if it contains elements of an employment contract under Section 43 of the LC.

Besides the essential elements of an employment contract, a manager's contract may also include other covenants of the parties not contrary to mandatory provisions of the LC and other labour-law regulations.

§ 2 Employment contract on home work or telework

Section 52 of the LC in force establishes quite a liberal legal model of home work and telework, which may be performed in an employment relationship on the basis of an employment contract. Current rules concerning home work and telework creates quite a wide scope for freedom of contract of the parties to an employment relationship.

Home work is based on an employment relationship where work is not performed at the employer's workplace, but rather in the employee's own home in or in a different agreed place. If the contracting parties agree on a different place as a place of performance of work in the employment contract, the employee should still have the status of a home employee even if he, in fact, does not work at home. Therefore, the status of a home employee is characterized by the fact that the place of performance of work is a place different than the employer's workplace.

Since it is an employment relationship, home employees are also covered by the rules on employment relationship with certain exceptions that are listed exclusively. Some of these exceptions are related to special rules concerning the labour-law relationship, working time and obstacles to work. Home employees and teleworkers are not covered by the rules of the LC concerning continuous daily rest and continuous weekly rest. Home employees and teleworkers are not entitled to wage for overtime work, wage surcharge for work on public holidays, wage surcharge for night work and wage compensation for performing work in difficult conditions. The LC allows a different agreement to be made between the employer and the employee (for example, that part of these wage surcharges or all of them, including wage compensation for performing work in difficult conditions, will be provided by the employer to the employee, although the employee is not directly entitled to them according to the law.

The change of the employee's status to a home employee or teleworker is also possible by amending the employment contract.

The contracting parties may agree that the status of a home employee or a teleworker will be granted to an employee in a fixed-term employment relationship for or in an employment relationship for an indefinite period. Similarly, home work or telework may also be performed by an employee in full term or partial term.

§ 3 Agreement on work performed outside employment relationship

Agreements on work performed outside of an employment relationship have been very frequent in practice until recently, mainly because they established no duties of payment into social funds. Agreements on work performed outside of the employment relationship constituted, until 1st January 2013, a considerably looser labour relationship between the employer and the employee than the employment relationship. Since employers in practice started to replace employment contracts with such agreements in great extent, a substantial legislative change occurred on 1st January 2013. The LC defines the content of such agreements in a way similar to an employment relationship. Still, these agreements do not establish an employment relationship but relationship based on labour – law. Most foreign countries do not have this type of agreement. This is one of the reasons why many foreign employers do not see the necessary difference between an employment relationship established by an employment contract and a looser labour-law relationship established by agreements on work performed outside of the employment relationship. Since 1st January 2013 this, originally considerably looser, labour-law relationship has become very similar to an employment relationship.

Except for the employment, other basic labour-law relations are those created upon agreements to work outside of the scope of employment, within which paid work is performed for remuneration. The agreements to work outside of the scope of employment can be characterized as atypical, supplementary employments. The agreements to work outside of the scope of employment present a specific contractual type of the Slovak and Czech labour law in the EU.

The agreements to work outside of the scope of employment can be considered a flexible component of the labour law, establishing a looser employment relationship with a wider contractual freedom than the employment enables. Through agreements to work outside the scope of employment, currently broadly used as atypical labour-law contracts, the employees are able to perform paid work alongside their employment, care for minors, study, etc. In the labour-law relationships established by the agreements to work outside of the scope of employment, the employees have lower protection and less rights than employees working in the regular employment. Pursuant to the LC and the courts' decisions, the agreements to work outside of the scope of employment should be concluded by the employers only in exceptional cases when it is not economical and practical for them to employ an employee in the regular employment.

Agreements on work performed outside of an employment relationship, along with the employment contract, create freer labour-law relationship. Up until now, employers in Slovakia used to replace by such agreements employment contracts; as such the agreements did not constitute any obligations for employers to contribute to social funds.

Such legal regulation is currently substantially amended. New legal regulation converges the content of labour-law relationships based on agreements on work performed outside of employment with that labour-law relationships based on the employment contract.

For labour-law relationships based on agreements of work performed outside of employment (for example, provisions of the LC concerning the employment relationship, particularly on working time [with certain exceptions such as regarding overtime or on-call duty and the performance of night work]), are to be used. Section 119(1) of the LC states that the minimum wage has to be applied with regards to agreements of work performed outside of the employment relationship, too. On the other hand, regulations on holidays do not apply. Agreements on work performed outside of the employment relationship as of 1st September 2012 create insurance obligations of the employer with respect to the relevant social funds, even though certain advantageous rates of levies in cases of employing of persons in the retirement age and of students are provided.

As described under Section 223(1) of the LC, in n order to perform their tasks or to provide for their needs, employers may conclude agreements with natural persons on work performed outside an employment relationship ("work performance agreements", "agreements on work activities" and "agreements on temporary jobs for students") for work that is limited in its results ("work performance agreement") or for occasional activities limited by the type of work ("agreement on work activities", "agreement on temporary work for students").

Labour-law relationships established by these agreements are covered by the provisions of the general part of the LC, provisions on occupational safety and health, several provisions on working time and provisions of the LC on minimum wage.

The working time of employees who perform work under agreements on work performed outside of an employment relationship must not exceed 12 hours within any 24-hour period and in the case of adolescent employees it must not exceed 8 hours within any 24-hour period. It is not permissible to order or agree to work stand-by and overtime work in the case of employees who perform work under agreements on work performed outside of an employment relationship. Such agreements may only be concluded with an adolescent employee if such shall not jeopardise his healthy development, safety, morality or vocational preparation. Such agreements may not be concluded for activities that are the subject of protection pursuant to copyright law. Disputes pursuant to such agreements shall be dealt with equally to disputes pursuant to employment relationships.

I. Work performance agreement

An employer may conclude a work performance agreement with a natural person if the extent of work (work tasks) for which the agreement is concluded is not in excess of 350 hours in a calendar year. The period of work shall include work performed by the employee for the employer pursuant to a different work performance agreement.

A work performance agreement shall be concluded in writing, otherwise this agreement is invalid. The work performance agreement must include the definition of the work tasks, agreed remuneration for performance of it, the period in which the work task is to be performed and the extent of work, a extent is not directly influenced by the definition of the work task. A written agreement on work performance shall be concluded on the day preceding the day of the work performance commencement at the latest. Remuneration for performance of a work task shall be due upon completion and submission of the work. The parties may agree that part of the remuneration shall be due upon performance of a determined part of the work task. The employer may appropriately reduce the amount of remuneration upon negotiation with the employee if the performed work does not correspond to the conditions as concluded.

II. Agreement on temporary job of students

An employer may conclude an agreement on a temporary job of students with a natural person who has the status of a secondary school pupil or a student in full-time higher education under applicable legislation who is under 26 years of age. Work can be performed under an agreement on the temporary job of students no later than the end of the calendar year in which the natural person reaches 26 years of age. Work under an agreement on the temporary job of students shall not exceed 20 hours per week on average. The average for the purposes of the maximum admissible working time shall be calculated from the whole period covered by the agreement up to a maximum of 12 months. An employer shall be obliged to conclude an agreement on the temporary job of students in writing, otherwise it shall be invalid. The agreement must state: the agreed work, the agreed reward for the work performed, the agreed extent of working time and the period for which the agreement is concluded. The employer shall be obliged to issue the employee with one copy of the agreement on the temporary job of students. An agreement on the temporary job of students shall be concluded for a determined period or for an undetermined period of time. The method of termination of the agreement may be agreed in the agreement. Confirmation of the status according to the Section 227 paragraph 1 shall constitute an inseparable part of the agreement. Immediate termination of the agreement may only be agreed to in cases where an employment relationship may be terminated immediately. If the method of termination does not follow directly from the agreement concluded, it may be terminated by the agreement of participants as of the agreed date, and unilaterally only by giving notice without stating a reason with a 15-day notice period beginning on the day when the written notice was delivered. This shall not apply if an agreement is concluded in the period from the end of study at secondary school or the end of the summer semester in higher education no later than the end of October of the same calendar year.

III. Agreement on work activity

Work activities may be performed for up to 10 hours per week on the basis of an agreement on work activities.

An employer must conclude an agreement on work activities in writing otherwise it shall be invalid. The agreement on work activities must state the agreed work, the agreed remuneration for work performed, the agreed extent of working time and the period for which the agreement is concluded. An agreement on work activities may be concluded for a definite or indefinite period. The agreement may include an agreement on the method of its termination. Termination of the agreement with immediate effect may be agreed to only for those circumstance in which an employment relationship may be terminated with immediate effect. If the method of termination of the agreement is not agreed to in the agreement itself, termination is possible by agreement of the contracting parties as of an agreed date, and may be terminated by a single party only with notice without stating a reason with a 15-day notice period starting from the date on which written notice is delivered.

§ 4 Agency work

Just like in the case of the standard labour-law relationship with an employment relationship with a real employer, agency work must, according to the LC in force, be performed in an employment relationship and on the basis of an employment contract. Just like other "real employers", temporary employment agencies hired their employees, until 1st January 2013, not on the basis of an employment contract, but on the basis of other forms of contract, even though, in fact, an employment relationship was involved. Therefore, the amendment to the LC in force since 1st January 2013 imposes a duty on temporary employment agencies to hire employees on a temporary basis only in an employment relationship and not in a different legal relationship.

Chapter 8

Modification of employment relationship

§ 1 Modification of content of employment relationship

Labour-law relationships under Slovak labour-law rules are based on the contracting principle, which means that the content of an employment relationship may, in principle, be changed only by agreement of the parties. This is one of the reasons why it is important that the employer and the employee agree on the type of work in the employment contract so that, for the employer, a narrow definition of the type of work agreed to is not too restrictive. The agreement on modification of the content of an employment relationship may only cover the rights and obligations established by a manifestation of will of the parties (for example, in the employment contract, or those resulting from default provisions of the LC or other labour-law regulations). The agreement on the modification of content of an employment relationship cannot modify the rights and obligations of the parties of an employment relationship resulting from mandatory provisions of the LC. This applies to the modification of content of an employment relationship on the basis of a legal act, which is the employment contract. Apart from the modification of content of an employment contract, change of an employment relationship may also include the change of the employer. Legal consequences in the case of a change of the employer are associated with a general succession of right and duties resulting from labour-law relationships.

The LC establishes written form of amendment to an employment contract, but its non-observance is not associated with the sanction of nullity of amendment to the employment contract. Non-observance of this duty may by sanctioned not only by imposing a fine, but also by an action for performance.

I. Transfer to different work

Unilateral transfer to different work is, under Section 55 of the LC, legally defined as an exception to the contract principle in labour-law relationships. Section 55 of the LC contains an exhaustive list of reasons for unilateral transfer to different work.

The first group of unilateral transfer to different work consists of reasons establishing the employer's duty to proceed to such transfer to different work. Non-compliance with this duty by the employer would be a breach of labour-law regulations, with a possibility of imposing sanctions by the work inspectorate. If the employer failed to transfer the employee to different work in these cases, the employee would not have to perform previous work anymore even if this work corresponded with the type of work agreed to in the employment contract with the employer. The employee's refusal to perform previous work cannot be regarded as a breach of work discipline.

The second group consists of reasons entitling the employer to transfer the employee to different work, but it is a right that may or may not be exercised by the employer.

Under Section 55 of the LC, the employer is entitled to proceed to unilateral transfer of the employee to different work for these reasons:

a) a medical opinion states that the employee's health condition has caused the long term loss of his ability to perform his previous work or if he can no longer perform such work as a result of an occupational illness or the risk of such an illness, or if he has already received the maximum permitted level of exposure in the work place as determined by a decision of a competent public health body,

b) a pregnant woman, a mother who has given birth within the last nine months or a breast-feeding woman performs work that such women may not be employed to do or which according to a medical opinion jeopardizes her pregnancy or maternal function,

c) according to a medical opinion or a decision of the public health body, it is imperative in the interest of protecting health of other persons against contagious diseases, (hereinafter referred to as "quarantine measure"),

d) it is deemed imperative by virtue of a legal ruling of court or other competent body,

e) by virtue of a medical opinion, an employee working at night is acknowledged unfit for night work,

f) a pregnant woman, a mother who has given birth within the last nine months and a breastfeeding woman requests a transfer to day work if she was assigned to night work.

Under Section 55(4) of the LC the employer may, without the consent of the employee, transfer the employee for a necessary period of time to work different than that as agreed upon, if so required for averting extraordinary events, or for mitigating the immediate consequences thereof. Work to which an employer transfers an employee pursuant to provisions of Labour Code must correspond to the employee's health capacity for work.

The duty to take account of the employee's capability and his qualification may be regarded as the employer's legal duty only if the employer has, at his disposal, work appropriate to the employee's capability and qualification that he intends to offer to the employee.

A. Long-term loss of health capability

An employee's long-term loss of health capability excludes the temporary incapability for work, which, under the Act No. 561/2003 Coll. on Social Insurance, lasts, in principle, no longer than a year, unless there is damage to the employee's health causing him long-term incapability to perform previous work. The employee's long-term loss of health capability may be caused not only by a long-term temporary incapability for work, but the damage to health may be so serious that, in a short time after its damage, it causes a long-term loss of health capability to the employee to perform previous work. If the employee suffers a long-term loss of capability for previous work and the employer does not transfer him to different work, the employee may refuse to continue working. This would be an obstacle to work on the employer's part, which would give the employee the right to wage compensation in the amount of their average earnings. The employee would be entitled to wage compensation even if the employer had demonstrated that there is no other appropriate work for the employee to be transferred to. In these cases, notice given by the employer for long-term loss of health capability and redundancy is possible. In this situation, the employee himself may also terminate the employment relationship by notice or immediate termination if, according a to a medical report, he cannot continue performing the work without a serious risk for his health and if the employer did not transfer him to other appropriate work within 15 days of submitting the report.

B. Achievement of maximum exposure permitted

Achievement of maximum exposure permitted is not a reason for transferring the employee to different work or to terminate an employment relationship by notice given by the employer under Section 63(1)(c) of the LC, if, before the transfer to different work or notice, a decision of the public health authority stated that the employee, given his health state, has suffered a long-term loss of capability for previous work or that he continues performing the work due to a risk for his health or an occupational disease.

C. Transfer of a pregnant woman, mother within 9 months of childbirth or breastfeeding mother

The employer's duty to transfer such a woman to different work exists also when the employee does not perform work included in the lists of types of work prohibited for pregnant women and mothers but there is a reason where performance of such work poses a risk to her pregnancy or maternity function, which requires a medical opinion.

D. Quarantine

The reason for transfer to different work is not the employee's incapability for previous work, but a necessity to avoid contagious diseases to be transmitted by the employee to other persons. Persons with suspected contagion may be put under quarantine. Quarantine means isolation, increased health supervision and medical surveillance. Persons are put under quarantine in the case of suspected contagion, if they must submit to increased health supervision. Quarantine consists of the prohibition of certain activities that might lead to spreading of the contagious disease, or in modification of working conditions at the employee's workplace. In case of application of quarantine, it is irrelevant whether the employee suffers from a long-term loss of capability for previous work. In this case, there must be a suspicion of contagion. Quarantine is imposed in connection with performance of epidemiologically critical activities (for example, activities associated with a risk of occurrence and spreading of contagious diseases). Such activities may only be performed by persons with appropriate health conditions and professional qualification. Health capacity with respect to the performance of epidemiologically critical activities is demonstrated by a natural person by means of a health certificate issued during the first medical examination by a physician who indicates, in the health certificate, its term of validity and health capacity for performing specific epidemiologically critical activities. Persons with a disease or suspected disease or contagion must be put under isolation on the basis of an order issued by a physician or a regional public health authority. Isolation is cancelled when there is no risk of spreading of contagion. Isolation takes place at home or at the infection department and in reserved rooms of non-infection departments of institutional medical facilities, in social service facilities or other facilities designated by the regional public health authority. Quarantine is associated in labour law with the legal consequence that the employee cannot, for certain time, perform any work, or it constitutes a reason for transfer to different work. According to the LC, it is an obstacle to work on the employee's part, who receives benefits under the Social Insurance Act. Conditions of returning to work are governed by Section 157 of the LC.

E. Final judicial decision

Apart from a final judicial decision, a final decision of a competent authority other than a court also imposes a legal duty on the employer to transfer the employee to different work. Unilateral transfer of the employee to different work is possible only if a final judicial decision or a final decision of a competent authority other than a court declares the necessity of unilateral transfer of the employee to different work. The employer must transfer the employee, in particular, in case of a sentence prohibiting certain activity for a certain period.

F. Transfer of an employee working at night

The employer's duty to transfer a woman from night work to day work applies to pregnant women (pregnant employees), mothers (employees) within 9 months of childbirth (mothers of children under nine months of age) and breastfeeding women during the entire breastfeeding period. These employees need not submit any medical opinion to the employer. In these cases a request of the woman (employee) is sufficient. The LC does not require the employee in such a position to submit a written request to the employer to transfer her to different work.

The statutory ground establishing the employer's legal duty to transfer the employee to different work is also the case where the employee working at night is, on the basis of a medical opinion, recognized as unfit for night work. With respect to this statutory ground of the employee's transfer to different work, no change of type of work or place of performance of work is required, but only a unilateral change of working regime from night regime to day regime, which is agreed to between the employee and the employee in written, oral or tacit form. Unilateral transfer of an employee working at night is characterized by the fact that he is, on the basis of a medical opinion, recognized as unfit for night work. The employer must transfer him even if the employee is ready to continue performing night work (for example, remuneration for performance of night work is more favourable for the employee). The employer's legal duty, however, depends on a medical opinion as a medical recommendation is not sufficient. Therefore, the employer's legal duty to transfer the employee to different work on unilateral basis can be fulfilled even if no change of the type of work or the place of performance of work of the employee agreed in the employment contract occurs.

G. Averting an exceptional event or mitigating its immediate consequences

The LC establishes only one legal ground establishing the employer's right to transfer the employee even without his consent for necessary time to different work. It is the necessity of averting an exceptional event or mitigating its immediate consequences.

II. Agreement on temporary allocation of employee

The labour-law relationship of the temporary performance of work by an employee with a different employer is characterized by the fact that its content, in comparison with the usual content of an employment relationship, consists in the circumstance that, during temporary allocation of an employee for performance of work with a different employer, the employee does not fulfil his main duty to work with respect to his employer, but rather, with respect to his hiring employer, who is not his real employer.

The labour-law relationship of the temporary allocation of an employee for performance of work with a different employer implies two legal acts – an agreement on temporary allocation of employee between the employee and the employer and an agreement between the employer and the entity hiring the employee on a temporary basis(for example, the hiring employer). No contract is concluded between the hiring employer and the employee allocated on a temporary basis.

A. Relationship between employee allocated on temporary basis and hiring employer

There is no employment relationship between the employee and the employer hiring him on a temporary basis. Rather, it is a *sui generis* labour-law relationship. On the the basis of temporary allocation, the employee must comply with the instructions of his temporary "employer". During the entire period of the temporary allocation, the employer's power is transferred to another entity hiring the employee on a temporary basis. However, executive employees of the employer hiring the employee on a temporary basis cannot make any legal acts on behalf of the employer allocating the employee on temporary basis with respect to such an employee.

Despite the fact that the labour-law relationship of the temporary allocation of an employee to different work with the hiring employer implies that the employee is, on a temporary basis, working for an entity different than his real employer. During temporary allocation, he fulfils his duty of obedience with respect to the hiring employer by complying with his instructions. The hiring employer acquires the right to issue working instructions.

These various forms of employment of employees are relevant from the perspective of legal consequences. If the employer employs his employees for performance of work in a different place, this employment relationship is governed by the general provisions of the LC. However, in case of the temporary allocation of employees, special provisions of the LC concerning the temporary allocation apply, which requires an intensive cooperation with employees as far as the change of type of work agreed upon is concerned.

Legal characteristics of the labour-law relationship of the temporary allocation of an employee for performance of work to a different employer include the following:

– during temporary allocation, the employee is integrated, on a temporary basis, in the staff of the hiring employer,
– the hiring employer is entitled to issue working instructions with respect to that employee,
– legal acts, with respect to the employee, during the temporary allocation are done by the real employer,
– termination of the labour-law relationship of the temporary allocation is governed by the agreement concluded between the employer and the employee,
– termination of the labour-law relationship of the temporary allocation does not terminate the employment relationship between the employee and the employer.

The employee's wage (salary) during temporary allocation and their travelling reimbursements are provided by the employer allocating the employee on temporary basis. Employers may also agree on the reimbursement of wage (salary). During the temporary allocation of an employee for the performance of work with a different employer, working conditions, wage conditions and conditions of employment of employees allocated on a temporary basis must be at least as equally favourable as wage conditions of other employees of the hiring employer.

The principle of equal treatment between allocated employees and comparable employees of the hiring employer applies to the full extent. Moreover, the legislator requires that the same level of working conditions, wage conditions and conditions of employment of employees allocated on a temporary basis as a minimum level (by using the term "at least").

B. Unilateral termination of temporary allocation

Unilateral termination of this labour relationship is possible only on the basis of conditions agreed upon by the parties, which means that, when establishing this labour relationship, the parties do not agree to the method of its unilateral termination, as the LC does not allow any of them to terminate temporary allocation unilaterally. In particular, the employee, when making an agreement on temporary allocation, need not know the legal consequences of missing agreement on unilateral termination of the temporary allocation when establishing this specific labour relationship. The absence of such an the agreement on unilateral termination of the temporary allocation of the employee may be, for example, when concluding an agreement on temporary allocation, wished by the employer himself in order to eliminate possible adverse consequences of unilateral termination of this relationship by the employee.

C. Right to damages

The employer's right to damages from the hiring employer results from a commercial-law contractual relationship, in which the contracting parties may also agree upon different conditions, including the right to damages to be paid to the employer if such damage was incurred by the employee when fulfilling work tasks for the hiring employer or in a direct connection with performance of work tasks for the hiring employer.

D. Temporary employment agency

A temporary employment agency is also entitled to perform the temporary allocation of the employee for the performance of work to a different employer within the meaning of Section 58 of the LC.

Just like in the case of a standard employer, the legal status of a temporary employment agency may be acquired not only by a legal person, but also by a natural person, who may perform it only in the legal form of an employment relationship.

The temporary allocation of employees is done for remuneration, which is charged by the agency and not to the employees themselves, but rather from the hiring employer. The licence to perform the activity of a temporary employment agency is granted by the Central Office for Work.

The amendment to the Act No. 5/2004 Coll. on Employment Services caused, as of 1st May 2013, a substantial limitation of fixed-term employment relationships. If a temporary employment agency has linked fixed-term employment contracts, the fifth of such consecutive employment contracts establishes, by operation of law, an employment relationship for an indefinite period with the hiring employer.

III. Transfer of undertaking or part of undertaking

The term transfer of undertaking or part of undertaking is not defined by the LC. According to current case law of the ECJ, transfer of undertaking or part of undertaking means the organized grouping of resources allowing pursuit of an economic activity with its own aim. The term transfer of undertaking must meet two conditions. There must be a change of employer and the economic entity transferred must maintain its identity. In contractual relationships, there must be a change of person responsible for the performance of activities, ensuring the observance of the employer's duties with respect to employees. Maintaining identity, as the second legal condition of transfer of undertaking, is characterized by performing the same (or similar) activities by the new employer and by maintaining the employees management, work organization, operational processes or available operational resources. The transfer of activities or tasks or a part thereof are also regarded as dissolution of the employer with legal succession under the LC, leading to the transfer of rights and duties resulting from labour-law relationships.

A. Concept of (part of) undertaking

With respect to the applicability of a transfer of undertaking or a part of it, in practice, it is necessary to verify in the case at hand first whether it is an "undertaking" or "part of an undertaking" and whether it is transferred to another owner. The traditional concept of undertaking is used primarily in commercial law, according to which an undertaking is an organizational unit in which the employer, using personal, material and immaterial resources, pursues a labour/technical objective that may not be limited to covering its own needs.

Maintaining identity of an economic unit

An economic unit, as the basic legal concept of transfer of undertaking, is, according to previous case law of the ECJ, represented not only by material, but also immaterial elements. These include, for instance, not only buildings or machines, but also the personal element and organizational element (know-how), production methods and stock inventory. It is a functioning and viable economic unit (*Spijkers*, C-24/85). The transferee of undertaking must take over an existing undertaking, in the activity of which it continues, or at least, can continue in an activity of the same or similar type. It is relevant whether a still existing economic unit was sold. An economic unit may include, in certain sectors, a unit based primarily on human labour. The employees themselves permanently connected by their common activity can constitute an economic unit. Such a unit maintains its identity after any transfer, when the new owner of undertaking not only continues the activity concerned, but also takes over an essential part of staff, given the number and qualification, that was deliberately used by the predecessor in this activity (*Sützen*). An economic unit should not be understood only as an activity. Its identity results also from other characteristics, such as staff, management, work organization, operational methods and operational instruments. In *Santner*, the ECJ built on its ruling in *Rygaard* and examined whether there was a transfer of a permanently established economic unit whose activity is not limited to only achieving a certain aim. According to the ECJ, the term economic unit should be understood as an organizational unit of persons and property intended for pursuing an economic activity with its own aim. Such an economic unit must be sufficiently structured and independent, but it need not necessarily include substantial material or immaterial resources (*Santner*).

Maintaining identity is characterized by performing the same activities by the new employer and by maintaining the staff, management, work organization, operational methods or available operational resources. One of the important criteria of maintaining identity of the economic unit transferred is a certain degree of similarity between the activities carried out before and after the transfer.

B. Employer's information duties

Under Section 29 of the LC an employer shall be obliged, no later than one month prior to the transfer of rights and obligations arising from labour-law relations, to inform the employee representatives, and if no employee representatives operate at the employer, the employees directly in writing on:

a) the date or proposed date of the transfer,
b) reasons thereof,
c) labour-law, economic and social implications of the transfer with respect to employees, and
d) projected measures of the transfer affecting employees.

With a view of achieving consensus, an employer shall be obliged, one month prior to implementation of measures affecting employees at the latest, to negotiate such measures with the employee representatives. Obligations stipulated shall also apply to the transferee employer.

C. Preservation of rights of employees

Rights and duties are transferred to the transferee. These are rights and duties resulting from an employment contract and from a labour-law relationship that existed on the date of the transfer. The basic labour-law consequence of the transfer of undertaking, business or a part thereof is the transfer of rights and duties resulting from labour-law relationships to the new employer, which must take place, by operation of law, as of the date of transfer. These rights are transferred automatically, by operation of law, due to the transfer of undertaking, and cannot depend on the intention of the transferor or transferee, or agreement of employees. The transfer of rights affects all rights resulting from an employment contract or a labour-law relationship that existed on the date of transfer. Rights and duties are transferred to the transferee at the moment of transfer of the undertaking or part of the undertaking. In this way, it was intended to avoid the possibility that the transferee refuses to employ the employees after the transfer or that the transferee agrees with the previous owner that the take-over of employees is excluded. This protection of employees applies only to employees who were, at the moment of the transfer of the undertaking, employees of the undertaking as the object of transfer.

The transfer of undertaking, business or part thereof cannot be, as such, a reason for dismissal of employees by the transferor or transferee. However, this provision does not preclude dismissals that may take place due to economic, technical or organizational reasons including changes concerning employees.

Depending on what part of the undertaking is transferred, the employees of this transferred part are protected against dismissal by the employer. Of course, protection against termination of the employment relationship does not apply to employees who are not employed in the transferred part of the undertaking, although they perform certain duties which involve the use of assets of the employer that is transferred (*Arie Batzen*, C-186/83).

Accordingly, the protection of employees in case of transfer of undertaking or a part thereof, consists in the fact that a change of ownership of undertaking or a part thereof or its lease cannot justify a dismissal by the employer.

The object of the transfer of rights and duties resulting from labour-law relationships consists of employment relationships, but the former employer with legal succession need not terminate employment relationships, provide a severance allowance and, once the owner changes, the new owner need not conclude new employment contracts. The new employer enters into all rights, duties and responsibilities. This new employer acquires not only obligations resulting from the concluded employment contracts, but also obligations from concluded collective agreements negotiated by previous employer, until termination of the collective agreement by notice or its expiry or until the date of a new collective agreement coming into force.

With respect to previous case law of the ECJ, the problem of collective agreements and the problem of the term working conditions were of major importance. The ECJ prefers an extensive conception of collective agreements. The term collective agreement, according to the case law of the ECJ, includes various types of collective agreements and undertaking agreements. Likewise, a wider interpretation of the ECJ applies to the interpretation of the term working conditions. Working conditions resulting from collective agreements should be interpreted extensively, preserving the purpose of the protection of employees in case of transfer of undertaking, whose legal position should not be deteriorated by the transfer of undertaking as compared to the legal position before the transfer of undertaking.

Only the collective agreement in force at the time of transfer is binding for the transferee. The provisions of the LC, just like the directive itself, do not protect hypothetical benefits resulting from possible amendments to collective agreements after a transfer of undertaking.

In the case of rights of employees resulting from collective agreements, the directive allows the Member States to limit or reduce the period of effect of the collective agreement in question. However, this limitation may not be shorter than one year from the moment of transfer of the undertaking or part of the undertaking.

The object of the transfer of rights and duties in connection with a transfer of the undertaking, business or a part thereof includes the rights of employees, acquired until the moment of transfer of undertaking, to old-age, invalidity or survivors' benefits under supplementary company pension schemes outside of the statutory social security schemes. For instance, in the case of the *Commission vs. Belgium* (C-237/84), the ECJ declared that Belgium had not transposed the Directive No. 77/187/EEC properly because its legislation did not protect the rights of employees to old-age benefits under supplementary pension schemes.

D. Protection against termination of employment relationship by employer

The transfer of undertaking as such cannot justify termination of the employment relationship by the employer. However, the prohibition of dismissal is limited only to dismissal justified only by the transfer of the undertaking. A transferee, who enters into the rights and duties of the former employer, may, with respect to the employees, exercise his right of notice, but this notice may not be justified by the transfer of the undertaking, but ratehr, must be justified by other economic, technical or organizational reasons. Accordingly, the transferee may implement, after the transfer of the undertaking, organizational, production or rationalization changes (mergers) in the acquired businesses.

Under Section 29a of the LC if a transfer results in significant changes in an employee's working conditions and the employee does not agree with the change, employment shall be deemed to be terminated by agreement pursuant to Section 63(1)(b) of the LC with effect from the date of the transfer. The employer shall issue the employee a written document concerning the termination of the employment relationship pursuant to the first sentence. An employee falling under the first sentence shall be entitled to a severance allowance pursuant to Section 76 of of the LC.

E. Continuing force of collective agreements

Apart from the working conditions agreed individually, after the transfer of the undertaking or its part, the rights and duties resulting from collective agreements continue to exist and such agreements may not be amended to the detriment of employees within one year.

F. Protection of functions of employee representatives

In case of transfer of the undertaking or its part, continuity of representation of employees by means of employee representatives must also be preserved. This applies only to cases where the transferred undertaking preserves its autonomy and continues to exist as an autonomous operational unit. This does not apply if necessary conditions for the renewal of designation or the election of employee representatives are met. If the term of office of the representatives of the employees affected by the transfer of the undertaking or part of the undertaking expires as a result of the transfer, the representatives of the undertaking continue to enjoy the protection provided by the laws, regulations, administrative provisions or practices of the Member States as provided to employee representatives upon expiry of their term of office.

Chapter 9

Termination of employment relationship

Whenever the LC is amended, the employers in the Slovak Republic try to make the existing legal model of the termination of the the employment relationship by the employer more flexible. The existing legal model of the termination of employment relationship by the employer appears to be protectionist with respect to employees. Unilateral termination of an employment relationship is, more than four decades since the codification of the LC, only possible in case of one of the exhaustively listed reasons. The LC also stipulates other substantive conditions that make it more difficult for the employer to terminate the employment relationship unilaterally by notice or immediate termination.

Termination of an employment relationship is, in a mandatory way, governed by Section 59 of the LC. According to this provision, an employment relationship may be terminated:
a) by agreement,
b) by notice,
c) by immediate termination, or
d) by termination within a probationary period.

An employment relationship concluded for a fixed period shall terminate upon expiry of the agreed period.

An employment relationship of an alien or stateless person shall terminate, unless terminated by other means, upon the day:
a) his residency within the territory of the Slovak Republic is due to terminate pursuant to an executable ruling on the forfeiture of the residence permit,
b) a verdict imposing the sentence of expulsion from the territory of the Slovak Republic on such person entered into force, or
c) of expiration of the period for which the residence permit on the territory of the Slovak Republic was issued.

An employment relationship shall also terminate upon the death of the employee.

§ 1 Agreement on termination of employment relationship

Just like in the foreign labour-law regulations, the agreement on the termination of the employment relationship is the most natural way to terminate the employment relationship. Agreement on the termination of the employment relationship is fully consistent with the fundamental contract principle in labour law. However, it is not the most common method of termination of the employment relationship in practice. At the time of restructuring changes, also due to the financial crisis, the most common method of the termination of the employment relationship is bynotice given by the employer.

The LC requires a written form of the agreement on the termination of the employment relationship, but its non-observance is, under Section 17 of the LC, not connected with the legal consequence of nullity of the legal act. An oral agreement on the termination of the employment relationship is valid, as well. If the employer does not observe the written form of the agreement on the termination of the employment relationship, he infringes labour-law regulations and may be sanctioned by the work inspection authorities.

The agreement on the termination of the employment relationship must contain the ground of notice if required by the employee or if the employment relationship is terminated due to organizational reasons or reasons concerning the employee's health (Section 63(1)(a) to (c) of the LC).

§ 2 Termination of employment relationship by notice

I. Notice

Notice as a unilateral legal act must be made in writing, under pain of nullity, and it must be delivered to the other party of the labour-law relationship.

An employment relationship may be terminated by giving notice on the part of the employer or employee. Notice must be given in writing and delivered to the other party, or otherwise it shall be invalid. An employer may only give notice to an employee for reasons expressly stipulated in this Act. The reason for giving notice must be defined in the notice in terms of fact, such that it may not be confused with a different reason, or the notice shall otherwise be deemed invalid. The reason for giving notice may not be subsequently amended. Where the employer gives notice to an employee by virtue of Section 63 of the LC, paragraph (1),letter b), he may not within 2 months create the wound-up work post anew and employ another employee to the same post. Notice that was delivered to the other party may only be revoked with his consent. Revocation of notice, and the consent to its revocation must be made out in writing.

II. Notice period

Since 2011 notice periods are distinguished by the LC depending on the total duration of the employee's labour-law relationship with a particular employer. Regulation of notice periods is of relatively cogent legal nature.

Recent amendment to the LC fundamentally changed the existing legal regulation of notice periods. The length of the notice period is set at a minimum, and thus allows an employer to agree with employees on a longer notice period within employment or collective contract. The statutory regulation of minimum duration of the notice period on the other hand protects the employee. In this way, the current text of the LC achieved a higher standard of harmonization with international commitments of the Slovak Republic, in particular with the European Social Charter, which requires Member States to ensure reasonable duration of notice period for employees. Slovak Republic ratified European Social Charter in 2008. As to the length of the duration of notice period, the basic period of notice is set for the employee and the employer for at least one month. An employee whose employment lasted at least one year and less than five years is entitled to a minimum two-month notice period. In case an employee worked for employer on the day of the delivery of notice for more than five years, such employee is entitled for a minimum three-month notice period.

In cases when notice is given by employee, he is entitled to a minimum 1-month notice period, if on the date of notification of notice the employee worked for employer for at least one year. In cases of employment relationships shorter than one year an employee has a legal right to a minimum one-month notice period.

As it is apparent from the above, the notice period depends only on the length of employment and not on the nature of notice, as it was under the previous legal regulation (for example, period of notice on the grounds of economic reasons was longer).

Under Section 62 of teh LC, where notice has been given, the employment relationship shall terminate upon expiration of the period of notice. The period of notice shall be a minimum of one month, unless this Act stipulates otherwise. The notice period for an employee who is given notice for the reasons stated in Section 63 of the LC paragraph (1) letter (a) or (b) or because the employee's health condition has, according to a medical opinion, caused the long term loss of his ability to perform his present work, shall be at least:
a) two months if the employer in the employment relationship has employed the employee for at least one year and less than five years as at the date of delivery of notice,
b) three months if the employer in the employment relationship has employed the employee for at least five years as at the date of delivery of notice.

The notice period for an employee, who is given notice for reasons other than those stated above shall be at least two months, if the employer in employment relationship has employed the employee for at least one year at the date of delivery of the notice.

For the purposes, the period of the employment relationship shall include the repeated fixed term employment relationships concluded with the same employer if they followed each other without break.

If notice is given by an employee who has been employed in the employment relationship by the employer for at least one year at the date of delivery of notice, the notice period shall be at least two months.

The notice period shall begin from the first day of the calendar month following the delivery of notice and end on the last day of the corresponding calendar month unless this act stipulates otherwise.

A. Monetary compensation in case when employee does not continue to work for employer until the end of notice period

Monetary compensation for an employee who does not continue to work for the employer until the end of notice period was first enshrined in the LC at the time of economic boom and low unemployment. Employers used this legal regulation to ensure that their employees didn't leave during the duration of notice period and before they were able to secure adequate replacement of employee. The amount of this monetary compensation, if it was agreed in writing with the employee in the employment contract, represented the amount of one average monthly salary of the employee. The amendment to the LC allows an increase in the monetary compensation directly based on the law.

According to the new legal regulation, if the employee does not remain in an employment relationship during the whole time of notice period, the employer is entitled to a monetary compensation of the amount which is calculated as a multiple of the notice period.

III. Participation of employee representatives in termination of employment relationship

The amendment to the LC re-embedded the participation of employee representatives at the unilateral termination of the employment relationship from the side of the employer (for example, in situations of notice given by employer or of immediate termination of the employment relationship by the employer). Participation by representatives of the employees is required in the form of a prior hearing of notice given by the employer or immediate termination of the employment relationship. Such prior hearing is set as a condition for the validity of notice or by the immediate termination of the employment relationship. However, the consent of the representative of employees with notice or immediate termination of the employment relationship is not considered as substantive requirement of notice or as the immediate termination of employment. The aim of the new legal regulation is to force the employer to not ignore employee representatives during giving notices or while immediate terminations of employment relationships.

However, if the social partner of the employer, the employee representatives, fail to discuss the request for termination of employment by notice or by the means of immediate termination within the statutory period, the LC creates the fiction that the consultation with employee's representatives took place. The LC provides for a 7-day period for negotiation on notice and for a 2-day period on immediate termination of the employment relationship, which begins from the day of receipt of the request by the employer.

IV. Invalidity of termination of employment

The issue of invalidity of the termination of employment is very important because it is a procedural guarantee of rights of employees, enshrined not only in Section 79.2 of the LC, but also in Section 14 of the LC, which provides for the judicial review of the rights of employees. The judicial review of the rights of employees is enshrined also in Code of Civil Procedure and in the Constitution of the Slovak Republic. According to the current legal regulation, the employee and also the employer may defend against invalid termination of the employment relationship in the preclusive period of two months. The possibility of judicial review of the invalid termination of the employment relationship remains, but the amendment to the LC sets differently from previous regulation, the question of financial demands of the employee in cases when the employer invalidly terminated the employment relationship. According to the previous regulation, in cases of invalid termination of employment by the employer, the employee could claim from the employer to pay wage compensation for a maximum of nine months if the total time for which remuneration should be provided exceeded nine months. If the total time for which an employee should get compensation had been longer than nine months, the employee could not get such compensation. This situation had been partially corrected by the mentioned amendment to the LC by allowing an employee to receive wage compensation for a maximum of 36 months, if the total time for which compensation should be provided exceeds 12 months.

V. New legal regulation of severance allowance at termination of employment relationship

Unlike in previous regulation, the most significant legislative amendment in the case of severance allowance at the termination of the employment relationship should be considered the reintroduction of concurrence of the notice period and severance allowance. According to previous regulation, such concurrence was not possible and the LC contained principle of "allowance or notice period".

Also according to new amendments to the LC, provision of severance allowance is possible in the case of the termination of the employment relationship by the employer for organizational reasons or for health reasons, but also in the case of agreement on termination of the employment relationship. The sum of severance allowance differs depending on the number of years of work conducted for employer.

The new legal model of allowance provided in relation to the number of years worked is less favourable for employees. Although previous regulation was based on the alternation of "severance allowance or notice period", the differentiation of the amount of allowance according to the number of years worked for the employer was significantly more favourable for employees. New regulation addresses the provision of allowance independent of the duration of the notice period, and links it to the sum of the number of years that the employee worked for the employer.

If the employment relationship lasted less than two years, the employee is entitled for severance allowance corresponding to the amount of the average monthly salary. Employees are eligible for severance an allowance corresponding to the amount of double average monthly salary if they worked for the employer for at least five years. For example, the employee is entitled to allowance of four average monthly salaries if the duration of employment was at least ten years and less than twenty years. If the employment lasted at least twenty years, the employee is entitled to an allowance of five average monthly salaries.

VI. Regulation of competing earning activities of employee

According to previous legal regulation, the employee was required to promptly notify the employer on his earning activity which may be of a competitive nature to the activities of the employer. According to the new legal regulation employee must ask the employer for prior approval to pursue such earning activity. At the same time, the amended LC establishes an irrefutable presumption in the sense that if the employer does not respond to the request of the employee within 15 days of its receipt, the employer's consent is considered to be provided. Unlike under previous legal regulation, the employer is now also entitled to withdraw consent for serious reasons and also in writing (Section 83(3) of the LC). Such withdrawal is required to be justified.

VII. Offer of other appropriate work

The substantive conditions of notice given by the employer include an offer of other appropriate work according to Section 63(2) of the LC.

The employer must offer the employee other appropriate work in the case of notice given for reasons of notice indicated in Section 63(1) of the LC, unless it is a notice for breach of work discipline or for a reason that justifies the immediate termination of the employment relationship or unless it is a notice for the insufficient fulfilment of work tasks. The employer cannot, in fact, offer other appropriate work if it is dissolved without legal succession or if the employer as a whole is relocated and the employee does not agree with the change of place of the performance of work as agreed with the employer in the employment contract.

Under former legislation, it was possible for social partners to agree, on the basis of a collective agreement, not only on the conditions of this duty of offer given by the employer, but also to exclude this duty of offer given by the employer. If a collective agreement was concluded that excluded the duty of offer given by the employer, the employer could give a valid notice to the employee without fulfilling his duty of offer with respect to the employee.

As of 1st January 2013, the LC excluded the possibility to cancel the offer of other appropriate work by means of collective agreements before applying a reason for notice.

Even though the LC does not require the offer of other appropriate work to be made in writing, with respect to legal certainty of both parties to the employment relationship and with respect to the employer's duty to demonstrate this fact in case of a judicial dispute, it is advisable to make it in writing. The employer must offer the employee other appropriate work before giving him notice. If this offer followed the notice, the notice would be void. The notice would also be void if the employer only offered the employee work for the time of substituting another employee.

Under Section 63(2) of the LC, the employer may give an employee notice, unless given on grounds of the unsatisfactory fulfilment of working tasks, for less serious breach of labour discipline or for reasons for which the immediate termination of the employment relationship is applicable. This is possibleonly in such case where:
a) the employer does not have the possibility to further employ the employee, not even for a reduced working time, in the place which was agreed to as the place of work performance,
b) the employee is not willing to shift to other work appropriate that was offered to him by the employer at the place of work agreed as the place of work performance or undertake the necessary training for this other work.

Appropriate work is also considered work for a reduced weekly working time, even though the employee was employed by the employer in an employment relationship for a stipulated weekly working time (for example, for a full term). The extent of the employee's work term in case of the offer of a reduced working time is not decisive.

Appropriate work may be any work in the place that was agreed upon in the employment contract as the place of the performance of work. This work need not correspond with the type of work agreed to by the parties in the employment contract. It will be any work that corresponds with the employee's health state, and, if possible, also with his qualification and skills. In case of a judicial dispute concerning the validity of notice given by the employer, the offer of other appropriate work must be made, but it must also be demonstrated that the employee refused this offer. The duty of offer of other appropriate work given by the employer is not considered fulfilled if it is an offer of other appropriate work only for a limited period (for example, during the taking of a maternal or parental leave by another employee).

VIII. Reasons for notice

The employer may terminate the employment relationship by notice only for reasons exhaustively listed in the LC. He cannot use any other reason for notice. The employer cannot validly waive, in advance, any of the reasons for notice or make an agreement with the employee that he will not use some of the reasons for notice with respect to the employee. The provisions of the LC concerning reasons for notice are mandatory, and therefore they cannot be modified on the basis of an agreement between the parties to an employment relationship.

Validity of notice may not be conditioned.

A reason for notice applied by the employer must be formulated in such a way that the real reason for notice is obvious. Insufficient specification of the reason for notice may also affect the validity of notice due to the lack of certainty.

The LC establishes not only the employer's duty to define the reason for notice in factual terms, but it also establishes a requirement concerning the method of defining it. The employer must define the reason for notice in factual terms in such a way that it may not be confused with a different reason for notice. A reason for notice is defined in factual terms in a way that eliminates confusion only if the factual circumstances of the reason for notice are defined in the notice in such a way that they, as a whole, establish an Act that may not be confused with other Acts. A reason for notice defined in factual terms is a reason including circumstances that, as a whole, may be brought under one of the factual situations listed in Section 63(1) LC.

Under Section 63(1) of the LC, the employer may give notice to the employee only for the following reasons:

a) if the employer or part thereof
   1. is wound up or
   2. is relocated and the employee does not agree with the change in the agreed location for performance of work,
b) if an employee becomes redundant by virtue of the employer or competent body issuing a written resolution on change in duties, technical equipment or reduction in the number of employees with the aim of securing work efficiency or on other organisational changes,
c) a medical opinion states that the employee's health condition has caused the long term loss of his ability to perform his previous work or if he can no longer perform such work as a result of an occupational disease or the risk of such an disease, or if he has already received the maximum permitted level of exposure in the work place as determined by a decision of a competent public health body,
d) an employee

1. does not meet the preconditions set by legal regulations for the performance of the agreed work,
2. ceases to fulfil the requirements pursuant to Section 42 paragraph (2) of the LC,
3. does not fulfil the requirements for the proper performance of the agreed work due to no fault of the employer, determined by the employer in internal regulations, or
4. does not satisfactorily fulfil the work tasks, and the employer has in the preceding six months challenged him in writing to rectify the insufficiencies, and the employee failed to do so within a reasonable period of time,

e) if there are reasons on the part of the employee, for which the employer might immediately terminate the employment relationship with him, or by virtue of less grave breaches of labour discipline. For less grave breaches of labour discipline, the employee may be given a notice if, with respect to the breach of labour discipline, he has been cautioned in writing within the previous six months as to the possibility of notice.

If the employer intends to give notice to an employee on the grounds of the breach of labour discipline, he shall be obliged to acquaint the employee with the reason for such and enable him to give his statement on this.

A. Reason for notice under Section 63(1)(a) point 1 LC

This reason includes two factual situations: either the entire employer or part of it is wound up.

If the entire employer entity is wound up (for example, it ceases to exist as a legal entity), the employer loses the objective possibility of continuing to employ his employees. Since the dissolution of the employer entity does not automatically cause termination of the employment relationship, until the date of dissolution of the employer entity, the employer must terminate the employment relationships of employees so that, by the date of the employer's dissolution, their periods of notice will have expired.

If the entire employer entity is wound up, the employer has no objective possibility of offering the employee other appropriate work (Section 63(2) of the LC). The termination of employment relationship by notice given by the employer for this reason is not covered by the protection period under Section 64 of the LC (prohibition of notice) or Section 66 of the LC concerning previous approval of the district office for work, social affairs and family, in case of a notice given to an employee with a health disability.

If the employer ceases to exist as a legal entity before the periods of notice of his employees have expired or before he has satisfied the statutory claims of the employees, the authority having dissolved the employer, must designate a new employer or a liquidator if the employer is liquidated, which must satisfy the claims of employees. The state must satisfy only the claims of employees of the employer entities having the legal status of public administration authorities.

In case of the dissolution of part of an employer entity, the employer may give notice to an employee only if he cannot offer him other appropriate work under Section 63(2) of the LC or if the employee refuses such work. In case of application of this reason for notice, the prohibition of notice under Section 64 of the LC does not apply.

B. Reason for notice under Section 63(1)(a) point 2 LC

The reason for notice under Section 63(1)(a) point 2 of the LC includes two factual situations: if either the employer or part thereof is relocated.

If the entire employer entity or a part thereof is relocated, the employer loses the possibility of fulfilling one of his fundamental duties according to the employment contract, is the duty to employ the employee in the place of performance of the work agreed. If the employee is not ready to work in a place of the performance of work other than that agreed in the employment contract or in the place of his residence, the employer may give him notice of termination.

C. Employee's redundancy

This is an extensively formulated reason for notice that allows the employer to apply a notice of termination even if the employer increases the total number of employees (for example, the employer foresees a change of qualification structure of his employees). In practice, this reason is often applied in cases where, due to organizational changes, the employee loses part of his work tasks. This reason may be applied when the organizational change is approved. Such a change must be approved in advance so that there is a sufficient period for applying the notice of termination and for the expiration of the period of notice. If the employer or a different competent entity approves an organizational change too late and its implementation follows shortly after its approval, it runs the risk of not being able to fulfil its fundamental duty with respect to the employee during the period of notice, which is to assign work to the employee according to the employment contract.

With respect to the legal nature of approval of the organizational change, according to the case law, it is not a legal act. This means that a party to an employment relationship may not ask the court to declare its nullity. Therefore, it cannot be challenged in court with an application for declaration of nullity of such approval. As far as the form of the approval of organizational change is concerned, the LC requires written form. Its non-observance is not sanctioned by nullity. Between the organizational change and the redundancy, there must be a causal link, which is to be demonstrated by the employer in case of a judicial dispute. Selection of the redundant employee is only a matter for the employer. Such a selection made by the employer may not be examined with respect to its correctness. However, in case of this reason for notice, the employer must not only offer the employee other appropriate work according to Section 63(2) of the LC, but he must also respect the protection period under Section 64 of the LC.

D. Employee´s health reasons

The employee's health reasons are, as a whole, not a sufficient reason for notice given by the employer. The employee's health reasons are legally relevant in applying notice of termination by the employer only if they are connected with a medical opinion. This applies not only to a long-term loss of health capability of the employee for his current work, but also to the reasons based on occupational disease or a risk of occupational disease. If the health reasons are not assessed in a medical opinion or a decision of the public health authority, the employer may not apply notice for these reasons even if the employee were not able to perform his previous work due to health reasons or if he had to stop performing previous work due to the protection of health. Such circumstances on the employee's part could result in him not being able to fulfil appropriately his working duties under Section 47 of the LC resulting from the employment contract. The reason for the application of notice by the employer is a long-term loss of health capability of the employee as opposed to the temporary incapacity for work, which, in contrast, protects the employee against notice given by the employer. A medical opinion for purposes of labour-law is issued by a physician designated by a medical facility pursuant to Section 16 of the Act No. 576/2004 Coll. on Healthcare. The employee's health condition in the medical opinion, at the time of delivery of notice, is decisive. If the medical opinion were to be revoked later, it would not affect the validity of notice given by the employer. Certification of a risk of occupational disease, occupational disease or attainment of the maximum permitted exposure time is issued in form of a decision by the public health authority. The LC does not provide explicitly when the condition of long-term incapacity for work occurs. The employee's incapacity may be regarded as long-term, also with respect to the Social Insurance Act, in principle, if it is longer than one year. A long-term loss of an employee's health capacity also establishes the employer's duty to transfer the employee to different work on unilateral basis. The employer either fulfils this legal duty or he may also apply a notice of termination for this reason. In case of the application of this reason for notice by the employer, there must be a long-term incapacity of the employee for his previous work. Long-term incapacity of the employee for his previous work exists not only if the law prohibits performance of certain work by him that he may not perform on a long-term basis, but also if, according to a medical opinion, given his health condition, he cannot perform certain work that was agreed upon in the employment contract. This concerns, in particular, cases where the employee becomes fully invalid.

E. Failure to meet prerequisites for performance of work

Section 63(1)(d) of the LC contains four reasons for notice. Although, in linguistic terms, the terms prerequisites and requirements are identical, for the purposes of notice given by the employer, the LC attributes a different legal meaning and content to these terms.

With respect to the failure to meet prerequisites under point 1, they must be established in generally binding legal regulations. Failure to meet prerequisites may occur at any time during the employment relationship (for example, also when the employee, at the time of establishment of the employment relationship, met the prerequisites established by legal regulations for the performance of work agreed and later, due to change of nature of work or increase of its technical level, he does not meet them anymore). Failure to meet prerequisites consists, in particular, in a failure to meet qualification prerequisites, unlike requirements that are, with respect to their content, formulated in a considerably more extensive manner. For the sake of clear distinction between failure to meet prerequisites established in generally binding legal regulations and requirements for due performance of work, failure to meet such requirements is, according to the LC, explicitly associated with requirements established by the employer in his internal regulation.

A special reason for notice is the failure to meet requirements under Section 42(2) of the LC that the employer, established in his internal regulation for executive employees, directly subordinates to the statutory body. It is election or designation, as a condition for conclusion of the employment contract. The reason for failure to meet such requirements is legally irrelevant.

F. Reason for notice under Section 42(2) LC

The factual situation concerning this reason for notice, which consists in failure to meet requirements under Section 42(2) of the LC, applies only to those employers that, in their internal regulation, have established election or designation as a requirement of the performance of the function of executive employee in direct managing power of the statutory body. If this issue is not regulated in the internal regulation of employers, they may not apply this reason for notice. Failure to meet requirements under Section 42(2) of the LC is understood as an objective situation where the employer's fault is legally irrelevant. It is a situation that occurs when an employee in direct managing power, according to the internal regulation, is recalled from the function according to special regulation or resigns from his function.

G. Failure to meet requirements for performance of work by the employee

These requirements for due performance of work should be determined by special regulation or by the employer himself in his internal regulation. Unlike in the case of prerequisites, it is required that the employer has not caused this situation by his own fault.

Requirements, unlike prerequisites, need not be established in legal regulations. However, unlike in the case of prerequisites, the employee does not meet requirements without the employer's fault. These requirements of the employer should be justified by the nature of the work performed. Such requirements include: appropriate social conduct, use of special clothes for performance of work, organizational abilities, special skills etc.

The substantive condition of notice consisting in written request, applies only to requirements consisting of the unsatisfactory fulfilment of work tasks. The period for using a written request of the employer is, under current legislation, six months. For an employer to give a valid notice, he must ask the employee to eliminate shortcomings within six months and such shortcomings must not have been eliminated by the employee in due time. A written request by the employer is regarded as a substantive condition of notice of termination and it must be delivered to the employee. This request of the employer must also indicate a period within which the employee should eliminate the shortcomings declared. The length of this period must be proportionate so that the employee may, in fact, eliminate unsatisfactory work results, otherwise notice given by the employer is void. Only when the employee, in due time, does not eliminate shortcomings in unsatisfactory performance of his work tasks, may the employer apply a notice of termination with respect to him.

The reason for notice may also be longer, because the LC does not impose a duty on the employer to apply these reasons within a specific statutory period. However, when the notice is applied, the reason for notice must exist. Duration of this reason for notice is not limited by the LC. In practice, it may be that the employee has been fulfilling his work tasks in an unsatisfactory manner already for a longer period of time and that the employer does not react to such situation. This fact is of considerable legal relevance for the employer, because, unlike in the case of the reason for notice consisting of a breach of work discipline, which must always be based on fault in order to constitute a sufficient basis for the employer's notice and this reason for notice must be applied by the employer in subjective and objective time-bar periods, the employer is not legally bound by any time-bar period.

Existence of this reason for notice depends on the objective situation. The employer must measure the employee's work results appropriately (for example, by means of work consumption standards). At the same time, the employer must have asked the employee for the elimination of shortcomings in writing in the last two months.

According to recent case law, if within six months, the employer asked the employee for elimination of shortcomings and the employee, within this period, does not fulfil his work tasks in a satisfactory manner again, the employer need not ask him repeatedly for the elimination of shortcomings at work.

H. Breach of work discipline

The LC establishes only two reasons for notice based on the breach of work discipline: a reason entitling the employer to terminate the employment relationship immediately and a less serious breach of work discipline. The first reason for notice covers the case when the employee performs an act establishing the employer's right to the immediate termination of employment relationship, but the employer chooses a notice of termination instead. A less serious breach of work discipline need not be continuous. Before applying this reason for notice, the employer must have, in the last six months, informed the employee of the possibility of notice in connection to a breach of work discipline. It follows that for the employer to apply notice of termination, the employee must have breached work discipline in a less serious manner at least twice. Upon the first less serious breach of work discipline, the employer warns him in writing and upon second breach of work discipline in a less serious manner, the employer may apply a notice of termination. Before applying a notice of termination due to the breach of work discipline, the employer must inform the employee of the reason for notice and allow him to present his opinion. The form of this opinion of the employee is not determined by the LC. It can be either written or oral. However, it must be mention that the correct evaluation of the degree of breach of work discipline depends mainly on the assessment of specific circumstances of the case. The court must always, in case of a dispute concerning the nullity of the termination of the employment relationship, with respect to specific circumstances of the case, examine whether the employee breached work discipline by fault, and, if so, decide the degree of the breach of work discipline in the case in question. These considerations of the court are not limited by any specific criteria or limits, but rather, the court only takes the specific characteristics of the case at hand in account. It follows that, when examining the intensity of the breach of work discipline, the court is not bound by the qualification of a certain act of an employee by his employer in his work rules (or another internal regulation).

A breach of work discipline by the employee may be defined as a breach of his duties, committed by fault, resulting from legal regulations, labour-law regulations, instructions of the employer, collective agreement or employment contract, or work rules. The employer may apply this reason for notice only within two months of the date when he became aware of the reason for notice (subjective time limit), but no later than one year from the date when the reason for notice occurred (objective time limit). If the employer became aware of the breach of work discipline by the employee within two months, he cannot apply notice during the one-year time-bar period. These periods are time-bar periods. Once they expire, the employer cannot apply the reason for notice in question. The time-bar period starts running at the moment of the delivery of notice. In case of several short or long absences of the employee, the two-month limit does not end earlier than two months after the date following the last absence caused by fault. If the employer became aware of an absence of the employee later, the limit starts running on the first day following the date when the employer became aware of the fact that it is an absence of the employee caused by fault.

Should the employee stop going to work without reason, his absences would be linked and they would justify not only a notice for breach of work discipline, but also the immediate termination of the employment relationship. The two-month subjective time limit for applying notice of termination, or the one-month limit for applying immediate termination of the employment relationship, would start running from the moment when the employer becomes aware that it was an absence from work caused by fault. The objective time limit would start running no later than the first day following the date when the absence ended.

Should the employer refuse to assign work to the employee without a reason (for example, he would stop fulfilling his fundamental legal duty resulting from the employment relationship), the employee could ask the employer to fulfil his duty, but he would not be obliged to require work to be assigned. The employee's inactivity in this respect cannot cause any adverse legal consequences to him.

Should the employer refuse to assign work to the employee even though the employee was ready to perform work, the employee would be obliged to start working again when the employer asks him to do so and declares that he is ready to assign work to the employee. Therefore, it is not a breach of work discipline if an employee, who was not asked by the employer to start working again, does not come to work and does not require work to be assigned.

A breach of work discipline is not only a breach of such duties in performing work committed by fault that result in the type of work agreed in the employment contract, but also a breach of the employee's duties committed by fault in performing other work for the employer from his own initiative. Breach of duties committed by fault consisting in performance of other work for the employer in contradiction to legal regulations, work rules, the employer's internal rules or instructions of executive employees is cosidered to be a breach of work discipline, too. The employee must observe work discipline not only in performing work according to the employment contract, but also in performing work that he has been transferred to. A breach of work discipline may be committed by the employee on a business trip, as well.

All cases of breach of work discipline by the employee must be committed by fault, at least in the form of negligence. Only such breaches of work discipline may justify legal consequences including notice of termination.

Fault is not defined by the Labour Code. For these purposes, fault must be understood as defined in the Criminal Code.

IX. Subjective and objective time-bar period

The objective time-bar period for applying notice of termination by the employer is set by the LC at two years only in the case of application of the reason for notice based on breach of work discipline. The subjective period for the purposes of applying notice of termination by the employer starts running as soon as the employer becomes aware of it. Such an employer needs not be in the function of the statutory body. It is sufficient to be any executive employee, which in most cases will be the immediately superior executive employee. A business plenipotentiary must be regarded as a representative of the employer and not as an employee because he should not be in an employment relationship. The moment when the employer became aware of a breach of work discipline by the employee from the business plenipotentiary should not be the moment when the employer became aware of it. Therefore, the business plenipotentiary, under labour-law regulations in force, is regarded as a person independent of the employer, as a representative and not an employee, although he has full powers to act, in principle, in all matters on the employer's behalf.

X. Prohibition of notice

The protection period is a period within which the employer may not apply a notice of termination with respect to an employee, even though one of the cases justifying notice of termination exists. The protection period (prohibition of notice) applies only with respect to notice given by the employer. It does not protect the employee against termination of the employment relationship on the basis of a legal fact. As far as the prohibition of notice by the employer is concerned, the situation when notice took legal effect (for example, its delivery), is relevant. If the employer applies notice against an employee before the protection period expires, the notice is void. The prohibition of notice applies only with respect to the employer. The employee may give a notice of termination of the employment relationship even if there are reasons on his part for which the employer could not terminate the employment relationship by notice. Under Section 64 of the LC, an employer may not give a notice to an employee within a protected period. This means:

a) within a period when the employee is acknowledged to be temporarily incapable for work due to disease or accident, unless deliberately induced or caused under the influence of alcohol, narcotic substances or psychotropic substances, and within the period from submission of a proposal for institutional care or from entry into spa treatment up to the day of termination thereof,

b) in the event of a call-up to perform extraordinary service during a state of crisis, from the date when the employee is called up to perform extraordinary service, from the date of delivery of the call-up order or when called up to start extraordinary service by mobilization order or mobilization notice, or if the employee has been ordered to carry out extraordinary service, until the expiry of two weeks from his demobilisation; this shall also apply with regard to the performance of alternative service pursuant to special regulations,

c) within the period of a female employee's pregnancy, when a female employee is on maternity leave, a female employee or a male employee is on parental leave, or when a lone female employee or a lone male employee takes care of a child under the age of three,

d) within the period when an employee is released for execution of a public function for a long term, or

e) within the period when an employee working at night is on grounds of medical opinion acknowledged as being temporarily incapable to perform night work.

If an employee receives notice prior to the commencement of a protected period in such a way that the period of notice should expire within this period, the employment relationship shall terminate upon expiry of the final day of the protected period, except in such cases where the employee announces that he does not insist on the extension of the employment relationship.

Spa treatment and institutional treatment of employee

Prohibition of notice applies with respect to an employee during the period from the beginning of spa treatment until its termination. Spa treatment refers to treatment that covered by health insurance, but also to spa treatment where only the examination and treatment of the employee is covered by health insurance.

The second reason of the protection period is the employee's institutional treatment. The employee's institutional treatment as a reason for the protection period is a legally relevant reason for the prohibition of notice given by the employer, from the moment of filing an application for institutional treatment until its termination.

A protection period, where prohibition of notice by the employer applies, is also justified by institutional treatment (therapy) of the employee, irrespective of what type of institutional treatment of the employee is involved. It is institutional care provided in hospitals and specialized treatment facilities.

A. Employee's temporary incapacity for work

The temporary incapacity for work protects the employee against notice given by the employer. However, such temporary incapacity may not have been caused by the employee intentionally or have been caused under the influence of alcohol, narcotic substances or psychotropic substances. If the employer wants to give a notice to an employee without risk of its nullity, he should, in his own interest, verify the cause of the existence of the temporary incapacity for work.

The protection period due to the employee's temporary incapacity for work always starts on the date when it is declared that the employee is temporarily unfit for work and always terminates on the date when his temporary incapacity for work ends.

If the employee himself gives notice and, during the protection period, becomes unfit for work, the period of notice is not interrupted due to the incapacity for work. Therefore, there is no general prohibition for the termination of the employment relationship, but only a prohibition of notice by the employer. For the assessment of validity of the employer's notice, it is crucial whether, at the time of delivery of notice, such legal facts existed that, under the LC, establish a prohibition of notice. Their objective existence is decisive, irrespective of whether the employer was aware of them at the time of applying notice.

B. Employee's pregnancy, maternity and parenthood

Pregnancy protects a woman against the possibility of applying notice of termination, also when the woman herself or the employer is not aware of the pregnancy. A parent on parental leave is also protected against notice given by the employer. Prohibition of notice given by the employer for this reason also protects employees haven taken a child into custody to replace the care of parents for a child whose mother has died.

Since the LC allows a male or female employee, after returning to work, to go back on parental leave, which is still formulated as his right, an objective situation is crucial for assessing their protection against notice. At the time of notice being applied by the employer, it will be decisive whether the woman is on maternity leave or the woman or the man is on parental leave. Legal interpretation in the sense of the return of a woman from maternity leave and of a man or a woman from parental leave leads to a loss of the protection against notice given by employer, has no statutory basis. Considerations concerning the notice to be or not to be given by the employer must be guided by the circumstance whether such persons are on maternal or parental leave.

C. Performance of public function by the employee

A reason for the protection period, where a prohibition of notice applies to the employer, is only a long-term release of the employee for the performance of a public function. The LC does not define the term long-term release of the employee for the performance of a public function. In case of a long-term release of the employee for the performance of a public function, the employee does not fulfil duties resulting from the employment relationship and he is released from performance of these duties for the performance of a public function. A function is a public function if it is defined by the term of office based on election or designation.

D. Employee's temporary incapacity for performance of night work

An employee is an employee working at night if he, during night time between 10 p.m. and 5 a.m., works at least three hours of his working time within 24 consecutive hours on a regular basis. An employee's temporary incapacity for the performance of night work is a reason of prohibition of notice given by the employer. This temporary incapacity for the performance of night work must be demonstrated by a medical opinion. Employee protection, in case of this reason, also applies to employees fit for the performance of work in daily working regime, nut temporarily unfit for the performance of night work.

XI. Exceptions from protection period

The possibility of terminating employment relationship by notice given by the employer during the protection period, legally formulated as an exception, results from the nature of these reasons for notice. The existence of such reasons either objectively precludes the employer from continuing to employ the employee, or those reasons involve cases of such a breach of work discipline, when the legislator follows the principle that employees breaching work discipline do not deserve increased protection.

There are two reasons for establishing the immediate termination of the employment relationship by the employer. The first being a final conviction of the employee of an intentional crime and the second reason being a breach of work discipline in a serious manner. For these reasons, the employer may also apply a notice with respect to the employee. In case of this reason for notice, when immediate termination of employment relationship is also possible, only employees on maternal (parental) leave during ordinary maternal (parental) leave (for example, during the period under Section 166(1) of LC) are protected. If the employer applied notice with respect to the employee for this reason before starting maternity leave or parental leave and the period of notice of such an employee should expire during maternity leave or parental leave, it will expire at the time of termination of maternity leave or parental leave.

If the employer applies, with respect to a woman, notice for serious breach of work discipline (for example, for a reason otherwise establishing his right to immediate termination of the employment relationship), notice is valid even if the woman is pregnant. Similarly, notice for this reason applied with respect to an employee who is temporarily unfit for work would be valid, as well. This also applies to other reasons of protection period, which, in these cases of termination of the employment relationship by notice given by the employer, do not protect the employee. Prohibition of notice by the employer does not apply if the employee, due to his own fault, does not meet the prerequisites for the performance of work agreed under special regulation (for example, withdrawal of driving licence). However, in this case, at least the employee's in form of negligence is required.

Notice for other breach of work discipline

Notice given by the employer for other breach of work discipline entitles the employer to apply, with respect to employees, notice also during the protection period, with the exception of a pregnant woman or an employee on maternity leave or parental leave.

Unlike the reason for notice under Section 64(3)(b) of the LC, in case of notice given by the employer for a reason under Section 63(1) of the LC, protection of the employee against notice given by the employer applies to the entire period of maternity leave and to the entire period of parental leave, as well as to the entire period of parental leave. If the employer applies notice before the start of the protection period for these reasons, the protection period is not extended until the time of termination of maternity leave or parental leave.

Prohibition of notice does not apply to the notice given by employer in case of dissolution of employer or his part. The same applies in case of relocation of the employer as a whole or his part, in case the employee does not agree with the change of place of performance work and for other types of breach of work discipline, unless the employee is pregnant or on maternity leave, or the parental leave.

Other cases where prohibition of notice does not apply

The prohibition of notice does not apply to cases of termination of fixed-term employment relationship, termination of employment relationship by agreement, termination of employment relationship during the probationary period and to notice given by the employee. For reasons when the employer could terminate the employment relationship immediately, notice can be given irrespective of the protection period, unless the employee is on maternity leave or parental leave (Section 166(1) of the LC).

§ 3 Notice given by employee

Notice must be, under pain of nullity, made in writing and it must be delivered.

Just like in case of the notice given by the employer, notice given by the employee must be, under pain of nullity, made in writing and it must be delivered to the other party.

§ 4 Immediate termination of employment relationship

Legal nature of immediate termination of employment relationship by the employer

The immediate termination of employment relationship by the employer is established by the LC as an exceptional method of termination of the employment relationship. Given the importance of the immediate termination of employment relationship for both parties, this reason should be applied in practice only in exceptional cases when it is not fair to expect the employer to continue to employ the employee after giving notice, including during the period of notice. In the case of immediate termination of the employment relationship, no periods of notice apply. The immediate termination of the employment relationship is a unilateral legal act aimed at terminating the employment relationship at the moment of delivery of its written declaration to the other party. Unlike notice as a unilateral addressed legal act, the immediate termination of the employment relationship takes place at the moment of delivery, without any period of notice. Unlike notice, the immediate termination of the employment relationship may not be revoked because the LC does not contain a special provision on the revocation of the immediate termination of the employment relationship.

The immediate termination of the employment relationship may be performed not only by the employer, but also by the employee. Since the immediate termination of the employment relationship implies a significant intervention in the legal position of both parties to the employment relationship, unlike in the case of notice, not only the employer, but also the employee may terminate the employment relationship immediately only due to statutory reasons listed exhaustively.

Under Section 70 of the LC an employer and an employee must make the immediate termination of the employment relationship in writing, wherein they must define the reason in terms of deed in such a way that no confusion with another reason shall be possible. This is to be delivered to the other party within the determined term or it shall otherwise be deemed invalid. The stated reason may not be subsequently changed.

The employer must apply the reason for the immediate termination of the employment relationship in a subjective time limit of two months from becoming aware of the reason establishing the possibility of the immediate termination of the employment relationship, but within the objective time limit of one year from the reason coming into being. With respect to the subjective time-bar period on the employer's part, it is sufficient that an immediately superior executive employee or a superior executive employee becomes aware of this reason, who is entitled to, with respect to this subordinate employee (with respect to whom the employment relationship is to be terminated immediately), impose work tasks and give him binding instructions. However, this does not apply where the reason for establishing the immediate termination of the employment relationship was caused by the employee together with the executive employee. For the subjective time-bar period to start, in this case, another executive employee, superior to the executive employee who caused, together with the subordinate employee must become aware of the reason for the immediate termination of the employment relationship.

The one-year period is an objective time-bar period, which starts from the date when the reason for the immediate termination of the employment relationship came into being.

Periods for application of the immediate termination of the employment relationship are substantive time-bar periods. Once they expire, the right to apply the immediate termination of the employment relationship expires.

The objective period may be used by the employer only if, during the subjective period, the entitled person did not become aware of the reason for establishing the possibility of the immediate termination of the employment relationship.

If the employer, during the two-month time-bar period, becomes aware of the reason for the immediate termination of the employment relationship and does not use his right, he cannot apply for the immediate termination of the employment relationship in the one-year objective period.

I. Immediate termination of employment relationship

Under Section 68 of the LC, an employer may terminate an employment relationship exceptionally, only in cases where the employee:
a) was in the last instance sentenced for committing an intentional criminal offence,
b) was in serious breach of labour discipline.

A. Conviction of an intentional criminal offence by final judgment

According to labour-law, regulation for the immediate termination of the employment relationship may be applied if the employee was in the last instance convicted of an intentional criminal offence, irrespective of the length of the prison term or whether such activity of the employee was associated with the fulfilment of work tasks or directly connected with their fulfilment. Moreover, it is irrelevant whether the employee was sentenced to imprisonment or other penalty. However, it must be an intentional criminal offence of the employee. A criminal offence is an illegal act, the characteristics of which are listed in the Criminal Code, unless provided otherwise in the Criminal Code (Section 8 of the Criminal Code). The LC does not distinguish, in connection with the reason for the immediate termination of the employment relationship, whether it is a minor offence or a crime. Nonetheless, distinction between minor offences and crimes as categories of criminal offences is also legally relevant for the application of the immediate termination of the employment relationship because one category of minor offences consists of criminal offences committed by negligence, which cannot establish a sufficient legal basis for the immediate termination of the employment relationship because they are not intentional criminal offences. Another category of criminal offences consists of intentional criminal offences for which the Criminal Code establishes a custodial penalty of not more than five years. This category of criminal offences, if committed by the employee, is, besides crimes, a reason for the immediate termination of the employment relationship by the employer.

The employer may apply the immediate termination of the employment relationship with respect to the employee for his lawful conviction of an intentional criminal offence only if the judicial decision sentencing of an employee for a custodial penalty is final. As such, taking the employee into detention is not a reason for the immediate termination of the employment relationship. Subsequent annulment of a final judicial decision in criminal proceedings on the basis of an extraordinary remedy does not affect the validity of the immediate termination of the employment relationship because the legal act must be evaluated according to the legal situation at the time it was made.

B. Serious breach of work discipline

The serious breach of work discipline is a reason for the immediate termination of the employment relationship. The intensity of the breach of work discipline, which is a sufficient legal basis for the application of the immediate termination of the employment relationship, is not defined by the LC. Legal qualification of the serious breach of work discipline depends on the circumstances of the case in question. Factors to be taken into consideration include not only the person of the employee, his working position, the degree of fault and the way of breach of work discipline, but also the time and situation concerning the breach of work discipline. The employer may specify cases of serious breach of work discipline in his internal regulation. However, when determining the validity of the immediate termination of the employment relationship, the court is not legally bound by such definition made by the employer.

This factual situation is mostly connected with a breach of work discipline caused by fault, or breach of the employee's fundamental legal duties listed in Section 81 of the LC. The serious breach of work discipline must be demonstrated by the employer and, with respect to the employee, it must be caused at least by fault in the form of negligence. It is a breach of legal duties by the employee resulting from generally binding legal regulations, the employer's internal rules, from the employment contract or collective agreement. The employee may also breach work discipline on a business trip, if this breach is connected with the performance of work in an employment relationship.

C. Breach of work discipline abroad

The employer may also terminate the employment relationship when the employee returns from abroad, if he committed a breach of work discipline abroad. In this case, there is an exception concerning the beginning of the subjective time-bar period for the immediate termination of the employment relationship because it is irrelevant when the employer really became aware of the breach of work discipline by the employee. The subjective time limit for the application of the immediate termination of the employment relationship starts from the date of the employee's return from abroad, which can be, in practice, not only later than the moment when the employer becomes aware of the reason for the immediate termination of the employment relationship, but also earlier. Also in this case, the one-year objective time-bar period for the application of the immediate termination of the employment relationship.

D. Prohibition of immediate termination of employment relationship

The LC establishes a prohibition of the immediate termination of the employment relationship by the employer with respect to categories of employees enjoying special protection. If there is a reason for the immediate termination of the employment relationship, according to the LC, the employer may terminate the employment relationship by notice.

In case of a lone employee caring for a child younger than 3 years of age, his level of legal protection against the immediate termination of the employment relationship is the same as in case of employees on maternity leave or parental leave. This special protection is also granted to an employee provided that he is caring for a close person with a serious health disability. The term close person is defined in Section 116 of the Civil Code. In case of these categories of employees, however, the employer may terminate the employment relationship by notice, except for a pregnant woman on maternity leave or an employee on parental leave under Section 166(1) of the LC (for example, during ordinary maternity leave). The employer may not immediately terminate the employment relationship with persons from these categories, even if, otherwise, they meet all the conditions for the immediate termination of the employment relationship by the employer.

The LC prohibits the employer to apply the immediate termination of the employment relationship in case of a person with a health disability, who, under current legislation, has the status of a person with a serious health disability, without the need to examine whether this person is receiving care in a social service facility or institutional care in a medical facility.

II. Immediate termination of employment relationship by the employee

Unlike notice, which can be given by the employee without any reason, the immediate termination of the employment relationship may be given by the employee only for reasons listed exhaustively in the law. The immediate termination of the employment relationship is accomplished with delivery of the declaration of the other party, (for example, at the moment of delivery without any period of notice). In order to ensure that employees use this legal act responsibly and do not disrupt the employer's operation, the LC allows them to terminate the employment relationship in this way only for reasons explicitly indicated in Section 69.

Under Section 69 of the LC an employee may immediately terminate an employment relationship, if

a) according to a medical opinion, he is unable to keep performing work without serious threat to his health and the employer has not transferred him to other work appropriate for him within 15 days from the submission of such opinion,

b) his employer has failed to pay him a wage or wage compensation, travel reimbursement, payment for on-call duty or alternative income in the event of the employee's temporary incapacity for work or part thereof within 15 days of payment becoming due,

c) his life or health is directly threatened.

An adolescent employee may also immediately terminate an employment relationship if he is incapable to perform work without jeopardising his morals.

An employee may immediately terminate an employment relationship only within a term of one month from the day he became acquainted with the reason for the immediate termination of the employment relationship.

An employee who immediately terminated an employment relationship shall be entitled to wage compensation for the amount of his average monthly earnings for a two-month notice period.

A. Serious threat to employee's health

The employee may immediately terminate an employment relationship, if according to a medical opinion, he is unable to keep performing work without serious threat to his health and the employer has not transferred him to other work appropriate for him within 15 days from the submission of such opinion.

The employee's health condition must be so bad that, for this reason, further performance of work would pose a serious risk to his health. This must follow clearly from a medical opinion, which must explicitly declare that the employee is unable to keep performing his work without a serious threat to his health. At the time of application of the immediate termination of the employment relationship by the employee, a medical opinion must be already issued that clearly declares that the employee is unable to keep performing work without a serious threat to his health. If the medical opinion were issued later, after application of the immediate termination of the employment relationship, the immediate termination of the employment relationship would be void. The employee's right to terminate the employment relationship immediately comes into being only upon expiration of the 15-day period after submission of a medical opinion unless the employee has been transferred to other appropriate work before hand. This period starts running on the first day after the submission of medical opinion. If the end of the period falls on a Saturday, Sunday or a public holiday, the last day of the period is the next working day.

If the employer, after submission of medical opinion, offers the employee other work within the type of work agreed to the employee, it is not necessary to amend the employment contract. However, if work outside of the scope of the type of work agreed, the parties should make an agreement to change working conditions under Section 54 of the LC. If the employee refuses other appropriate work offered, he cannot the terminate employment relationship himself anymore because the reason for the immediate termination of the employment relationship has ceased to exist. In this case, the employer acquires the duty of unilateral transfer to other work under Section 55(1)(a) of the LC. The employer acquires this duty at the moment of the delivery of medical opinion to him. This legal situation does not entitle the employer to assign previous work to the employee. At the same time, there is scope for application of reason for notice given by the employer under Section 63(1)(a) of the LC. This procedure should only be applied by the employer if he does not manage to make an agreement with the employee to change the working conditions agreed under Section 54 of the LC.

This 15-day period does not mean that the employee must perform work posing a serious risk to his health during this period. If the employer does not transfer him to different work immediately after the submission of medical opinion, there is an obstacle to work on the employer's part, for which the employee must receive wage compensation in the amount of their average earning. If the employer failed to comply with his duty to transfer the employee to other work within 15 days of the submission of medical opinion, the employee would be entitled to terminate the employment relationship immediately.

B. Imminent threat to employee's life or health

Under Section 69(1)(c) of the LC, another reason for the immediate termination of the employment relationship by the employee is the imminent threat to life or health of the employee. Differences between this reason and the reason regulated in Section 69(1) of the LC (a) consist in their content and method of application. An imminent threat to the employee's life or health is a reason for the immediate termination of the employment relationship by the employee; the employee does not need any medical opinion for this purpose. However, it cannot be ruled out that such an opinion will be procured by the employee for the sake of legal certainty. The imminent threat to the employee's life or health, as a special case of the immediate termination of the employment relationship by the employee, need not be caused by the character of the work performed. Rather, it applies to non-standard situations in connection with work performed (for example, there is a situation at the workplace that is contrary to rules on occupational health and safety). The legal basis of application of this reason by the employee is also an instruction of the employer given to the employee for performance of certain work tasks in contradiction to rules on occupational health and safety. In case of such situation, the employee could refuse to comply with the instruction given by his employer without the risk that non-compliance with the instruction would be regarded as a breach of work discipline. It is obvious that this legal situation would allow the employee to either not comply with the employer's instruction or to terminate the employment relationship immediately even if he concluded himself that work under these conditions poses an imminent risk to his life or health.

In this case, an imminent threat to the employee's life or health is required. However, it will not only be an imminent threat to the employee's life, but also an imminent threat to the employee's health. Given the fact that "employee's health" is used in the singular, it may be inferred that this reason for the immediate termination of the employment relationship requires the existence of an imminent threat to the employee's life or health.

Assessment of the situation of an imminent threat to health will be, in a possible judicial dispute, a matter for the expert, even though the employee's action as such will be marked by the subjective perception of the situation of imminent threat.

The employee may use his right to the immediate termination of the employment relationship within the one-month subjective time-bar period, which starts running from the date when he becomes aware of the reason for the immediate termination of the employment relationship. However, this one-month period for application of the employee's right to the immediate termination of the employment relationship because he is unable to keep performing previous work without a serious threat to his health starts running no earlier than 15 days after submission of medical opinion. For this time, the employer must offer other appropriate work to the employee. This applies also in the case where the employer, after submission of medical opinion, announces before expiration of the 15-day period, that he does not have any other appropriate work for him or that he will not enable him to perform other appropriate work for other reasons. This applies also in the case where the employee knows from the beginning that the employer will not transfer him to other appropriate work because he knows that the employer has no such work. Only upon expiration of 15 days after the submission of medical opinion does the case exist where the employee is entitled to the immediate termination of the employment relationship.

C. Failure to pay wage or wage compensation

The employee may also terminate the employment relationship immediately if the employer failed to pay him even a part of the wage (salary) or wage (salary) compensation within 15 days of the due date. The reason for the immediate termination of the employment relationship by the employee exists in case of every late payment of wage (for example, always after 15 days of payment becoming due). Other payments, even though they are not payments of wage, are placed by the legislator on the same level. These payments include travel reimbursement, payment for on-call duty or compensation of income in the event of the employee's temporary incapacity for work. According to the Act No. 462/2003 Coll. on compensation of income in the event of the employee's temporary incapacity for work, as amended, this compensation is a special payment provided by the employer for calendar days from the first day of the employee's temporary incapacity for work, no longer than until the tenth day of the employee's temporary incapacity for work.

If a specific date of payment is agreed by the parties in the employment contract or collective agreement, the 15-day period within the meaning of Section 69 of the LC, after which the employee may terminate the employment relationship immediately, starts running on the first day following the day of wage becoming due as agreed.

If the date of payment is not agreed upon by the parties in the employment contract or collective agreement, statutory rules on wage becoming due under the LC apply. The 15-day period, after which the employee is entitled to terminate the employment relationship immediately, starts running on the first day of the month following the month during which wage should have been paid to the employee.

Failure to pay even a part of wage is also a reason for the immediate termination of the employment relationship by the employee. If the employer does not provide wage and other wage benefits under Section 69(1)(b) of the LC for a longer time, the reason for the immediate termination of the employment relationship exists after 15 days of every single payment becoming due.

For the employee, it is a very serious reason, on the basis of which the legislator allows him to terminate the employment relationship immediately. The employee is entitled to terminate the employment relationship immediately for this reason also when the employer fulfilled his duty, but later, after the due date, even if, at the time of the late fulfilment of this duty by the employer, the employee had not applied the immediate termination of the employment relationship.

The time for application of the reason for the immediate termination of the employment relationship by the employee is immediately connected with the date of wage or salary becoming due.

D. Risk to morals

An adolescent employee (up to 18 years old) may terminate his employment relationship immediately if he is unable to perform work without jeopardising his morals. The LC does not define the term "jeopardising his morals". This situation need not be caused by fault by the employer (for example, there can be a working environment jeopardising the adolescent employee's morals). This reason for the immediate termination of the employment relationship depends on the objective situation jeopardising the morals of an adolescent employee that may be assessed objectively by the competent court. The objective situation jeopardising the employee's morals also has a subjective element. Beyond doubt, cases may occur where the situation at the workplace objectively jeopardises the morals and, despite this, with respect to the employee's personal characteristics, such a situation at the workplace does not jeopardise the adolescent employee's morals. Whether this situation exists depends on an assessment of the circumstances of the case at hand. Risk to morals is, under the LC associated with the condition that employee cannot perform work for this reason.

E. Wage compensation as satisfaction for immediate termination of employment relationship

Wage compensation in the amount of the employee's average earning for the two-month period of notice is a satisfaction for the employee terminating the employment relationship immediately without a period of notice for a serious reason.

§ 5 Termination of fixed-term employment relationship

A fixed-term employment relationship may be terminated by expiration of the period agreed by the parties. During this period, agreed by the contracting parties, the fixed-term employment relationship may also be terminated by means of other statutory methods listed in Section 59 of the LC (for example, on the basis of an agreement, notice, immediate termination of the employment relationship, termination of the employment relationship during the probationary period or the employee's death). This also applies to nationals of third countries working as employees in an employment relationship.

The employment relationship ends upon the expiration of the period (for example, on the basis of a legal event without the need for any legal act aimed at its termination). If the duration of a fixed-term employment relationship was agreed upon by the parties alternatively, the employment relationship ends on the basis of the event that occurs earlier. The employment relationship ends by expiration of the period also if its termination falls within the protection period. Before its termination, the employer is not obliged to offer the employee other appropriate work or to take care of his new employment.

However, before expiration of the period, agreed the fixed-term employment relationship may also be terminated by means of other methods listed in the LC.

The employment relationship does not end upon the expiration of the term agreed if, at the time of its establishment or modification, the statutory conditions for establishment of a fixed-term employment relationship are not met or the fixed-term employment relationship was not established by a written employment contract.

I. Reclassification of employment relationship into employment relationship for indefinite period

The LC also foresees situations where the fixed-term employment relationship originally agreed upon turns into an employment relationship for an indefinite period. This happens if the employee, after expiration of the period agreed, continues to perform work and the employer knows it. This employment relationship turns into an employment relationship for an indefinite period, unless agreed otherwise by the parties, with all statutory limitations of its termination, as foreseen by the LC in particular on the employer's part. Continuation of work with the employer's knowledge, however, does not mean that further performance of work by the employee must be known to the statutory body itself or its members. Such person may be any executive employee superior to the employee (for example, the next superior executive employee). Continuation of work takes place with the employer's knowledge and it is not impeded by the employer (member of statutory body or another executive superior employee). However, if such an executive employee clearly indicates to the employee that he does not agree with the further performance of work, the employment relationship should not turn into an employment relationship for an indefinite period. The employment relationship is reclassified from a fixed term to an indefinite period only if the employer knows about the further performance of work and does not forbid him to continue working explicitly or in a different manner ("with the employer's knowledge").

Reclassification of a fixed-term employment relationship into an employment relationship for an indefinite period does not take place if the employer, after the termination of the period of duration of the employment relationship, explicitly forbids the further performance of work by the employee.

§ 6 Termination of employment relationship during probationary period

An essential element of the termination of the employment relationship during the probationary period is a declaration of a party clearly indicating the termination of the employment relationship during the probationary period. Unlike notice, termination of the employment relationship during the probationary period does not require any reason on the employee's or employer's part. In case of the termination of the employment relationship during the probationary period, the LC provides that the employment relationship is terminated on the date indicated in the declaration of the party as the date of the termination of the employment relationship. If such date is not indicated in the declaration of the party, the legal act is not void for this reason and the date of termination of the employment relationship is deemed to be the date of delivery of the declaration to the other party.

The employer may terminate the employment of a pregnant woman, a mother who has given birth within the last nine months or a breastfeeding woman only in writing, in exceptional cases not relating to her pregnancy or maternal function, giving appropriate reasons in writing. Otherwise, the termination shall be invalid unless it is stipulated otherwise below. Written notification on the termination of an employment relationship shall be delivered to the other party, as a rule, within the minimum of three days prior to the day the employment relationship is to terminate.

I. Peculiarities of termination of employment relationship during probationary period with respect to special categories of employees

On the basis of the new Directive 2010/18/EU on parental leave, the Directive 92/85/EEC on protection of mothers, as well as the prohibition of discrimination in the entire area of labour-law relationships, in case of the termination of the employment relationship during the probationary period with a pregnant employee, mother of a child within 9 months of childbirth or a breastfeeding woman, the employer must indicate reasons for the termination of the employment relationship during probationary period. A breastfeeding woman enjoys this protection throughout the breastfeeding period, even if breastfeeding takes longer than 9 months after childbirth. Non-observance of this legal duty by the employer causes nullity of the termination of the employment relationship during the probationary period. Non-observance of the three-day indicative period prescribed by the LC concerning written notification of the termination of the employment relationship during the probationary period does not lead to nullity of the legal act. Its non-observance is a breach of labour-law regulations with the possibility of applying labour-law sanctions.

The employment relationship during the probationary period may also be terminated by the immediate the termination of the employment relationship. The other party must be notified of the legal act of the termination of the employment relationship before the probationary period expires, otherwise, termination of the employment relationship during the probationary period is void.

If the probationary period was not agreed in due form (for example, only in oral form, or in a written employment contract, but only after establishment of employment relationship), the employment relationship may only be terminated according to other methods listed in Section 59 of the LC.

§ 7 Collective redundancies

The LC has regulated the legal model of collective redundancies since 1996.

For the time being, the LC of the Slovak Republic is built on one of the definitions of collective redundancies as enshrined in Directive 98/59/EC, which derives collective redundancies from the number of employees.

Under Section 73 of the LC, collective redundancy occurs if an employer or a part of an employer terminates the employment relationship by notice for the reasons stipulated in Section 63 paragraph (1) letter (a) and (b) of the LC, or if the employment relationship is terminated by another method on reason not relating to the person of the employee within 30 days:

a) of at least ten employees of an employer who employs more than 20 and less than 100 employees,
b) of at least 10% of the total up expenses of employees of an employer who employs at least 100 and less than 300 employees,
c) of at least 30 employees of an employer who employs at least 300 employees.

With a view to reaching an agreement, the employer shall be obliged, at least one month prior to the commencement of collective redundancies, to negotiate with the employee representatives, and if there are no employee representatives in the workplace directly with the affected employees, measures enabling avoidance of collective redundancies of employees, or reduction thereof, mainly negotiate the possibility of placing them in appropriate employment at the employer's other work places, also subsequent to preceding preparation, and measures for mitigating the adverse consequences of collective redundancies of employees. To this end, the employer shall be obliged to provide the employees representatives with all the necessary information and to inform him in writing, in particular as to:

a) the reasons for the collective redundancies,
b) the number and structure of employees to be subject to termination of employment,
c) the overall number and structure of employees employed by the employer,
d) the period over which collective redundancies shall be effected,
e) the criteria for the selection of employees to be subject to termination of employment.

The employer shall at the same time deliver a copy of the written information with the names, surnames and addresses of permanent residence of the employees whose employment relationship it intends to terminate to the Office of Labour, Social and Family Affairs for the purposes of finding a solution to the problems associated with the collective redundancy.

Subsequent to negotiations on collective redundancies with the employees representatives, the employer shall be obliged to deliver written information on the outcome of negotiations to:

a) the Labour Office, and
b) the employees representatives.

The employees representatives may submit comments relating to collective redundancies to the Labour Office.

With regard to collective redundancies, the employer may give notice to employees for reasons as stipulated of the employment relationship by agreement for the same reasons, upon expiry of one month from the day of delivery of written information at the earliest.

If an employer violates the obligations stipulated by an employee subject to the termination of an employment relationship within the scope of collective redundancies, the employee shall be entitled to wage compensation at the minimal amount of a twofold of his average monthly earnings pursuant to Section 134 of the LC.

For the purposes of collective redundancy, an organisational unit of the employer that has the status of a branch plant registered in the Commercial Register under applicable special regulation is deemed to be a part of the employer.

In addition to smaller legislative changes brought by recent amendment of the LC, a substantial legislative change should be considered the provision of Section 73.13, according to which for the purpose of collective redundancies, the organizational unit of the employer with no legal personality is considered as an integral part of the employer. In this way, the LC allows for the situation in which legal obligations of the employer with legal personality in the event of collective redundancies may be performed by the organizational units of the employer (branches). Such newly regulated status particularly suits employers with a complex organizational structure, who used to have great difficulty in meeting their notification obligations on collective redundancies related to Labour Offices.

§ 8 Nullity of termination of employment relationship

The issue of nullity of the termination of the employment the relationship is very important because it is the procedural guarantee of the rights of employees, enshrined not only in Section 79(2) of the LC, but also in Section 14 of the LC, which establishes the the right to judicial protection of the rights of employees. The guarantee of judicial enforcement of rights of employees is also established by the Civil Procedure Code and the Constitution of the Slovak Republic.

Under legislation in force, not only the employee, but also the employer, may challenge a void termination of the employment relationship in a two-month time-bar period.

In the case of void termination of the employment relationship, relative nullity exists and it may only be invoked by the party affected by the reason for nullity. It is an exception to the principle of absolute nullity of legal acts. The provisions of the LC on the nullity of the termination of the employment relationship are mandatory.

Disputes concerning the void termination of the employment relationship are decided by the courts. The rights resulting from the void termination of the employment relationship may be exercised by both parties of the employment relationship in a two-month time-bar period, which starts running from the date when the employment relationship should have ended.

Rights resulting from the void termination of the employment relationship concern only the cases of the termination of employment relationship on the basis of a legal act. The party to the employment relationship against whom the legal act declaring the nullity was made in order to terminate the employment relationship, may invoke his right in court so that the court rules on the nullity of the termination of the employment relationship. Nullity must be determined by the court.

Until final ruling of the court, the employment relationship is regarded as validly terminated. Therefore, the termination of the employment relationship is void only if its nullity was declared in a judicial decision. Without a judicial decision in the matter of the nullity of the termination of the employment relationship, the terminated employment relationship is deemed validly terminated. If the employer terminates the employment relationship by notice during the probationary period, by immediate termination or by agreement, and the employee is satisfied that it is a void termination of the employment relationship, until the court rules, both contracting parties must abide by special provisions of the LC concerning the nullity of the termination of the employment relationship, which serve as a *lex specialis* with respect to other labour-law regulations.

The two-month period for bringing an action for the nullity of t the ermination of the employment relationship is a substantive time-bar period. Once it expires, the right to bring an action for the nullity of termination of the employment relationship expires. The court examines this time limit of its own motion. Since it is a substantive time limit, on the last day of the period, the application for the termination of the employment relationship must be filed in court. It starts running from the date when the employment relationship should have ended by the termination challenged in court. The period starts running only if the notice or declaration of the immediate termination of the employment relationship was delivered, which is a substantive condition of validity.

I. Termination of employment relationship by employee

The basic prerequisite for invoking rights resulting from the void termination of the employment relationship by the employer is that the employee must inform the employer that he wishes to continue working for the employer. This also applies in the case of void termination of the employment relationship by the employee.

A. Form of notification

If the employer wishes that the employee continues working in an employment relationship, he should file an application in the court asking for a declaration of nullity of the termination of the employment relationship and also inform the employee that he wishes that the employee continues working. The form of notification of the employer or the time limit for such notification are not defined by the LC. If the employer makes such notification in writing, he should deliver it to the employee in person, because it is a document that concerns the termination of the employment relationship. An employee who has not started working, even though the employer informed him that he wishes that the employee continues working, must compensate the loss caused by this to the employer from the date of the delivery of this notification to the employee. The employee must compensate loss incurred by the employer until the date when the employee started working again or until a final judicial decision declaring the nullity of the termination of the employment relationship is rendered. The employer's right to damages is limited by the limitation period under Section 106 of the Civil Code. Before invoking his right to damages in court, the employer has the right to damages only for one month before invoking his right.

If the employer asked the employee to start working, he must assign work to him and pay him for the work performed. This performance of work is, by operation of law, terminated at the moment when the judicial decision on the nullity of the termination of the employment relationship becomes final. If the employee caused loss to employer by his action, provided that other prerequisites of liability exist, he is liable for damages.

B. Fiction of termination of employment relationship by agreement

If case of a void termination of the employment relationship by the employee, if the employer does not wish that the employee continues working, the fiction applies that the employment relationship ended upon expiration of the period of notice by agreement, if void notice was given, or on the date when the employment relationship should have ended in case of a void immediate termination of the employment relationship or a void termination during the probationary period. The LC allows the parties to agree on the termination of employment relationship in a manner a different from the legal fiction of agreement. If the parties wish to use the possibility of making the different agreement, they should make a written agreement derogating from statutory rules. In case of the termination of the employment relationship by agreement on the basis of fiction, the employer cannot claim damages from the employee.

II. Termination of employment relationship by employer

If the legal act aimed at the termination of the employment relationship was made by the employer and it was addressed to the employee, who considers the legal act to be void, his further action depends on whether he wants to continue working for the employer (for example, if the court declares for example, nullity of for example, termination of for example, employment relationship), or if he decides to work for another employer. If the employee decides to stay in an employment relationship with the employer, for the employment relationship to continue, the employee must inform the employer that he wishes to continue working for him and, in a two-month time-bar period, file an action for for example, nullity of for example, termination of for example, employment relationship with the competent court.

A. Employee's written notification

The employee's written notification addressed to the employer, in the sense that he wishes to continue working for him, is made in writing and it produces legal effects from the moment of delivery. Non-observance of the written form of notification does not cause its nullity. If the employee's notification is made in oral form, it produces legal effects from the date when the employer became aware of it. The employee may modify his notification repeatedly.

If the employer makes, with respect to the employee, two legal acts aimed at the termination of the employment relationship (for example, a notice and subsequently immediate termination of the employment relationship), the employee should, with respect to each of these legal acts (if he wishes to stay in an employment relationship with the employer), inform the employer that he wishes to continue working for him.

A notification of the employee, in the sense that he wishes to continue working for the employer, is also an action for the nullity of the termination of the employment relationship filed against the employer.

B. Continuation of work

When the employee declares his wish to continue working for the employer, the employer either starts assigning work to him until the final judicial decision, or he does not assign work to him. In such situations, the employer provides wage compensation to the employee. The fact that the employer allows the employee to continue working does not mean that he agrees with the employee with respect to the nullity of the termination of the employment relationship. Work is assigned by the employer according to the employment contract. For the period of work until settlement of the judicial dispute, the employee receives wage.

C. Wage compensation

If the employer gives a void notice to the employee or in case of void immediate termination of the employment relationship or void termination during probationary period, and if the employee has informed the employer that he wishes to continue working for the employer, his employment relationship continues and the employer must pay him wage compensation if he does not assign work to him according to the employment contract. This compensation is equal to the average earning from the date when the employee informed the employer that he wishes to continue working until the date when the employer allows him to continue working or until the court renders a ruling on the termination of the employment relationship under Section 79 of the LC. The employee is entitled to wage compensation, if statutory prerequisites are met, until the court ruling declaring the nullity of the termination of the employment relationship becomes final. Such wage compensation awarded to the employee must be paid, at the latest, at the moment when the employer allows the employee to continue working or until the moment of the valid termination of the employment relationship.

When the employee announces that he wishes to continue working after the employer's declaration of termination, the employer must provide wage compensation because he is obliged to continue assigning work according to the employment contract to the employee. This compensation has the legal nature of satisfaction for the loss caused by the employer. Wage compensation is paid to the employee in these cases only if the employee wishes to work or is able to work. If the employee cannot perform work (for example, because of temporary incapacity for work or due to taking of maternity leave or parental leave or for a different obstacle to work without the right to wage compensation), he is not entitled to wage compensation in these cases. Similarly, wage compensation is not paid to an employee if, after the void termination of the employment relationship, he applied for old-age pension, which was awarded to him. The employee has this right to wage compensation only if the court declares the nullity of the termination of employment relationship. If the court does not declare the nullity of the termination of the employment relationship, the employee must return the wage compensation provided by the employer on the legal basis of unjustified enrichment. Wage compensation may be claimed by the employee in court even if the court has not yet declared the nullity of the termination of the employment relationship. The right to wage compensation is not a recurrent payment. The court may only award wage compensation in the amount due at the time the ruling was rendered and it cannot be awarded to the employee for the future. The employee's right to wage compensation is subject to limitation under the Civil Code in the general three-year limitation period. If the employer refuses to assign work to the employee once the court ruling declaring the nullity of the termination of the employment relationship has become final, it is an obstacle to work on the employer's part, which entitles the employee to wage compensation in the amount of the employee's average earning.

The employer's application for denial of wage compensation to the employee or its decrease

The employer has a right to wage compensation from the date when he informs the employer that he wishes to continue working until the time when the employer allows him to continue working or when the court rules on the termination of the employment relationship. It is a special provision governing the rights of an employee with whom the employer terminated the employment relationship in a void manner. General provisions of the LC on wage compensation do not apply to labour-law claims of employees of this kind.

Under previous legislation, in case of the void termination of the employment relationship by the employer, the employee could obtain wage compensation from the employer wage compensation for no more than nine months if the entire time for which should be provided exceeded nine months. If the entire time for which the employee should obtain wage compensation as "damages", even substantially, exceeded nine months, the employee could not obtain higher wage compensation. This legal situation is partially improved by the amendment to the LC in favour of employees, by allowing the employee to obtain this wage compensation for no more than 36 months if the entire time for which wage compensation should be provided to the employee exceeds 12 months.

In order to decrease or deny wage compensation after 12 months, the employer must apply for such decrease in court.

With respect to procedure, without such application, the court cannot deny or decrease wage compensation, rather, an application for the appropriate decrease of wage compensation is necessary. In contrast, in the case of an application of the employer for the decrease of wage compensation, the court may only decrease wage compensation, but not deny it. When ruling on the decrease of wage compensation, the court is not bound by the extent of the decrease claimed by the employer. The employer's application for the decrease or denial of wage compensation may not be made as a separate application for court proceedings, but only in the proceedings in which the employee invokes his right to wage compensation due to the void termination of the employment relationship by the employer.

The termination of the employment relationship may also be based on a judicial decision (Section 240 of the LC) if the court rules that it is not possible to fairly require from the employer to continue employing the employee. However, the court cannot rule on the termination of the employment relationship retrospectively (for example, from the date of effect of notice), but the employment relationship should only be terminated on the date when the court decision becomes final.

The termination of employment relationship in this way, on the basis of court decision, is possible only if the employer terminates the employment relationship in a void manner and the employee does not wish to continue working, but files an application with the court claiming declaration of the nullity of the termination of the employment relationship.

If the employee, for example due to incapacity for work, is unable to perform the work assigned according to the employment contract, he is not entitled to wage compensation even if he declared before that he wishes to continue working for the employer. The court may award wage compensation only if it is due at the time that the court ruling is rendered.

D. Fiction of termination of employment relationship by agreement

If, on the basis of a final decision, the nullity of the termination of the employment relationship is declared, but the employee announces that he does not wish to continue working for the employer, on the basis of fiction, the employment relationship is terminated by agreement. This legal situation exists not only when the employee explicitly announces that he does not wish to continue working for the employer, but also when, after delivery of a declaration of termination from the employer, the employee does not react (for example, he does not inform the employer that he wishes to continue working for him). Fiction of agreement applies only if the parties have not agreed otherwise.

§ 9 Legal regulation of provision of severance allowance upon termination of employment relationship

Under the Slovak LC, severance allowance is provided only upon termination of the employment relationship for economic reasons or for a health reason on the employee's part. The current legal model for the provision of severance allowance is formulated in such a way that severance allowance may be provided not only in case of notice given by the employer, but also in case of the termination of the employment relationship by agreement. In case of notice given by the employer, as well as in case of the termination of the employment relationship by agreement, severance allowance represents a certain compensation of material loss caused by a social risk on the employee's part not caused by his fault.

Under Section 76 of the LC if the employment relationship is terminated with notice for the reasons set out in Section 63 paragraph (1) letters (a) or (b) or because the employee's health condition has, according to a medical assessment, caused the long term loss of his ability to perform his previous work, the employee shall be entitled to a severance allowance at the termination of the employment relationship equal to at least:

a) his average monthly earnings, if the employee's employment relationship lasted at least two years and less than five years,
b) two times his average monthly earnings, if the employee's employment relationship lasted at least five years and less than ten years,
c) three times his average monthly earnings, if the employee's employment relationship lasted at least ten years and less than twenty years,
d) four times his average monthly earnings, if the employee's employment relationship lasted at least twenty years.

If the employment relationship is terminated by agreement for the reasons set out in Section 63 paragraph (1) letter (a) or (b) of the LC or because the employee's health condition has, according to a medical assessment, caused the long term loss of his ability to perform his previous work, the employee shall be entitled to a severance allowance at the termination of the employment relationship equal to at least:
a) his average monthly earnings, if the employee's employment relationship lasted less than two years,
b) two times his average monthly earnings, if the employee's employment relationship lasted at least two years and less than five years,
c) three times his average monthly earnings, if the employee's employment relationship lasted at least five years and less than ten years,
d) four times his average monthly earnings, if the employee's employment relationship lasted at least ten years and less than twenty years,
e) five times his average monthly earnings, if the employee's employment relationship lasted at least twenty years.

If an employer terminates an employee's employment relationship by notice or by agreement on the reasons that the employee must no longer perform his work as a result of an occupational accident, occupational disease or the risk of such a disease, or that the employee has already received the maximum permitted level of exposure in the work place as determined by a decision of a competent public health body, the employee shall be entitled to a severance allowance equal to at least ten times his monthly earnings. This shall not apply if an occupational accident was caused by the employee breaching, through his own fault, legal regulations or other regulations for ensuring occupational safety and health or instructions for ensuring occupational safety and health despite having been duly and demonstrably familiarized with them and had knowledge of them and and compliance with them was systematically required and regularly checked, or if an occupational accident was caused by the employee under the influence of alcohol, narcotic substances or psychotropic substances and the employer could not prevent the occupational accident. If, after the termination of the employment relationship, an employee again takes up an employment relationship with the same employer or the employer's legal successor before the end of the period for which a severance allowance is provided, the employee shall be obliged to return the severance allowance or a proportionate part thereof if the employer and employee do not agree otherwise. A proportionate part of the severance allowance shall be determined according to the number of days from the return to employment until the expiry of the period resulting from the provided severance allowance.

As follows from the above, the LC explicitly also establishes the provision of severance allowance upon the termination of the employment relationship by agreement with another amount of severance allowance. Unlike severance allowance upon the termination of employment relationship by notice given by the employer under Section 76(1) of the LC, in the case of the termination of the employment relationship by agreement, the LC differentiates the amount of severance allowance to a greater extent and allows for the provision of severance allowance in the amount of average monthly earning also to those employees whose employment relationship with the employer lasted less than two years and. It also allows employees to obtain severance allowance in the amount of five times the average monthly earning if the employee's employment relationship lasted at least twenty years.

The amount of severance allowance is established as a minimum amount, which can be increased not only in the collective agreement, but also in the employment contract. Severance allowance upon the termination of the employment relationship may also be provided according to the LC also for reasons other than statutory ones. Whether the employer will also provide severance allowance for reasons other than statutory ones depends in particular on the employer and his economic situation. In such cases, it is recommended to establish these possibilities in the collective agreement or work rules and not to proceed with respect to every employee individually, which could result in a breach of the principle of equal treatment of employees.

§ 10 Discharge benefit upon termination of employment relationship

Upon first termination of the employment relationship, after becoming entitled to an invalidity pension, old-age pension or early old-age pension, the employee is entitled to a discharge benefit, provided that he applies for such pension before the termination of the employment relationship or within ten days from its termination.

The LC establishes only the minimum amount of discharge benefit in the amount of at least the employee's average monthly earning. A higher amount of discharge benefit may be established by a collective agreement in the case of the first termination of the employment relationship after becoming entitled to a pension. If the employer and the social partner agree a higher discharge benefit for the employees in the collective agreement, such an obligation of the employer constitutes, just like in the case of severance allowance, the normative part of the collective agreement that may be invoked by the employee in court.

Unlike severance allowance, the discharge benefit is to be provided, under the legislation in force, to the employee once, upon the first termination of the employment relationship after becoming entitled to an old-age pension, early old-age pension or invalidity pension.

Chapter 10

Employee's legal duties

Pursuant to current legislation, the employee must maintain work discipline. This duty constitutes, according to Section 47 of the LC, the content of the employee's employment obligation. In compliance with this generally formulated duty, the employee must respect a whole range of duties resulting from various provisions of the Labour Code (for example, Sections 81, 82 and 83 of the LC), from other labour regulations, employer's internal rules and collective agreements.

§ 1 Duty to work responsibly and properly

The legal quality and content of the employee's duty to work responsibly and properly should be according to his forces, knowledge and skills, be examined rather from the perspective of objective requirements related to the result of the employee's working activity (for example, requirements concerning the quantity of work performance are contained in work consumption rules) as opposed to subjective requirements (for example, the employee's knowledge and skills).

§ 2 Duty to follow instructions of superiors issued in accordance with legal regulations

The essential purpose of the employer's instructions is to specify the content of the employee's working activity, which is defined in more general terms, in particular in the employment contract, or results from generally binding legal regulations. An important instrument of the immediate control of the working process are, in particular, the employer's instructions specifying the employee's work tasks. Instructions may only be issued within the scope of powers of the entity entitled to issue them. The personal scope of the right to issue instructions results from generally binding legal regulations and internal organization rules. Executive employees are entitled to issue instructions within the scope of their powers, generally determined in Section 9 of the LC. If the employer's instruction is contrary to legal regulations, it may not be regarded as exercise of a right anymore. Given the fact that it is an instruction contrary to the law, it does not establish the employee's legal duty. The employee's duty to follow the instructions of his employer that are in compliance with legal regulations is enshrined in Section 81(a) of the LC and it is one of the fundamental legal duties of every employee, irrespective of his function. The employee's duty to follow his employer's instructions is also enshrined in Section 47(1)(b) of the LC, according to which the employee is obliged and according to the employer's instructions, to perform the work in person according to the employment contract in a determined working time, and to maintain work discipline. This legal duty of the employee characterizes both the employee's obligation and the employment relationship. The employee's legal duty to follow his employer's instructions is coupled with the right of the employer and his executive employees (within the meaning of Section 9 of the LC) to determine and impose work tasks on the employer's subordinate employees, to organize, direct and control their work and give them binding instructions for that purpose. The employee's legal duty to follow his employer's instructions is defined in Section 81(a) of the LC as pertaining exclusively to such instructions of the employer that are in compliance with legal regulations. If the employer issues an instruction that is contrary to legal regulations, the employee is not obliged to comply with such an instruction. Refusal to comply with the employer's instruction that is contrary to legal regulations is not a breach of legal discipline and, accordingly, it cannot justify any sanctions imposed by the employer on the employee. By complying with the illegal instruction, the employee would breach his fundamental duty to comply with legal regulations relating to the work performed by him. This duty stems from Section 81(c) of the LC and is formulated in the Labour Code as the employee's fundamental duty.

§ 3 Duty to use working time

As far as compliance with this fundamental employee's duty is concerned, his timely arrival at the workplace and his exact departure from the workplace is essential, since the employee's duty to be at the employer's disposal is the fundamental prerequisite of work performance. With respect to its content, it is a duty to arrive at the workplace and be present there in a state suitable for performing work. The employee's failure to come to work due to his personal incapacity caused, for example by using alcohol, may be regarded as a serious breach of work discipline. This duty of the employee concerns the full use not only of his working time, but also of production means for performing the entrusted work.

§ 4 Duty to comply with legal regulations and other regulations relating to work he performs if he was properly informed thereof

The first group of duties concerns compliance with generally binding legal regulations relating to the work performed. The employer need not inform the employee of their content. Indeed, the due performance of work according to the employment contract necessarily implies the knowledge of generally binding legal regulations and their ignorance cannot excuse the employee. The employee's work duties relating to the work he performs also result from other regulations, from internal regulations and from collective agreements. Under the Labour Code, the duty to comply with these regulations is conditioned by the employer's duty to inform the employees of their content.

§ 5 *Duty to comply with rules of treatment during temporary inability to work*

The duty to comply with the rules of treatment determined by the examining physician during the employee's temporary inability to work is, under Section 81(d) of the LC, a legal fiction of work duty. During the temporary inability to work, the employee is not present at work. The legal fiction of the employee's legal duty, as used in the LC, allows the employer to check on the employee even outside the workplace.

By enshrining this duty of the employee, the scope of duties of executive employees has been extended. These employees must check the performance of work duties of their employees even outside of the employer's workplace. The duty of executive employees to do "field work", or to visit the employee's home, also has its constitutional limits and it may not be exercised to the full extent without the employee's agreement. Denial of this agreement by the employee as such cannot be regarded as a breach of work discipline, since it does not imply a breach of rules of treatment. In case of a conflict between the employee's constitutional right to privacy and his duty to comply with the instructions of his superior executive employees, the natural person's constitutional right to privacy should prevail.

§ 6 *Duty not to act in contradiction to justified interests of employer*

The employee's duty not to act contrary to justified interests of the employer is enshrined in Section 81(e) of the LC. It is a fundamental duty of the employee formulated in a negative way. It relates not only to ordinary, but also to executive employees. Its essence consists in abstaining from such behaviour of the employee that might be considered contrary to the employer's justified interests. Such activity may include paid, but also unpaid activity of the employee. Such activity must also correspond with the employer's scope of activities (see also Section 83 of the LC). A breach of this duty of the employee committed by fault (for example, in form of abusing information for another undertaking), may be, according to case-law, depending on the legal consequences caused, qualified as such a breach of work discipline where the employer may even exercise his right to immediate termination of the employment relation.

§ 7 *Duty to respect business secret*

According to Section 81(f) of the LC, the legal duties also include the legal duty to maintain confidentiality in matters that the employee has become acquainted with in the course of employment, and which, in the interests of the employer, may not be disclosed to other persons. The LC defines this legal duty separately, even though it is a specific legal form of a more generally formulated duty of the employee provided for in Section 81(e) of the LC, pursuant to which the employee may not act in contradiction to justified interests of his employer. The employer should make sure that the employee, as a party to the employment relationship, knows what the object of the business secret is that the duty of confidentiality relates to. The scope of defining the content of business secret depends on the employer himself. He may define its content in more detail (for example, in the work rules). Not every breach of the employee's duty of confidentiality under Section 81(f) of the LC will be a breach of trade secret under Section 17 of the Commercial Code. The legal differences concerning the employee's duty of confidentiality in matters that he has become acquainted with in the course of employment, unlike Section 17 of the Commercial Code, constitute the framework of the labour-law relationship and of the employment relationship. Section 17 of the Commercial Code defines the term "trade secret" for commercial-law relationships. However, that does not mean that a breach of trade secret cannot have any labour-law consequences. If a person is employed and he breaches a trade secret under Section 17 of the Commercial Code, he also breaches his fundamental labour-law duty enshrined in Section 81(e) of the LC. On the other hand, not every breach of the employee's duty of confidentiality in matters that the employee has become acquainted with in the course of employment and which, in the interests of the employer, may not be disclosed to other persons, will also be a breach of trade secret. Although the employer is, in principle, entitled to require, during the duration of the employment relationship, the employee to comply with this duty to maintain business secret, it must be also said that this legal duty of the employee results directly from the LC, irrespective to his contractual obligation to maintain business secret, which is reflected in the content of the employment contract. This duty is a legal duty of all employees. As follows from Section 81(f), the LC defines the duty to maintain business secret as one of the fundamental legal duties of the employee, which, if breached by fault, cannot be regarded as a serious breach of work discipline. Therefore, in case of a breach of business secret committed by fault, the employer is entitled, during the employment relationship, to jeopardize the employee's existence by notice or immediate termination of the employment relationship, but he may not use other means of guaranteeing the rights and duties resulting from labour-law relationships than those provided for in the LC. Apart from the possibility of notice or immediate termination of the employment relationship, if material loss is suffered by the employer, the employee's breach of duty committed by fault may also be penalized by establishing the employee's liability for damage, even if the employment relationship has been terminated in the meantime. Any breach of business secret by the employee is also a breach of the employee's fundamental duty not to act in contradiction to the employer's justified interests. The possibility of making an agreement concerning the employee's confidentiality, even beyond the duration of employment relationship, is still a major issue for the employers. The LC is based on the idea that the rights and duties of the employment relationship are limited by the duration of the employment relationship. However, this does not apply to legal relationships based on liability, if they arise as a consequence of a breach of rights and duties during the employment relationship. The possibility of limiting the employee by means of the duty of confidentiality even beyond the duration of the employment relationship is closely intertwined with the constitutional right to freedom of business or another paid activity. This constitutional right may only be limited on the basis of the law. For the time being, the LC provides no legal basis for establishing the employee's duty of confidentiality beyond the duration of the employment relationship.

§ 8 Duty to respect prohibition of smoking imposed in workplaces

The Act No. 377/2004 Coll. on Protection of Non-Smokers defines the use of tobacco products as a specific type of drug addiction, which must be dealt with by the employer at the workplace, not only with respect to the protection of the health of non-smokers, but also of all employees. The legal duties of employees in this field include the duty to respect of the prohibition of smoking imposed in workplaces. A breach of this duty committed by fault may be regarded as a breach of work discipline, which may subsequently lead to the termination of the employment relationship by notice given by the employer pursuant to Section 63(1)(e) LC. Apart from the possible liability for material loss based on labour law enforced in particular against the employer's employees, the Act on Protection of Non-Smokers also relies on special sanctions in the form of fines. The fines for breaches of the Act on Protection of Non-Smokers are imposed by several authorities.

§ 9 Limitation of employee's competing activity

I. Performance of competing activity during employment relationship

The performance of a competing activity by employees can be a serious threat to the employ-er's interests. Therefore, under the LC in force, the performance of a competing activity by the employee is conditional on the employer's agreement. The employee must, under Section 83 of the LC, before taking up the competing activity, ask the employer for his prior written approval. The LC in force establishes an irrefutable legal presumption if the employer does not react to the employee's request within 15 days of its service, in which case, the employer's approval is deemed to have been given. The employer is entitled, even after giving the employee his prior written approval of the competing activity, to withdraw this approval due to serious reasons in writing (see Section 83[3] of the LC). This withdrawal must include relevant reasons.

II. Limitation of performance of employee's competing activity beyond employment relationship

The right to perform paid activity is one of the fundamental human rights enshrined in the European Social Charter and in the Constitution of the Slovak Republic. This right may be limited by the law only to the necessary extent, while respecting the principles of legality, legitimacy and proportionality. Limitation of the employee's competing activity after the termination of the employment relationship is allowed by the LC only under certain circumstances and exclusively on the basis of a mutual agreement of the employee and the employer. The agreement of contracting parties on the limitation of the employee's competing activity after the termination of employment relationship is allowed only in case of activities in which the employee could, during the employment relationship, obtain information that, if abused, could cause the employer substantial damage. The extent of such information should be defined by the employer, in his own interest, in an internal regulation. The principle of proportionality applies. Therefore, the employee's limitation by the employer beyond the necessary extent could be restricted or annulled by the court. The limitation of employee's competing activity after the termination of the employment relationship must be contained in the employment contract itself, otherwise the agreement on limitation of the employee's competing activity after the termination of the employment relationship is void.

The LC does not specify the object on the limitation of the employee's paid activity after the termination of employment relationship. At the time of making such an agreement, it should be clear to the employee what information or knowledge is involved, which is not normally available and the use of which in favour of another employer, after the termination of the employment relationship could cause damage to the former employer.

A. Remuneration for performance of a competing activity by the employee

Since it is a limitation of the employee's paid activity after the termination of the employment relationship, the employer must give the employee an adequate pecuniary compensation of at least 50% of the average monthly wage for every month of limitation of the employee's paid activity. In the collective agreement, the employer may agree with the social partner on a minimum rate of adequate pecuniary compensation given by the employer, provided that the statutory minimum is respected (for example, 50% of average monthly wage for every month of performance of the employee's obligation).

B. Adequate pecuniary compensation in case of a breach of the employee's obligation

Should the employee fail to adhere to his obligation, he must give the employer an adequate pecuniary compensation mutually agreed upon with the employer in the employment contract, which may not be higher than the pecuniary compensation which would have to be provided by the employer himself to the employee for the limitation of the employee's competing activity after the termination of the employment relationship.

The obligation not to perform another paid activity after the termination of the employment relationship may only be cancelled by the employer, only during the employment relationship. The LC explicitly requires written form of cancellation, under pain of nullity. Pursuant to Section 83a(6) of the LC, the employee's obligation expires on the first day of the calendar month following the month in which withdrawal was delivered to the other party or on the last day of the employment relationship if it is sooner.

The employee may terminate the obligation not to perform a competing activity after termination of employment relationship if the employer fails to pay him pecuniary compensation within 15 days of the due date.

§ 10 Duties of employees under the rules on occupational safety and health

These duties include, in particular, the duties to respect legal regulations on occupational safety and health, to respect other rules and instructions on occupational safety and health, to respect the principles of safe work, to protect the health at work and to ensure the safe conduct at work and to determine working procedures that he has been duly and demonstrably informed of. These duties are fundamental duties. If rules concerning the work performed by the employee are concerned, they are also a necessary prerequisite of the performance of work. The employee must comply with these rules irrespective of whether he has been duly informed thereof. Compliance with other regulations, instructions and principles concerning occupational safety and health requires that the employer duly informs the employees there of:

- to act so that compliance with duties concerning occupational safety and health is ensured;
- to use the protection instruments assigned as instructed and to take care of them;
- to take part in training organized by the employer in the interest of occupational safety and health and to submit to tests and medical examinations provided for by the law,
- to inform his superior without any undue delay or, from time to time, to the competent trade body, representative of employees for occupational safety or the competent authority of work inspection and the authority for protection of health of any shortcomings that may jeopardize occupational safety or health, in particular immediate and serious threat to life or health, and take part in their elimination according to this capacities;
- to submit to examinations performed by the employer or the competent state administration authority in order to determine whether the employee is under the influence of alcohol, narcotics or psychotropic substances; the category of the employer's employees and other persons entitled to instruct an employee to submit to an examination must be defined by the employer in the work rules or in an internal regulation issued in agreement with the representatives of employees;
- not to use alcohol, narcotics or psychotropic substances at the employer's workplaces and outside such workplaces during working time, not to work under such influence and to respect the prohibition of smoking imposed in workplaces;
- the duty not to use alcohol at the employer's workplaces and outside such workplaces during working time does not apply to employees whose work involves exceptional use of alcohol. The employee's duty not to use alcohol, narcotics or psychotropic substances is associated in particular with occupational safety and health. Prohibition of using alcohol applies to the employee's workplace both during working time and leisure time of the employee. During working time, the prohibition of alcohol and other stupefying substances applies also outside of the employer's workplaces. Should the employee breach this duty, the employer might refuse to assign further work to him or he could send the employee home and qualify his absence at work as absence in the legal sense.

The employee has the right to refuse to perform work, to leave the workplace to resort or to a safe place, if he has a justified fear that his life or health of life or health of others is imminently and seriously threatened and, if possible, to take measures to eliminate the consequences of such threat.

The LC qualifies the employee's participation in training on occupational safety and health as the performance of work for which the employee is entitled to obtain wage.

Chapter 11

Legal regulation of working time

§ 1 General characteristics

Working time is essential to the employee. The length of working time determines the overall quality of life of the employee. The basic purpose of labour-law regulation on the length of working time is to protect the employee's health and to enable his personal development. Therefore, it is not by accident that the labour-law regulation on working time was at the origin of labour law and it is still one of the most important elements i n the development of labour law at the European and global level.

Another characteristic of the development of legal regulation on working time not only in the Slovak Republic, but also in other countries that acceded to the EU on May 1st, 2004, is a massive increase of overtime work and on-call duty. With respect to the amount in overtime work actually performed and the statutory maximum overtime work allowed, the Slovak Republic occupies one of the first places in the European Union.

From the perspective of the right to human dignity and the real risks of its breach, first of all, it must be observed that the limit of overtime work has been increased from 400 hours a year in certain categories of employees up to 550 hours a year. In this respect, one may ask who benefits from our European primacy in overtime work.

When the amendment to the LC was being drafted, employers claimed that this legal instrument would increase the employment rate, with 550 hours of overtime work being approximately 1/4 of the employment obligation of an unemployed person. Does such extent of overtime work create elementary conditions for the quality of life of the employee, his family and his children?

As far as the length of weekly working time is concerned, it is necessary to mention the resolution of the European Parliament of 8st October 2008, which finally refused the Council's common position for the further liberalisation of the Working Time Directive and explicitly stated that approval of this proposition would be antisocial. The European Parliament refused any concessions and insisted on a 48-hour weekly working time including overtime with no exceptions. The European Parliament considers the Council's common position of June 2008 as a 'return to the 19th century'. Furthermore, it explicitly states that 'unlimited deregulation is the cause of destruction and its consequences include the current global financial crisis. Opt-out cannot continue forever, because it is against protection of life and health of employees and occupational safety and it also enables social dumping.[34]

Despite this clear resolution of the European Parliament, the Slovak LC extended the opt-out system beyond the category of healthcare workers to two lines of executive work positions.

According to Article 22 of Directive 2003/88/EC, it is an exception from the maximum extent of weekly working time, which is set by the directive at 48 hours a week. This exception is called 'opt-out', which means that the employee concerned opts out from the normal working time limits. This exception enshrined in Article 22 of Directive 2003/88/EC allows the Member States to derogate from the maximum length of weekly working time. Unlike the extent of weekly working time set in Section 85 of LC at 48 hours, a longer weekly working time set at 56 hours a week is possible. It is an average weekly working time, which includes weekly working time, overtime and idle on-call duty of the employee performed at the employer's workplace. According to new legislation, the increased extent of weekly working time set at no more than 56 hours applies not only to healthcare workers, but to all executive employees of the employer in two executive levels. These are executive employees directly controlled by the statutory body and executive employees that are subordinate to those executive employees. The specific definition of executive employees of these two executive lines can be formulated by the employer in his internal regulations. The status of healthcare workers is regulated by healthcare regulations.

Working time can have, in the future, major positive or negative impacts on the quality of life of employees, on the safety and protection of life of employees and on the special constitutional protection of children and family. Therefore, working time is essential to the employee. The length of working time determines the overall quality of life of the employee. The basic purpose of labour-law regulation on the length of working time is to protect the employee's health and to enable his personal development. Therefore, it is not by accident that the labour-law regulation of working time was at the origin of labour law and it is still one of the most important elements of development of labour law on the European level. The length of working time directly determines the extent of the employee's rest. The real length of working time directly affects the employee's personal and family life and has a positive or negative impact on combining the employee's work and family life.

Working time is, moreover, an essential element of flexibility in labour-law relationships. The labour law of the Slovak Republic is characterized by quite a high level of liberalization of legal regulation of working time, which is regulated primarily by the LC and partially by special acts (for example, the legal regulation of working time for employees in the transport sector).

§ 2 Legislative changes of regulation of working time as of 1st January 2013

The LC of the Slovak Republic is based on the 48-hour maximum weekly working time enshrined in Directive 2003/88/EC concerning certain aspects of the organization of work-

---

34 European Parliament's resolution of 8 October 2008

ing time. At the same time, as an EU Member State, the Slovak Republic must comply with the minimum rest period after the work is done.

One of the particularities of the flexibility of employment relationships in the Slovak Republic prior to its social democratic reform was mostly the particularly high range of overtime at a total of 400 hours per year, which includes 150 hours of mandated overtime and another 250 hours of overtime. The same extent of agreed overtime remains even after the reform of labour law.

The problem of Slovak legislation in the area of working time is that for reduced daily and weekly rest after work is done, adequate rest periods in accordance with the current case law of the ECJ are not provided. The employer is not required to compensate employees for rest periods without undue delay, but the actual provisions of the LC allow for rest periods at the long term (30 days at daily rest periods and within eight months at weekly rest periods).

Another problem of Slovak legislation regulating working time is the constant pressure of businesses to expand the personal and material scope of the opt-out system. Until 31st December 2012, opt-out was allowed by the LC not only for healthcare workers but also to a broadly defined category of managers. Recent amendment to the LC narrowed the personal scope of the opt-out system and since 1st January 2013, the LC allows opt-out to be applied only to healthcare workers.

Despite adopted legislative changes in the area of working time, the LC leaves for the future possibility to conclude full time employment contracts also in relation to several employers and the maximum weekly working time of 48 hours is considered in relation to every employer separately. Section 50 of the LC states that the rights and obligations of concurrent employments are to be considered quite separately, with the exception of adolescent employees younger than 18 years of age.

Previous legislation application practice has proven that the account of working time and flexi-account are helpful tools which can be used in order to avoid the reduction of employees in times when the employer is facing economic problems and its employees are not sufficiently used. This legal instrument of the organization of working time is left untouched by LC untouched. However, its implementation is bound exclusively on the agreement with employee representatives or by collective agreement. Working time account shall not be introduced only on unilateral decision of the employer without agreement with the employee representatives or without a collective agreement.

A special feature of the introduction of a working time account is up to a 30 month schedule period.

Reduced daily rest after work is possible even after the reform on enumerated grounds. Legislative formulation of these enumerated grounds in Section 92 of LC is so wide that the application practice often leads to the reduction of the daily rest period up to 8 hours after the work is done. The granting of compensatory rest periods did not meet, and even after the reform is not in accordance with Directive 2003/88/EC on certain aspects of working time, and the current case law of the ECJ. Even after the reform of labour law legislation is allowing for flexi-account for working time and a very liberal legislation on flexible working time remained in the text of LC.

§ 3 Concept of working time

Working time as a concept designates the time during which the employee is at the disposal of the employer, performs work and discharges obligations pursuant to the employment contract. Under current case law of the ECJ, the concept of working time is a concept of EU law, and therefore it cannot be interpreted differently in various Member States. According to Directive 2003/88/EC, working time means is defined as any period spent at or outside of the employer's workplace, during which the employee carries out the tasks determined by the employer or is ready to carry out such tasks. This definition of working time, in connection with the definition of rest period, implies that the performance of overtime work must also be included in the working time, since it is clearly not a rest period. Unlike the concept of working time, a work shift is part of weekly working time excluding overtime work, during which the employee must work on the basis of a predetermined timetable of work shifts.

Working time includes breaks at work provided in the interest of occupational safety and health as well as adequate break periods for eating, if the work cannot be interrupted under Section 91(1) of LC.

In principle, for defining the concept of working time, it is irrelevant whether the employee actually works during the working time, takes part in education, or does not work, because he is waiting for material, provided that he is at the employer's disposal for the performance of work. Travelling to work and back is not regarded as the performance of work.

§ 4 Length of working time

Unlike the concept of working time, the concept of length of working time is a limitation of the period of the performance of employee's work agreed upon, as defined in the employment contract. In this sense, the employee's work within the length of working time agreed upon is a synallagmatic duty with respect to the employer's duty to pay for the work performed. The duration of the duty to work is defined by the contracting parties in the employment contract both in terms of duration of the employment relationship and in terms of the length of working time.

I. Stipulated weekly working time

The stipulated weekly working time is essential to the employee. The employer may not, in principle, ask the employee to perform work beyond the stipulated weekly working time, except for overtime work. The stipulated working time directly determines not only the definition of overtime work, but also the calculation of the length of paid holiday or its limitation, the employee's right to additional paid holiday or breaks at work for breastfeeding. The length of stipulated weekly working time in a one-shift operation is set by the LC at no more than 40 hours a week. More favourable rules on stipulated weekly working time apply to employees in a two-shift operation (38 ¾ hours) and an even more favourable stipulated weekly working time applies to employees in a three-shift operation and a continued operation (no more than 37 ½ hours a week).

II. Maximum daily working time

Maximum daily working time is not explicitly established by the LC. However, Article 3 of Directive 2003/88/EC establishes a minimum daily rest period of 11 hours. It follows that the daily working time cannot, in principle, exceed 13 hours. The LC establishes only the maximum daily length of a work shift. The maximum length of a work shift in case of an uneven distribution of working time is 12 hours a day. However, the length of daily working time can be derived from the statutory determination of the minimum length of the employee's daily rest after work, which is set at 12 hours in Section 92 of the LC.

A. Maximum working time for adolescent employees

The LC establishes the maximum statutory weekly working time in each employment relationship separately. On the basis of the maximum weekly working time defined, Section 85(7) of the LC establishes the maximum daily working time for adolescent employees, implementing the requirements of Directive 94/33/EC. Unlike Section 85(4) of the LC, no exceptions are allowed.

A common feature of the legal regulation of the maximum weekly working time for adolescent people over 16 years and adolescent people under 16 years is that it is established with respect to the person of the adolescent employee (for example, the maximum weekly working time cannot be exceeded, even if they worked for several employers). For this purpose, working time with several employers is added.

B. Working time of healthcare workers (opt-out)

Under Section 85a of the LC, the average weekly working time of an employee including overtime work may exceed 48 hours for a period of four consecutive months in the case of a healthcare employee under special regulation. The average weekly working time of an employee falling under the first sentence including overtime work may not exceed 56 hours.

It follows from the position of Section 85a in the structure of the LC that the increased extent of weekly working time agreed upon may be applied both as unevenly distributed working time and as evenly distributed working time. The extent of the possible extension of weekly working time based on an agreement between the employee and the employer itself implies that, in practice, it will be applied in the legal form of unevenly distributed working time. According to the latest case law of the ECJ (*Fuß III*), an employer may not force an employee to work in an extended weekly work mode exceeding the maximum weekly working time set by the directive at 48 hours including overtime work. The breach of voluntary character is associated with liability consequences on the employer's part.

Apart from the above, the extended weekly working time is governed by all provisions of the LC on the statutory limits of performing overtime work, night work and of performing on-call duty.

In case of the above legal model of weekly working time, the extent of weekly working time in a scheduling period of no more than four months may not exceed 56 hours, the employee is entitled to withdraw his consent. The competent authority (labour inspection) may, in case of a threat to occupation safety and health, restrict or prohibit performance of such work in a longer extent of weekly working time.

§ 5 Even distribution of working time

Under Section 86 of the LC, evenly distributed working time means that the extent of working time in one week is the same or its difference does not exceed three hours and working time in individual days may not exceed nine hours. The maximum length of a work shift in the case of even distribution of working time is nine hours, excluding breaks for eating, rest periods and overtime work. The LC defines evenly distributed working time in a mandatory manner. Parties to an employment relationship may not derogate from the definition of evenly distributed working time by an agreement. The weekly distribution of working time is a matter for the employer, who decides on the distribution after negotiating with the representatives of employees and informs the employee thereof at least one week in advance, and with validity of at least one week (see Section 90(9) of the LC). The LC does not specify how the employer should exercise his right. It may be inferred from other provisions of the LC concerning working time that a 5-day working week is the basis, that the working time of the same work shift may be divided (Section 90 of LC) and the existing legal model of legal regulation of work on rest days (Section 94 of the LC) must be applied. Of major importance is the distribution period set at four weeks, during which the average working time may not exceed the limit for stipulated weekly working time, even if (for example, in one or two weeks), the limit for the stipulated weekly working time is exceeded. Such extent of stipulated working time does not include overtime work.

§ 6 Uneven distribution of working time

Under Section 87 of the LC, the mode of distribution of working time must be regarded as the employer's power to be exercised after agreement with the representatives of employees or after agreement with the employees themselves in case of the uneven distribution of working time with a distribution period of no more than four months. The generally formulated legal condition is that the employer is entitled to distribute the working time unevenly only if the character of the work or operating conditions do not allow him to distribute working time evenly. Under current legislation, the LC requires the employer to fulfil condition of establishing unevenly distributed working time consisting in the character of the work or operating conditions of the employer. These conditions of establishing unevenly distributed working time are determined alternatively, rather than cumulatively. Unevenly distributed working time need not be established for all employees of the employer. It may also be established for a specific part of the employer's staff (for example, for corresponding organizational units or types of work). In case of unevenly distributed working time, employees younger than 18 years may not work longer than 8 hours in 24 hours.

I. Agreement with representatives of employees in case of distribution period longer than four months

In case of a distribution period longer than four months, an individual agreement between the employer and the employee on the uneven distribution of working time is possible only if there are no employee representatives at the employer's workplace. Therefore, if there are employee representatives at the employer's workplace, an individual agreement between the employer and the employee on the uneven distribution of working time is impossible. In this case, the LC also requires that the work activities concerned are characterized by a different need for work during the year.

A stricter labour-law regulation of the uneven distribution of working time with a distribution period extended up to 12 months is required by Directive 2003/88/EC concerning certain aspects of the organisation of working time itself, which does not allow for an individual agreement between the employee and the employer.

II. Agreement with categories of employees enjoying special protection

Weekly working time may be unevenly distributed by the employer only on the basis of an agreement with the employee in the cases of an employee with a health disability, a pregnant woman, a woman or man permanently caring for a child younger than three years of age or a lone employee permanently caring for a child younger than 15 years of age.

III. Working time account

Under Section 87a of the LC, a working time account as a special method for the uneven distribution of working time is a special legal model of unevenly distributed working time. Working time account means that in the case of a greater need for work, the employee works more hours than his stipulated weekly working time and in case of a lesser need for work, the employee works less than his stipulated weekly working time or does not work at all. At the same time, the average stipulated weekly working time for the distribution period of no more than 12 consecutive months may not be exceeded. A peculiarity of this legal instrument is that the employee receives wage even if he is not working or is working less than his stipulated weekly working time and, on the other hand, his work is not considered to be overtime work when he is working more than his stipulated weekly working time.

Working time account may be introduced by the employer only on the basis of the agreement with employee representatives. The agreement with the employee representatives may not be replaced with the employer's unilateral decision.

A. Agreement on introducing a working time account

A prerequisite of introducing a working time account is the employer's agreement with employee representatives. Employees must respect such an agreement. The agreement on introducing a working time account agreed between the employer and the employee representatives must be made in writing. Otherwise, it is void under Section 17(2) of the LC. An employer who has no trade organization may, under Section 233a of the LC, also conclude a working time account with a works council or works representative.

Apart from the employer's agreement with employee representatives, the employer must, in the case of a working time account concerning special categories of employees, also conclude an individual agreement. This applies to employees with a health disability, a pregnant woman, a woman or man permanently caring for a child younger than three years of age or a lone employee permanently caring for a child younger than 15 years of age. With respect to introducing a working time account, the distribution period is very important, which is defined by the LC as a maximum of 12 consecutive months. The specific length of the distribution period should be agreed upon by the employer with the employee representatives because it is an essential element of introducing a working time account with the employer concerned.

Within the duration of the working time account, as far as the legal character is concerned, working time is detached from remuneration for work. The introduction of a working time account allows the employer, in a period with a lessor need for work, to assign work in a lesser extent than the stipulated weekly working time and, in a period with a greater need for work on the employer's part, it allows the employer to assign work to the employee in a lesser extent than his stipulated weekly working time without the employee's consent.

If an employer implements a working time account, he must keep records of the employee's working time, employee's paid wage account and a difference account. In the difference account, the employer should record the difference between the employee's stipulated weekly working time and actually worked working time every week, as well as the difference between the wage actually paid and the wage to which the employee is entitled.

B. Employee's right to constant wage in case of application of working time account

The employee's protection in the case of the application of a working time account consists in particular in his right to constant wage, which corresponds with the stipulated weekly working time. If, until the employment relationship is terminated, during the application of a working time account the employer pays a lower wage to the employee than that resulting from the working time account, the employer must pay the rest of the wage to the employee.

C. Return of wage paid upon termination of employment relationship

The employer may require the wage paid to be returned by the employee if the employee has not worked the entire working time corresponding with the period of application of the working time account, in the case of notice given to the employer under Section 63(1) (d) and (e) of the LC, as well as in the case of the immediate termination of the employment relationship by the employer. In case of other types of termination of the employment relationship, the employer is not entitled to recover the wage paid not covered by the time worked by the employee. Under the LC, the employer is entitled to claim the return of the wage paid to the employee, which may be enforced in court by the employer. Nonetheless, he is not obliged to claim the return of the wage paid.

§ 7 Flexible working time

According to current Slovak legislation, the legal model of flexible working time is very liberal and it provides a wide legal margin for the contracting parties.

The employee's flexible working time is the operational time, which consists of optional working time and basic working time. Operational time is the total working time that the employee must work during the relevant flexible working period determined by the employer. Optional working time is a time segment during which the employee himself may choose the beginning and/or the end of working time. Basic working time is a time segment in which the employee is obliged to be in the workplace. Between the two segments of flexible working time, there is a time segment during with the employee must be present in the workplace. The employee is entitled to choose the beginning and end of working time himself only within the optional working time. He does not have this option in basic working time when he must be at the employer's disposal as decided by the employer himself.

The LC allows for the introduction of a daily flexible working time, weekly flexible working time and also a four-week flexible working time. It also allows for other flexible periods than four weeks (for example, longer than four weeks). This applies not only to the even distribution of working time, but also to the uneven distribution of working time.

The length of a work shift in the case of the application of flexible working time may not exceed 12 hours. In the case of a daily flexible working time, the employee must work the determined length of an entire work shift every day, which may not exceed 12 hours. He chooses the beginning of the work shift himself.

In the case of a weekly flexible working time, the employee chooses not only the beginning of the work shift, but also its end. In the case of a weekly flexible working time, the employee has no specific length of a daily work shift, but only a period of mandatory presence in the employer's workplace (basic working time). The rest of the weekly working time is worked by the employee as he decides. However, he must work the entire weekly working time determined in a week and the length of his work shift may not exceed 12 hours.

In the case of a four-week flexible working time, the employee chooses the beginning of the work shift and its end. He must be present in the workplace during the basic working time. The working time determined by the employer for a four-week period must be worked within four weeks. The length work of a shift may not exceed 12 hours.

§ 8 Employee's right to different regulation of working time

Different regulation of working time may be agreed upon by the employer with the employee in the employment contract or it may be allowed by the employer upon the employee's request during the employment relationship. In the former case, the employer is legally bound by the different regulation of working time in the employment contract, which he cannot modify unilaterally. This applies not only to cases where the employer agrees with the employee on a different regulation of determined weekly working time when concluding the employment contract, but also in the case of the modification of working conditions agreed upon in the employment contract under Section 54 of the LC. If the employer allows for the different regulation of determined weekly working time upon the employee's request, he is entitled to cancel it unilaterally if the condition for allowing it no longer exists (change of operating circumstances).

Under Section 164(2) of the LC, if a pregnant woman, a man or a woman continuously caring for a child younger than 15 years of age requests a reduction in working time or other suitable modification of working time, the employer is obliged to grant their request if it is not prevented by compelling operational reasons.

§ 9 Work on public holidays

For work performed on public holidays, the employer provides a wage surcharge to the employee. Work on a public holiday, which is a working day, performed by the employee is not regarded as overtime work. Work on public holidays may be regarded as overtime work only if the employee, according to the timetable of work shifts, should not have worked, because he had a day of continuous rest in the week (normally Saturday or Sunday). Since the employee had worked a full weekly working time in the previous days, work performed on a public holiday is overtime work. In the case of the performance of work being ordered on a public holiday, the same conditions apply to the employer as if it were a rest day; however, apart from the possibilities of ordering work on rest days, the employer is entitled to order performance of work on a public holiday, also in the case of continuous operation and work necessary for watching the employer's property.

§ 10 On-call duty

The basic feature of on-call duty is the performance of necessary work that must be performed in justified cases outside of the scope of the work shift schedule. If the employer fails to respect this basic legal feature of on-call duty, he is in breach of the law. A breach of labour-law regulations could also cause sanctions imposed on the employer (fines imposed by the work inspection). This would apply, for instance, if the employer ordered on-call duty for performing his daily tasks, which can be performed in normal working time within the scope of the work shift schedule. Similarly, an employer would breach the law if he ordered performance of on-call duty on a regular basis, even if no necessary tasks were involved.

During the on-call duty, the employee does not work, but he is ready to work, being at his employer's disposal. If work is performed, the employee is entitled to a wage (salary). If performance of work within the scope of on-call duty exceeds the extent of stipulated working time, it is overtime work and it is included in overtime work limits. The employer may order on-call duty or agree with the employee on the performance of on-call duty. If the employee does not respect the on-call duty ordered, he breaches work discipline. Beyond the maximum statutory limit of on-call duty, the employer may agree with the employee on the performance of on-call duty. An agreement on performing on-call duty need not be made in writing. If an employee refuses to conclude an agreement on performing on-call duty beyond the maximum statutory limit, he does not infringe work discipline. The LC distinguishes active on-call duty, which is performed at the employer's workplace and is qualified as working time and idle on call duty, which is performed in a determined place outside the employer's workplace and not included in the working time.

On-call duty of transport employees are governed by special regulations.

I. Extent of on-call duty

The employer is entitled to order on-call duty unilaterally up to 8 hours a week and 100 hours a year. An employee may be ordered to perform on-call duty work only for the type of work that he must perform under the employment contract. On-call duty work for a type of work other than that agreed upon in the employment contract may only be agreed upon with the employee. With respect to the on-call duty work agreed with the employee beyond the statutory limit, the LC does not impose statutory limits concerning its total scope. Even in case of on-call duty work agreed with the employee, the employer's necessary tasks must be involved.

II. Limitation of scope of on-call duty under a collective agreement

The LC allows contracting parties to limit the scope of on-call duty work that may be agreed upon with the employee in collective agreements. Should social partners limit the scope of on-call duty work in a collective agreement, an employment contract establishing a greater extent of the employee's on-call duty work would be void in this part, under Section 231 of LC. The extent of on-call duty work stipulated in the collective agreement would be binding in this case.

III. Prohibition of ordering on-call duty

The employer may not order adolescent employees to perform on-call duty work. On-call duty work may not even be agreed upon with adolescent employees by the employer. Moreover, on-call duty work may not be ordered by the employer to a pregnant woman, a woman or man permanently caring for a child younger than three years of age or a lone woman or man permanently caring for a child younger than 15 years of age.

IV. Different remuneration of on-call duty

Depending on whether on-call duty work is performed by the employee in the employer's workplace without working or in a different place than the employer's workplace, the LC provides for different remuneration. Remuneration of on-call duty work is regulated by the LC only on the level of statutory minimum. More favourable remuneration may be stipulated in collective agreements. Individual degrees of the difficulty of work for the purposes of remuneration of on-call duty should be regulated, in particular, by collective agreements. This procedure in remunerating on-call duty work is consistent with the ECJ ruling in *Vorel* (C-437/05), which declares that it is correct for an EU Member State to apply legislation that, for the purposes of the employee's remuneration with respect to on-call duty work performed by the employee in his workplace, takes account of various periods when the work is actually done and periods when the work is not done even if the employee is ready to do it. In this way, the ECJ showed that it regards on-call duty work performed at the employer's workplace as working time, but, on the other hand, remuneration of on-call duty is a matter for the EU Member States. In case of on-call duty work performed at the employer's workplace, the employee has the right to compensation in the amount of minimum wage. If, work is performed during on-call duty, it is the performance of work and not on-call duty work and the employee has a right to wage. If no work is performed during on-call duty, this time is not included in the weekly working time.

§ 11 Overtime work

According to the LC, overtime work is any work exceeding the length of working time stipulated in the employment contract, performed by order of the employer or with his consent beyond the determined weekly working time and performed outside the scope of the timetable of work shifts. Under the LC, it is work beyond the determined weekly working time resulting from the predetermined distribution of working time, and performed outside of the scope of the timetable of work shifts.

I. Agreement with employee representatives on conditions of overtime work

The conditions and extent of overtime work is determined by the employer after agreement with the employee representatives. An individual agreement between the employee and the employer on agreed overtime work beyond the stipulated maximum of 150 hours a year should not be contrary to the agreement between the employer and employee representatives operating at the employer's workplace concerning the conditions and scope of overtime work. If such an individual agreement between the employer and the employee were included by the parties in the employment contract and the agreement of social partners in the collective agreement were more favourable for the employees, the employment contract would be void in that part pursuant to Section 231(1) of the LC.

II. Risky work

In case of an employee who performs risky work, overtime work cannot be ordered, but the employer may agree with the employee on its performance. Thus, the LC exceptionally allows, also in case of risky work, overtime work based on the agreement with the employee if urgent repair work is required or under exceptional circumstances, if there is a risk threatening life or health or if there is a threat of a loss of great extent. This overtime work is not include in the number of hours of maximum extent of overtime work per year.

§ 12 Night work

Under Section 98 of the LC, night work is work performed within the time period between 22:00 and 06:00 hours. After 6 a.m., the employer must provide a wage surcharge to the employee for night work.

The employer does not have the right to distribute the working time so that the employee works in night shifts in two consecutive weeks unless agreed upon with the employee. Under the LC, such an agreement need not be made in writing. For the sake of legal certainty, however, the employer should make such an agreement with the employee in writing, also with respect to the inspection performed by the work inspection authorities.

Exceptionally, the employer may distribute the working time so that the employee works in night shifts in two consecutive weeks if the character of work or operational conditions do not permit them to distribute the working time in a different manner.

The character of work and the operational conditions are, in case of every employer, more or less different. Their assessment and evaluation must be based on objective criteria. These must be causally linked with creating an objective impossibility to distribute the working time so that the employee does not work in night shifts in two or more consecutive weeks.

This method of distributing working time is subject to negotiations with the employee representatives, who should make sure that the employer does not circumvent the purpose of the law or that he does not infringe it directly. If such situations arise in the practice, the employee representative may initiate an inspection of the observance of labour-law regulations by the competent work inspectorate, which may impose quite a wide range of fines on the employer.

The LC does not allow for the constant performance of night work even if the employee agrees to such constant performance of night work. This interpretation is consistent with the ILO Recommendation to the ratified ILO Night Work Convention No. 171/1990, which provides that if a work change includes night work, two consecutive shifts in full working time should never be performed except for cases of force majeure or accident, or cases of imminent accident.

The limitation on the performance of continuous night work would also be contrary to the objective of Directive 2003/88/EC concerning certain aspects of the organization of working time, which is the protection of life and health of employees. This directive explicitly provides that there is a need to limit the duration of periods of night work and to provide for employers who regularly use night workers to bring this information to the attention of the competent authorities for occupational safety and health.

I. Prohibition of ordering night work

The employer may not order adolescent employees to perform night work. The performance of night work may not even be agreed with them. Exceptionally, under Section 174(1) of the LC, adolescent employees older than 16 years of age may perform night work not in excess of one hour if it is necessary for their vocational training. In these cases, the night work of the adolescent employee older than 16 years of age must be linked directly to his work during the day according to the timetable of work shifts. A pregnant woman, a mother who has given birth within the last nine months or a breastfeeding woman may perform night work, but if they decide not to perform it, their employer must transfer them to daily work. In the case of such request, they are entitled to such transfer without having to submit a medical report.

§ 13 Special duties of the employer concerning documentation of working time

The LC does not specify how the employer should keep documentation of the working time. It depends on specific conditions of the employer and from the decision of the employer himself. Above all, it depends from the employer what on of documentation of working time he chooses to keep. Documentation of working time is not the same as documentation of attendance. Furthermore, the employer must also keep separate documentation for the active part of on-call duty and the idle part of on-call duty. The LC also outlines how the employer should comply with this duty in order to record the beginning and end of the time segment during which the employee performed work or on-call duty based on order or agreement.

The workplace need not be the same as the place of the work performance stipulated in the employment contract. The workplace is usually defined in a much narrower way. At the beginning of the working time, the employee must be present at his workplace in a state apt for performing work. If the employee needs to wash or change clothes before the performance of work, this time is not included in the working time.

On the other hand, under Section 90(10) of the LC, the employer may, upon negotiation with the employee representatives, determine the time necessary for personal hygiene upon completion of work, which is included in the working time of employees. In the documentation of overtime work, the employer must record any overtime work, even if overtime work is not included in the maximum extent of overtime work allowed in a year, but also overtime work for which the employee obtained alternative time-off. Overtime work must also be recorded if the employee's wage agreed upon in the employment contract also reflects overtime work.

With respect to the verification of illegal work and illegal employment, the work inspection authority keeps, under Section 5(3)(s) of the Labour Inspection Act, a public register of natural and legal persons punished with a fine for infringing the prohibition of illegal employment and, under Section 6 of that Act, it reports the cases of illegal work and illegal employment to the Social Security Agency, Central Agency for Work, Social Affairs and Family, the Competent Agency for Work, Social Affairs and Family, Public Procurement Office and, in case of an alien performing illegal work, also to the Police Corps office. These duties of inspection authorities concerning illegal work should motivate the employers to fulfil their statutory duties in the performance of dependent work or employment.

The employer must:
- keep records of agreements on works performed outside of the employment relationship in the sequential order of their conclusion,
- keep working time records of employees performing work on a basis of an agreement on the temporary job of students.

I. Employer's reporting duty

Besides the notification duty, the employer also has a reporting duty under the Illegal Work Act, which establishes reporting duties of employers concerning persons insured in the pension scheme and affiliates of the pension insurance, but also employees insured in the accident insurance scheme.

II. Employer's registration duty

Under the Social Insurance Act (Section 231), the employer must register in the register of insured persons and affiliates of the pension scheme:

a) an employee under Section 4(1) of the Act for Sickness Insurance, pension insurance and unemployment insurance before such insurance comes into being, no later than the beginning of the performance of the employee's activity and to deregister an employee under Section 4(1) of the Act no later than the day following the end of such insurance, to cancel registration in the register of insured persons and affiliates of the pension scheme, if there was no insurance relationship, and to report any changes concerning the above circumstances;

b) an employee under Section 4(2) of the Act for Accident Insurance before the labour-law relationship comes into being, no later than the beginning of the performance of work, and to deregister, under Section 4(2) of the Social Insurance Act, from the register of insured persons and affiliates of the pension scheme no later than the day following the termination of the labour-law relationship, to cancel registration in the register of insured persons and affiliates of the pension scheme, if there was no labour-law relationship, and to report any changes concerning the above circumstances. The deadline for fulfilling the above duties of the employer is met even if the form is sent within the deadline by fax or e-mail or if the information is sent by a short message service (SMS).

Chapter 12

Rest periods

§ 1 Breaks at work for rest and eating

An employer must provide an employee whose work shift is longer than six hours with a break for rest and eating of 30 minutes, which is not included in the working time. An employer shall be obliged to provide an adolescent employee whose work shift is longer than 4.5 hours, with a break for rest and eating of 30 minutes. Breaks at work for eating and rest in the case of flexible working time are provided within the basic working time after three hours from the beginning.

The length of breaks at work for rest and eating is set by the LC at 30 minutes. If the employer wanted to extend the break for rest and eating on the basis of an agreement with the employee, he would have to make an agreement with the employee representatives. He could act autonomously if he had no social partner in the workplace.

Motor vehicle drivers are entitled to a safety break of at least 30 minutes after 4 hours of driving if no continuous daily rest after work follows. Just like other categories of employees, motor vehicle drivers have, no later than after 6 hours of work shift, a break for rest and eating of 30 minutes. If the total work shift of motor vehicle drivers is longer than 9 hours, they are entitled to a break for rest and eating of at least 45 minutes, which can be divided into two parts of at least 30 minutes and 15 minutes.

§ 2 Safety breaks at work

Unlike breaks at work for eating and rest, which are not include in the working time, safety breaks at work are included in the working time and the employee receives wage (salary) for such breaks at work. The employer's duty to provide the employee with safety breaks at work results from special regulations (transport regulations).

The employer's duty to provide the employee with safety breaks at work is established either by a special regulation or are established by collective agreements or the employer's internal regulation. Safety breaks at work should not be taken during breaks at work for eating and rest.

§ 3 Breaks at work for breastfeeding

Under Section 170 of the LC an employer must provide a mother who breastfeeds her child special breaks for breastfeeding in addition to breaks in work. A mother who works for the fixed weekly working time is entitled to two half-hour breaks per child for breast-feeding until the child reaches sixth months of age, and in the succeeding six months, one half-hour break for breast-feeding per shift. Breaks for breastfeeding may be combined and provided at the beginning or end of the shift. However, where working with a shorter working time, for at least half of the fixed weekly working time, the mother is entitled to only one half-hour break for breast-feeding per child until the end of the sixth month of the child's age.

§ 4 Continuous daily rest

Under Section 92 of the LC, the employer must arrange working time in such a way that, between the end of one shift and the beginning of another shift, an employee has the minimum rest of 12 consecutive hours within 24 hours, and a adolescent employee, at least 14 consecutive hours within 24 hours.

Such rest period may be reduced to eight hours for an employee older than 18 years of age in continuous operations and with work batches when performing urgent agricultural work, when performing urgent repair work concerning the averting of a threat endangering the lives or health of employees and in the case of extraordinary events. If an employer shortens the minimum rest period, he must additionally provide the employee with continuous equivalent rest as compensation within 30 days.

I. Conditions of reducing daily rest after work

The unilateral reduction of continuous daily rest to 8 hours is possible only for reasons stated exhaustively. The reduction of continuous daily rest is totally excluded with respect to adolescent employees. The reduction of daily rest after work to 8 hours on the basis of an agreement between the employee and the employer is not allowed. Should the employer reduce daily rest after work, he must additionally provide the employee with continuous equivalent rest as compensation within 30 days. This duty of the employer does not depend on the employee's request.

§ 5 Continuous rest in a week

Determination of a continuous rest in a week is made by the employer's. The LC imposes a certain legal procedure on the employer, which must be respected. It imposes a duty on the employer to provide the employee with weekly rest after work of two consecutive days of continuous daily rest, which may not be divided, but must be continuous and fall on a Saturday and Sunday or Sunday and Monday. Such determination of weekly rest need not be separately agreed upon with the employee. However, since the distribution of working time is involved, the employer consults, in the case of evenly distributed working time, such distribution with employee representatives and, in the case of unevenly distributed working time, the employer makes an agreement with the employee representatives.

The employer must arrange working time in such a way that weekly rest after work may be provided as indicated above and he must provide continuous weekly rest after work in two consecutive days on other days of the week. If the employer, due to the character of the work or the operating conditions, cannot provide weekly rest after work in this way, alternative legal models of weekly rest after work apply, which are subject to the agreement between the employer and the employee representatives and, if there are no employee representatives at the employer's workplace, other methods of providing continuous rest in a week must be agreed upon by the employer and the employee. The relevant method of determining continuous rest in a week depends primarily on the nature of the work performed and the operating conditions on the employer's part, even though these essential legal terms are not defined by the LC. They depend, to a considerable extent, from the object of the employer's activity.

Should the employer make an agreement with the employee younger than 18 years in order to reduce his weekly rest after work to 24 hours, such an agreement would be void because of a contradiction with the law. The agreement between the employee and the employer to shorten weekly rest after work need not be made in writing under pain of nullity.

I. First model of application of continuous rest in a week

The first model of providing continuous rest in a week implies a rest period of two entire days for the employee, which should fall on a Saturday and Sunday or a Sunday and Monday. This legal model of providing continuous rest in a week should be applied anytime that the nature of the work performed and the employer's operating conditions allow this. An employee younger than 18 years must always be granted continuous rest in a week according to the first legal model enshrined in Section 93(1) of the LC.

Provision of weekly rest after work according to this model does not require an agreement between the employer and the employee representatives or an agreement between the employer and the employee. However, in the case of unevenly distributed weekly working time, such working time may be unevenly distributed by the employer only with the consent of an employee with a health disability, a pregnant woman, a woman or man permanently caring for a child younger than three years of age or a lone employee permanently caring for a child younger than 15 years of age (see Section 87(3) of the LC).

II. Second model of application of continuous rest in a week

The second model of providing continuous weekly rest under Section 93(2) of the LC is possible only in cases where the application of the first model under paragraph 1 is not possible due to the nature of the work performed or due to operating conditions on the employer's part. If the above conditions are met, the employer may provide an employee older than 18 years of age with continuous rest in a week in the same extent as under Section 93(1) of the LC, but on different days of the week than those listed under paragraph 1.

Section 93(2) of the LC is mandatory; therefore, it may not be excluded by an agreement between the employee and the employer. The legal model of continuous rest in a week different than that under Section 93(1) of the LC must be respected by the parties to the employment relationship. Other procedures would be contrary to the law and might be subject to fines imposed by the competent work inspectorate. In the case of the uneven distribution of working time, the agreement between the employer and special categories of employees under Section 87(3) of the LC is required.

This model of providing weekly rest after work does not require an agreement between the employer and employee representatives or an agreement between the employer and the employee except for special categories of employees in the case of the uneven distribution of working time under Section 87(3) of the LC.

III. Third model of application of continuous rest in a week

The third model of distributing working time in a week with a lesser extent of weekly rest, with a 24-hour continuous rest in a week, may only be applied if the employee's working time can be arranged neither under Section 93(1) of the LC nor under Section 93(2) of the LC. In case of application of this legal model of providing continuous rest in a week reduced to 24 hours, the LC requires that it falls on a Sunday and it also requires the employer to provide the employee with alternative continuous rest in the week within eight months of the date when continuous rest should have been provided during the week. Accordingly, in the case of application of the third legal model of providing continuous rest in a week, the employer must provide the employee, within 8 months, with a compensation of the rest in a week reduced to 24 hours. In the case of application of this model, the agreement between the employer and the employee representatives is necessary and in cases where there are no employee representatives at the employer's workplace, this model of weekly rest after work requires an agreement between the employer and the employee. In case of an employee younger than 18 years, provision of weekly rest after work on the basis of this legal model is not allowed. In the case of the uneven distribution of working time with special categories of employees, the employer must make an agreement under Section 87(3) of the LC.

IV. Fourth model of application of continuous rest in a week

The fourth model of providing continuous rest in a week is possible as an alternative legal solution for the employer if continuous rest in a week, given the character of work and operating conditions, cannot be provided by the employer under Section 93(1) of the LC, Section 93(2) LC or Section 93(3) of the LC.

Obviously, the employer cannot choose it as the first model without examining whether it is not possible, given the character of work and the employer's operating conditions, to apply consecutively the first, second or third model of providing continuous rest in a week. The basic feature of this model of providing continuous rest in a week, unlike the third model, is that the employer need not provide compensation for it to the employee even if it is provided only in the extent of 35 hours that should fall on a Sunday and a part of either the day preceding or following Sunday. In the case of application of this legal model of providing weekly rest after work, agreement between the employer and the employee representatives is necessary and in cases where there are no employee representatives at the employer's workplace, an agreement between the employer and the employee is required, provided that the employee is older than 18 years of age. The uneven distribution of working time necessarily requires the employer's agreement with special categories of employees under Section 87(3) of the LC.

V. Fifth model of application of continuous rest in a week

The fifth model of providing continuous rest in a week is, under current legislation, possible only if, given the character of work or the employer's operating conditions, it is impossible to provide continuous rest in a week under Section 93(1) to (3) of the LC. The length of this rest in a week is set by the LC only at 24 hours only once in two weeks, which should fall on a Sunday, with a necessary compensation of this reduction of weekly rest within four months of the date when it should have been provided. This model of providing of weekly rest after work cannot be chosen by the employer as the first one and in the case of an inspection by the work inspection authorities, he must prove that, due to the character of work or the operating conditions, he could not arrange the working time under paragraphs (1) to (3) and he could not provide the employee with continuous rest in a week according to the first, second or this legal model. Agreement on the uneven distribution of working time is necessary if special categories of employees under Section 87(3) of the LC are involved.

§ 6 Rest days

Under Section 94 of the LC, work on rest days cannot be required by the employer from the employee and he may not order it. Rest days may be defined as continuous time-off, which may not be divided into parts. They are provided together for all employees, in principle once a week. Public holidays, unlike the days on which continuous rest in a week falls, are fixed by the Act No. 241/1993 Coll. This Act distinguishes national public holidays (Section 1 of the Act No. 241/1993 Coll.) and other public holidays (Section 2(2) of the Act No. 241/1993 Coll.). National public holidays according to this Act are 1st January, 5th July, 29th August, 1st September and 17th November. Other public holidays, which are also rest days, are 6st January, Good Friday, Easter Monday, 1st May, 8th May, 15th September, 1st November, 17th November and the 24th December to the 26th December.

The employer may order the employee to work also on rest days only if:
- the work is necessary,
- this work is exhaustively listed in the LC,
- it is ordered on an exceptional basis (it may not be ordered regularly); ordering such work must be consulted by the employer with the employee representatives.

All exhaustively listed cases of the employer's possibility to order performance of work also on rest days are limited in the sense that the work must be necessary (for example, it cannot be any work). At the same time, it must be work that cannot be performed on working days.

Chapter 13

Paid holiday

§ 1 General characteristics

The right to paid holiday is a constitutional right and it is an exclusively personal right that may not be transferred to another natural person. Paid holiday has personal character and therefore, on the employee's death, his right to paid holiday ceases to exist. His heirs acquire only the right to wage compensation for the paid holiday not taken. The right to paid holiday cannot be validly waived by the employee. If he did so, his legal act would be void for this reason.

Unlike other types and forms of rest after work, the employee's annual paid holiday should be a continuous time-off, during which the employee receives wage compensation in the amount of the average monthly wage from his employer. Slovak labour law, besides annual paid holiday, also regulates paid holiday for days worked in the interest of the employee himself, so that he does not lose his right to paid holiday if he does not work as long as is required for annual paid holiday.

§ 2 Types of paid holiday

I. Annual paid holiday

An employee who, during the continuous duration of an employment relationship with the same employer, performed work for the employer for at least 60 days in the calendar year is entitled to annual paid holiday.

If the employee worked with the employer for 60 days in the calendar year, but his employment relationship with this employer was not continuous during the entire calendar year, he is entitled to a proportionate part of annual paid holiday of one twelfth of annual paid holiday for each whole calendar month of continuous duration of the same employment relationship. The continuous duration of the employment relationship includes the termination of the former employment relationship and the immediate beginning of a new employment relationship of the employee with the same employer. This legal qualification of the continuous duration of the employment relationship is favourable especially for those employees who again establish an employment relationship with the same employer for a fixed term.

The condition of working 60 days for the purposes of annual paid holiday need not be met by the employee in every calendar year. According to the case law of the ECJ, the employer cannot require a certain number of days to be worked in an employment relationship every calendar year, although the employment relationship lasts longer (for example, several years). A day worked within the meaning of Section 101 of the LC is any day on which the employee worked the greater part of his shift. Times of shifts worked in various days cannot be cumulated.

II. Paid holiday for days worked

An employee who has not worked with the same employer at least 60 days in the calendar year, does not have the right to annual paid holiday, but he is entitled to paid holiday for days worked equal to one twelfth of annual paid holiday for each 21 days worked in the pertinent calendar year. This type of paid holiday is special in the sense that, unlike annual paid holiday, it can be reduced only due to unexcused missed work.

Under Section 103(1) of the LC the basic extent of paid holiday is at least four weeks.

The paid holiday of an employee who at the end of the relevant calendar year, will be at least 33 years of age is at least five weeks.

The basic extent of paid holiday is at least four weeks, irrespective of the employee's age and the duration of employment relationship.

The paid holiday of an employee who at the end of the relevant calendar year, will be at least 33 years of age, is at least five weeks. Under current legislation, it is irrelevant whether the employee was employed before turning 33, which eliminates the character of paid holiday based on merits and emphasizes the importance for health and rest of the employee after the work during the entire year or a part of it.

The LC fixes paid holiday in weeks. A week of paid holiday means seven consecutive calendar days, irrespective of which calendar day is the first day of the paid holiday. Therefore, it is a normal week, not a calendar week.

The employer may increase the extent of paid holiday. This may be agreed not only in collective agreements, but also in employment contracts or other individual contracts which is, in this part of the employment relationship, considered as a modification of the employment contract under Section 54 of the LC. The LC does not exclude cases of the paid holiday being extended by the employer by means of the employer's internal regulation. This applies, in particular, to cases where the employer has no social partner and he prefers to extend the paid holiday collectively, according to certain criteria (for example, working conditions). If the employer agrees to a longer paid holiday on an individual basis in employment contracts, he should be very careful in order not to infringe the equal treatment principle. The length of paid holiday should be, under Section 43 of the LC, part of the employment contract.

III. Supplementary paid holiday

Supplementary paid holiday is a special type of paid holiday that can be considered as a certain compensation for an employee working in difficult working conditions. It allows the employee, during a paid holiday longer than other employees have, to recover from work, which means that it is, at least in part, intended to protect his health.

The right to supplementary paid holiday results directly from the LC. It is examined separately, independently of conditions for other types of paid holidays.

Employees working underground over the whole calendar year in the extraction of minerals or driving tunnels or passages have the right to supplementary paid holiday.

IV. Proportionate part of annual paid holiday

The employee has the right to a proportionate part of paid holiday only if his employment relationship with the employer did not last the entire calendar year and he worked at least 60 days. Annual paid holiday and proportionate part of annual paid holiday is more favourable for the employee compared to paid holiday for days worked because it is only reduced after 100 days of excused absence at work in the case of obstacles to work, which are not considered, with respect to the purpose of paid holiday, as the performance of work. Paid holiday for days worked corresponds with one twelfth of annual paid holiday for each 21 days worked.

A. Proportionate part of paid holiday in case of termination of employment relationship

For the purposes of calculating the proportionate part of paid holiday, it is necessary to distinguish between the termination of the employee's employment relationship where the employee does not enter immediately into a new employment relationship (for example, he retires) and cases of the change of employment where, after termination of one employment relationship during the month, the employee enters into an employment relationship with another employer. If there is no change of employment and the employee's employment relationship with the employer ends, he may receive a proportionate part of the paid holiday for the corresponding month only if the employment relationship terminated with the employer on the last day of the month.

B. Proportionate part of paid holiday in case of changing employment

An employee is also entitled to a proportionate part of annual paid holiday in the extent of one twelfth of annual paid holiday for the month during which he changed his employment provided that the termination of e the mployment relationship with the former employer and the commencement of the employment relationship with the new employer are immediately linked. Of course, it must be a different employer. This condition is also met if, between the termination of one employment relationship and the commencement of another employment relationship, there are rest days (for example, days on which continuous rest in a week falls) and public holidays. If one employment relationship is terminated and a new employment relationship with the same employer begins, the conditions for acquiring the right to paid holiday are evaluated as if it were the same employment relationship, which applies only for the purposes of paid holiday.

§ 3 Extent of paid holiday

Under Section 103 of the LC, the basic scope of paid holiday is at least four weeks. The paid holiday of an employee who at the end of the relevant calendar year, will be at least 33 of age is at least five weeks. The basic extent of paid holiday is at least four weeks, irrespective of the employee's age and the duration of the employment relationship.

Under current legislation, the paid holiday of an employee who at the end of the relevant calendar year, will be at least 33 of age is at least five weeks. It is irrelevant whether the employee was employed or for how long his employment relationship lasted. Likewise, under current legislation, replacement periods, which were relevant for acquiring the right to paid holiday of at least five weeks, are irrelevant. The LC fixes the length of paid holiday in weeks. A week of paid holiday means seven consecutive calendar days, irrespective of which calendar day is the first day of the paid holiday. Therefore, it is a normal week, not a calendar week.

One week of an employee's paid holiday represents the number of working days that the employee must work under the timetable of work shifts, whether his working time, distributed in individual weeks, is stipulated or individually agreed. For example, in the case of employees with a regular 5-day working scheme in a week, a week of paid holiday represents five working days. In the case of a regular 4-day working scheme in a week, a week of paid holiday represents four working days.

Even though the length of paid holiday is fixed in weeks by the LC, the employee may also take it in parts shorter than a week (for example, in working days). The transfer of the extent of paid holiday to working days is also necessary in the case of a proportionate part of paid holiday and in the case of reduction of paid holiday where the employee has no entire calendar weeks.

The LC defines the extent of paid holiday as a minimum extent and fixes it at four weeks.

I. Increase of extent of paid holiday

The employer may increase the extent of paid holiday. This may be agreed not only in collective agreements, but also in employment contracts or other individual contracts which are, in this part of the employment relationship, considered as a modification of the employment contract under Section 54 of the LC. Paid holiday may also be extended by the employer in an agreement concluded between the employer and the works council or the employee representatives under Section 233a of the LC, which may be concluded by the employer if there is no trade organization at his workplace. The LC does not exclude cases of the paid holiday being extended by the employer by means of the employer's internal regulation. This applies, in particular, to cases where the employer has no social partner and he prefers to extend the paid holiday collectively, according to certain criteria (for example, working conditions). If the employer agrees to a longer paid holiday on an individual basis in employment contracts, he should be very careful in order not to infringe the equal treatment principle.

II. Extent of paid holiday in particular cases

The extent of paid holiday of certain groups of employees is influenced in particular by the type of work performed by them. The paid holiday of the headmaster of a school, the director of a school upbringing and education facility, the director of special educational facilities and their deputies, a teacher, a teaching assistant, a vocational training instructor and an educator shall be at least eight weeks. An amendment to the LC regulates these special categories of employees according to categories of educational employees under Act No. 317/2009 Coll. This type of paid holiday can also be extended, because it is regulated by the LC as a minimum extent.

§ 4 Reduction of paid holiday

Under Section 109 of the LC, the reduction of paid holiday means that if an employee satisfies the condition of working at least 60 days in a calendar year with the same employer, he is entitled to annual paid holiday, but, in particular due to obstacles to work on his part (which are, for the purposes of paid holiday, not considered as the performance of work), but also due to unexcused missed work shifts, his annual paid holiday may be reduced. Even if paid holiday is reduced, the employer must provide an employee whose employment relationship with the employer lasted the entire calendar year, with paid holiday of at least one week and at least two weeks in case of an adolescent employee. Under current legislation, it is not a legal duty, but a right of the employer to reduce paid holiday, which he does not have to use. The reasons for reducing paid holiday by the employer are listed in the LC exhaustively. Paid holiday is reduced, in particular, due to obstacles to work on the employee's part, which are not considered as the performance of work for the purposes of paid holiday, but also due to the performance of extraordinary service during a state of crisis or alternative service during wartime or in a state of war, due to the taking of parental leave under Section 166(2) of the LC and also due to the long term leave for the performance of a public function or a trade union function.

The extent of the reduction of paid holiday in these cases is one twelfth for the first 100 working days missed and by a further one twelfth for each additional 21 working days missed. All working days missed in the calendar year are cumulated. Paid holiday is reduced only when the total extent of such obstacles to work in the calendar year reaches the limit of 100 days. Paid holiday for days worked and supplementary paid holiday is not reduced for the reasons listed above. Another reason for reducing paid holiday is the unexcused missing of work shifts by the employee (absence) when the employer may, but does not have to reduce paid holiday. The legal qualification of unexcused missed work shifts must be done by the employer after consulting with the employee representatives. If there are no employee representatives at his workplace, the employer himself is entitled to assess whether it is an excused missed work shift or an unexcused missed work shift and consequently he may, but does not have to reduce paid holiday of the employee. For every unexcused missed work shift, the employer is entitled to reduce the employee's paid holiday in the extent of 1 to 2 days.

Another method, which is less favourable for the employee, applies to reducing paid holiday if the employee serves a prison term. The extent of this reduction is one twelfth for every 21 work shifts missed for this reason. The same extent of the reduction of paid holiday applies to detention, if the employee was finally sentenced or acquitted the indictment, or if criminal prosecution against him was terminated only due to the fact that he is not criminally responsible for the crime committed or that he was granted pardon or amnesty.

In the case of reducing paid holiday due to obstacles to work or unexcused missed work shifts, the employer must provide an employee, whose employment relationship lasted during the entire calendar year, with paid holiday of at least one calendar week. In case of adolescent employees, paid holiday in the extent of at least two calendar weeks must be provided. This limitation of the employer in determining the minimum extent of paid holiday does not apply where there is a reduction of paid holiday for serving a prison term or for the detention of the employee.

§ 5 Employer's right to determine the taking of paid holiday

Even though the right to paid holiday is a constitutional right, the time of taking paid holiday is determined exclusively by the employer. The form of the employer's decision determining the time of taking paid holiday is not stipulated by the LC. It is a right of the employer, which he must exercise with regard to the employee's justified interests. The employer's right to determine the taking of paid holiday by an employee applies to all types of paid holiday and to the entire extent of paid holiday that the employee is entitled to. If the employee himself decides to take paid holiday without it being determined by the employer, he breaches work discipline and he may also be sanction by the employer's notice for the breach of work discipline.

In order to determine the taking of paid holiday, the employer drafts every calendar year, with prior consent of the employee representatives, a plan of taking paid holiday. The employer may change the time of taking paid holiday by the employee. It is also a right of the employer that can cause the employer to be responsible for expenses incurred by the change of the time of taking paid holiday.

If there is no trade union organization, works council or employee representative at the employer's workplace, the employer determines the taking of paid holiday himself.

The employer may also determine the taking of paid holiday, even if the employee has not yet met the conditions for paid holiday, if it may be presumed that these conditions will be met by the end of the calendar year or before the termination of the employment relationship.

I. Employer's duties

The LC establishes certain duties of the employer with respect to determining the commencement of paid holiday. The employer must, when determining the time of taking paid holiday:

– announce the time of taking paid holiday to the employer no later than 14 days before the commencement of paid holiday,
– if the employee is taking paid holiday in several parts, at least one part should consist at least of two weeks unless agreed to otherwise between the employer and the employee,
– in case of an employee whose employment relationship with the employer lasted the entire calendar year, the employer must determine the taking of at least four weeks of paid holiday in the calendar year,
– paid holiday may not be determined for a period when the employee is recognized as temporarily unable to work due to illness or accident or when an employee is on mater-

nity leave or parental leave. In the case of other obstacles to work on the employee's part, the employer is entitled to determine the taking of paid holiday only on the request of the employee himself.

II. Collective taking of paid holiday

The employer is entitled, after agreement with the employee representatives, to determine the collective taking of paid holiday provided that it is necessary for operational reasons on the employer's part and compatible with the interest of employees. In the case of collective taking of paid holiday, the employer must take the justified interests of employees into account. The necessary operational reasons and the compatibility with interests of employees must be assessed according to the circumstances of the case at hand. The collective taking of paid holiday should be possible only in case of employers who, due to their object of activity or character of services provided, cannot determine the individual taking of paid holiday without a risk of damage on their part.

According to current legislation, the LC allows for the determination of the collective taking of paid holiday also for three weeks in case of serious operational reasons provided that it is announced by the employer at least six months in advance. It follows from the above that such an employer should not draft the plan of paid holiday of employees earlier, so that he does not have to, with legal consequences, change it even before the expiry of the six-month deadline, which he has for announcing the collective taking of paid holiday to employees.

Apart from the above, the employer may, in artistic professions, determine the collective taking of paid holiday for up to four weeks and in the case of employees of professional artistic, ensemble or determine the collective taking of paid holiday to the full extent in the case of activities associated with the performance of musical works. Even though, in principle, the collective taking of paid holiday of employees cannot be longer than two weeks, under current legislation, the employer may, in case of serious operational reasons on his part, determine the collective taking of paid holiday for up to three weeks. However, he must announce his decision to the employees at least six months in advance. In theatres and other artistic institutions performing musical works, the collective taking of paid holiday may be determined in full extent. Even during the collective taking of paid holiday, the employer must assign work to employees who, for various reasons, do not meet the conditions for paid holiday. This work must correspond with the type of work defined in the employment contract. If the employer could not, for various reasons, assign work to an employee according to the employment contract, it would be an obstacle at work on his part. For the entire time of assigning no work, he would have to pay the employee wage (salary) compensation if he did not agree to the performance of different work with the employee.

Under Section 111(2) of the LC, the employer may, after agreement with employee representatives, determine the collective taking of paid holiday provided that it is necessary for operational reasons. The collective taking of paid holiday, under paragraph (2) of the LC, may not be determined for more than two weeks unless provided otherwise. In the case of serious operational reasons that are announced to employees at least six months in advance, the collective taking of paid holiday may be determined for three weeks. The collective taking of paid holiday in professional artistic ensembles may not be determined for more than four weeks. In theatres and other artistic institutions performing musical works, the collective taking of paid holiday may be determined in full extent. The employer is entitled, after agreement with the employee representatives, to determine the collective taking of paid holiday provided that it is necessary for operational reasons on the employer's part and it is compatible with the interest of employees. In the case of the collective taking of paid holiday, the employer must take the justified interests of the employees into account. Necessary operational reasons and compatibility with the interests of employees must be assessed according to the circumstances of the case at hand. The collective taking of paid holiday should be possible only in case of employers who, due to their object of activity or character of services provided, cannot determine the individual taking of paid holiday without a risk of damage on their part.

A. Extent of collective taking of paid holiday

The LC changes considerably the extent of collective taking of the paid holiday in favour of the employer. Even though, in principle, the collective taking of paid holiday of employees cannot be longer than two weeks, under current legislation, the employer may, in the case of serious operational reasons on his part, determine the collective taking of paid holiday for up to three weeks. However, he must announce his decision to the employees at least six months in advance. In the case of professional artistic ensembles, the collective taking of paid holiday may not be determined for more than four weeks. Unlike under former legislation, in theatres and other artistic institutions performing musical works, the collective taking of paid holiday may be determined in full extent. Even during the collective taking of paid holiday, the employer must assign work to employees who, for various reasons, do not meet the conditions for paid holiday. This work must correspond with the type of work defined in the employment contract. If the employer could not, for various reasons, assign work to an employee according to the employment contract, it would be an obstacle to work on his part. For the entire time of assigning no work, he would have to pay the employee wage (salary) compensation if he did not agree to the performance of different work with the employee.

Previous regulation of paid holiday according to the LC left the determination of time of paid holiday to the discretion of the employer. In practice, there were frequently situations when the employer has not taken paid holiday until the end of the following calendar year. Hence, the reform of the LC responds to these situations as well as to the current case law of the ECJ and it confers the power to take paid holidays into the hands of the employees themselves. According to the amended provisions of Section 113(2) of the LC, if the employee does not take paid holiday until 30th June of the following calendar year so that the employee can complete it until the end of calendar year, the employee can draw his (her) paid holiday. The employee is required in this case to notify the employer in writing and at least 30 days in advance of the paid holiday. This period may be shortened with the consent of the employer.

Chapter 14

Remuneration for work

§ 1 General characteristics

Under current legislation, the term remuneration for work performed is not unified in labour-law relationships. In the case of the employment relationships of entities falling within the scope of the application of the LC (for example, or the business sector), the remuneration for work is designated as wage in the LC.

The level of remuneration for work performed in the Slovak Republic is low in comparison with the majority of EU Member States. With respect to the level of remuneration for work performed in the employment relationship, the Slovak Republic is one of the last EU Member States, only followed by Latvia, Bulgaria and Romania. Another problem of the current level of the remuneration for dependent work in employment relationships is that it does not create good prerequisites for providing old-age pensions that would guarantee elementary existence conditions for pensioners. Economists have calculated that, under the current model of old-age pensions in the Slovak Republic, a monthly wage of up to 700 euros does not even guarantee a minimum existence for a future pensioner. It means that he will depend on social assistance benefits.

Cheap labour is one of the reasons why many foreign businesses are attracted to the Slovak Republic. It is a major priority of business plans of foreign businesses.

The general characteristics of the remuneration of dependent work in employment relationships of businesses include the fact that the LC establishes no maximum limits of remuneration, not only with respect to tariff wage, but also various wage surcharges. The LC establishes only minimum levels of such wage benefits. Wage benefits beyond the minimum statutory level are usually subject to collective negotiations between social partners. Collective agreements, in this part, constitute a normative part, which establishes employee's rights enforceable in court.

Employers with no trade union organizations at their workplace may regulate the remuneration of their employees in their wage rules, which must respect the prohibition of discrimination. The employer's wage rules should be, according to current and abundant case law of the ECJ, legally correct and consistent with the equal treatment principle.

§ 2 Minimum wage, wage conditions

Even though current rules of the LC concerning remuneration are very liberal and create a wide scope for contractual freedom of parties to employment relationships, the level of minimum wage is still regulated by statute. Businesses propose solutions aimed at repealing the Minimum Wage Act every year and argue that it could decrease unemployment. The argument that an employer would hire more employees if he did not have to pay them the statutory level of minimum wage is questionable, since even now many employers infringe the Minimum Wage Act and pay such wage also in the case of more qualified work so that the employee receives a part of the wage in the amount of a minimum wage officially and a part of wage, which is not subject to income tax paid by the employer and social security payments, is paid by the employer to the employer 'in cash'. Such action of employers is not rare and it puts employees in a very unfavourable position when it comes to their future rights in the case of illness during the employment relationship or to the level of future old-age pensions.

The wage may not be lower than the minimum wage established by Act No. 663/2007 Coll. on Minimum Wage, as amended. It is the lowest possible amount of remuneration for work in labour-law relationships, which is paid not only to employees in the business sector, but also to employees working in the public interest receiving a salary for their work. The provision on minimum wage also applies in the case of remuneration based on agreements on work performed outside of employment relationships. If the employee does not reach the level of minimum wage, the employer must provide him with a wage surcharge. The provision of the LC concerning minimum wage restricts the contractual freedom of parties to employment relationships when negotiating the amount of wage in an employment relationship and providing remuneration for work performed on the basis of agreements on work performed outside of employment relationships. Unlike the LC, the Act on Remuneration of Work Performed in Public Interest (public service sector) does not provide the scope for the contractual freedom of parties to employment relationships when determining the functional salary, but it accepts the fact that the remuneration of employees must be at least the minimum statutory wage. Minimum wage does not include wage (salary) benefit for overtime work or for work on a public holiday, for work on Saturdays and Sundays, for night work or wage compensation for a more difficult performance of work. In the collective agreement, a wage higher than the minimum statutory wage may be agreed. In this case, the employer is bound by the higher minimum wage agreed upon in the collective agreement. In accordance with former legislation, the LC allows wage conditions to be agreed upon not only in the collective agreement, but also in the employment contract.

If the employee's wage in the calendar month in terms of hours worked does not achieve the amount of minimum wage, the employer will provide the employee with a surcharge corresponding with the difference between the wage achieved and the amount of minimum wage established for the degree of the workplace in question.

§ 3 Wage conditions according to the Labour Code

Remuneration of employees according to the LC is carried out only on a contractual basis. Wage conditions are, under Section 43 of the LC, a necessary part of the employment contract, unless agreed to in the collective agreement. The LC does not establish any upper limits of wage, but it does restrict the freedom of contract of parties to employment relationships by means of a minimum statutory wage. According to current legislation, Section 43(3) of the LC states that if wage conditions are not agreed upon in the employment contract and the provisions of the collective agreement that the employment contract refers to have lost effect, the wage conditions agreed in the collective agreement apply until new wage conditions are agreed upon in the collective agreement, no longer than 12 months.

The LC implicitly states what must be considered as wage conditions. They include, in particular, forms of remuneration, the amount of basic part of wage and other parts of benefits provided for work and the conditions of providing them. The basic part of the wage is the main part paid to the employee according to the time worked or the performance achieved. For the purposes of defining wage conditions in the employment contract, it is necessary to indicate the amount of hourly wage or monthly wage (amount of basic part of wage).

As far as the form of remuneration is concerned, the employer should indicate the amount of hourly wage or monthly wage, task wage or proportionate or mixed form of wage. in the employment contract (collective agreement). The conditions of providing other parts of wage concern, in particular, special parts of wage. These include the criteria that must be met for the employee to acquire the right to a specific part of wage in the specific amount. The LC does not impose a duty on the employer to agree, in the employment contract, specific amounts of other parts of wage.

I. Wage amount in the employment contract and collective agreement

Wage conditions may be agreed to either in the employment contract or in a collective agreement. This applies, in particular, to more favourable rules contained in the work rules, but also to those based on an individual unilateral decision of the employer, which is important mainly for employers with no trade union organizations at their workplace and no collective agreement concluded. More favourable wage conditions of employees can be regulated, for example, in a different agreement with employee representatives, but also in an internal wage regulation of the employer (for example, in the work rules). If the employer proceeds in this way, it does not automatically mean that he is not bound by the duty under Section 43 of the LC to agree to the wage conditions with the employee in the employment contract.

§ 4 Wage in kind

Wage in kind may be provided to the employee only with his consent and under the conditions agreed upon with him, only beyond the minimum wage. The wage up to the level of minimum wage must be provided in monetary form. It means that wage in kind can constitute only a part of the wage if the employee receives a wage higher than the minimum wage for his work from the employer. Wage in kind may be agreed upon between the employer and the employee either in the employment contract or in an amendment to the employment contract. The agreement between the employer and the employee may also be contained in a different contract (agreement), which, given its character and legal consequences may be regarded as an amendment to the employment contract. Under the LC, it is valid even if not made in writing. If the agreement of parties were contained in the employment contract, it should be made in writing, even though non-observance of the written form would not cause the nullity of legal act. Similarly, this applies to amendments to the employment contract, which, according to Section 54 of the LC, must be made by the employer in writing. Its validity is not conditioned by observing the written form. A collective agreement cannot replace the agreement between the employer and the employee concerning the provision of wage in kind in the employment contract or an amendment to such a contract. The extent of providing wage in kind must correspond with the employee's personal needs and the benefit of the employee and his family (ILO Convention No. 95 on the protection of wages).

Wage in kind may not be provided in the case of employees working in public interest.

§ 5 Wage in foreign currency

An employee performing work abroad pursuant to the employment contract may be provided with wages or part thereof in a foreign currency. The currency conversion of wages from euro to a foreign currency is executed according to the foreign exchange rate set and announced by the European Central Bank or the National Bank of Slovakia which is in effect on the date preceding the date set for the payment of wages in compliance with Section 130(2) of the LC or on another agreed day. Wage in foreign currency may be provided by the employer to the employee only if the employee works abroad pursuant to the employment contract; no explicit request of the employee or a specific agreement between the parties is required. With respect to the requirements of Section 43(5) of the LC, the parties should do so in the employment contract or in its amendment. An employment contract or its amendment under Section 43 of the LC may be, however, made only with the consent of both parties (the employer and the employee) with respect to the type of foreign currency and the part of wage paid in such currency, the duration of the performance of work abroad, other benefits associated with the performance of work abroad or the conditions of the employee's return from abroad. As far as the provision of wage in foreign currency is concerned, it need not be the currency of the state where the employee is working but also a currency agreed by the parties.

The provision of wage in foreign currency does not apply to cases where the place of the performance of work is not, according to the employment contract, agreed upon. It applies not only to the temporary performance of work, but mainly to foreign business trips for which the employee receives travel reimbursement pursuant to Act No. 283/2002 Coll. on Travel Reimbursement, as amended.

§ 6 Payment term of wage

Under Section 129 of the LC, a wage is due in arrears for a monthly period, by the end of following calendar month at the latest, unless agreed otherwise in the collective agreement or in the employment contract.

The wage (salary) is paid to the employee always after work has been performed. The wage (salary) is due by the end of following calendar month at the latest, unless agreed to otherwise in the collective agreement or in the employment contract. The LC allows the parties to agree upon the payment term of wage differently in the collective agreement or in the employment contract if the work for which the wage is to be paid has already been performed. If the payment term of the wage is not agreed differently, the wage is due in arrears for a monthly period, by the end of the following calendar month at the latest. If the payment term of the wage is agreed differently by the parties (for example, on the 15th day of the calendar month), the period for enforcing it starts, with respect to the computation of time, on the first day following the payment term agreed. If the contracting parties do not make use of the option to agree upon the payment term of wage differently, the period for enforcing the right starts on the first day of the month following the payment term of wage (for example, only after termination of the following calendar month). Provisions on payment of wage need not apply to employees performing home work to the full extent. Payment of wage may be agreed, in their case, also for the delivery of every work assigned and completed.

I. Transfer of wage to the employee's account

Under current legislation, the employer is not entitled to require the employee to open an account with a financial institution for the purposes of transferring the wage in a cashless payment system. This method of wage payment may be agreed upon with the employee.

The employee is entitled to require the employer to send his wage to several accounts in one or several financial institutions. The payment of wage into several accounts is done by the employer on the basis of an agreement with the employee or on the basis of the employee's request. The employee request need not be made in writing, as indicated under the LC. The LC imposes a prohibition on the employer to limit the employee with respect to the free disposal of the wage paid.

§ 7 Wage and wage surcharge for overtime work

The Slovak Republic is currently one of the EU Member States with the highest rate of overtime work. Many employees are eager to work overtime because the surcharges for overtime work help them to survive despite the low basic wage. The performance of overtime work is remunerated by the wage achieved and a wage surcharge equal to at least 25 % of the average earning provided that no alternative time-off has been agreed upon between the employer and the employee. The wage achieved and a wage surcharge equal to at least 35 % of the average earning, is provided for overtime work if risky work is performed by the employee. The performance of overtime for risky work would have to be agreed upon by the employer and the employee first. The amount of wage surcharge need not be derived from the employee's average earning (for example, with a fixed amount), but in monetary terms, it may not be lower than 25 % of the employee's average earning. The employee's right to a higher wage for overtime work is acquired after overtime work is completed only if no alternative time-off instead of wage increase has been agreed upon between the employer and the employee.

An employee does not have a right to a wage surcharge for overtime work for which he is taking alternative time-off and in the case that overtime work is reflected in the amount of wage. Once the employee has taken alternative time-off, he has no right to a wage surcharge because he has taken alternative time-off.

I. Alternative time-off based on an agreement between the employer and the employee

Taking of alternative time-off for overtime work may be agreed upon between the employer and the employee, in particular with respect to the term of taking alternative time-off, which increases the flexibility of labour-law relationships. Only if the employer and the employee do not make an agreement concerning the taking of alternative time-off for overtime work, the employer must, under the LC, provide the employee with alternative time-off no later than twelve months following the month during which overtime work was performed. Individual agreement between the employee and the employer concerning alternative time-off should also include the term when the employer will allow the employee to take alternative time-off. Only if the employer does not provide the employee with alternative time-off for overtime work does the employee has a right to wage surcharge for overtime work.

II. Overtime work reflected in the amount of wage

The employer may reflect the overtime work in the amount provided to the employee only with respect to executive employees directly subordinated to the statutory body and to the category of highly specialized employees, who need not have the legal status of executive employees.

If the employer foresees this possibility of reflecting overtime work in the amount of wage, he should always agree to this with the employee when making the employment contract. During the employment relationship, the employer may not do so unilaterally.

If the employer makes use of this possibility, he must respect the fact that the inclusion of overtime work in the amount of wage provided to the employee is allowed by the LC only up to the statutory maximum of overtime work, which is 150 hours a year. Up to this extent, the employer may also order the employee to perform overtime work unilaterally. The employer is not entitled, even on the basis of an agreement with the employee, to provide wage reflecting overtime work beyond 150 hours a year.

The employees whose wage already reflects the performance of overtime work up to the statutory limit of 150 hours a year, have no right to wage achieved for overtime work or wage surcharge for overtime work, or alternative time-off.

If the employer has made an agreement with the employee that the amount of wage reflects any overtime work (for example, not only statutory, but also agreed), such an agreement would be void as contrary to the law and the criterion of partial nullity of legal acts under the Civil Code would apply. In this case, the statutory maximum of overtime work would apply.

§ 8 Wage and wage compensation for public holiday

Foreign businesses should be aware of the fact that they must provide employees in an employment relationship with a wage surcharge for work on public holidays. With respect to information concerning the performance of work on public holidays, foreign businesses should also know that in the Slovak Republic, work is performed in the production sector and in the trade sector also on Sundays and public holidays. On public holidays and Sundays, all shopping centres and small shops are open. On public holidays and Sundays, work is performed in bigger or smaller constructions. Even though the current legal model of work on public holidays and Sundays allows employers to order an employee to work unilaterally only in exhaustively defined cases, employers often circumvent the law by making an 'agreement' with employees concerning work on public holidays and Sundays. Employees often have no other option if the employer insists on the performance of work on public holidays and Sundays. They want to keep their job and they can also want to receive a wage surcharge from the employer for work on public holidays and earn more than their low basic wage.

For work performed on public holidays, wage surcharge for work performed on public holidays is provided, irrespective of whether the public holiday is a working day, Sunday or a different day of continuous rest in a week. In the case of coincidence of overtime work and work on public holidays as quite independent rights, the employee is entitled to the wage surcharge for overtime work and the wage surcharge for work on a public holiday.

For work on a public holiday, the employee receives the wage achieved and a wage surcharge equal at least to 50 % of the average earning unless alternative time-off has been agreed upon between the employer and the employee. A higher wage surcharge for work on a public holiday may be agreed upon by the contracting parties in the employment contract or it may be enshrined in the collective agreement or in a different internal work regulation of the employer (wage rules, work rules). Taking of alternative time-off may not be ordered by the employer unilaterally. An individual agreement between the employee and the employer, which may be not only written, but also oral, may not be replaced by a collective agreement, work rules, the employer's individual instruction or a different internal regulation of the employer. Unlike the employee's right concerning the period of taking alternative time-off for overtime work, the employee is, when taking alternative time-off for work performed on a public holiday, entitled to a wage compensation equal to his average earning.

I. Wage agreed as reflecting work on public holidays in the case of executive employees

The LC allows the employer to agree with executive employees in the employment contract a wage reflecting any work performed on public holidays. In this case, the executive employee has no right to a wage surcharge or alternative time-off for work on public holidays. However, he is entitled to wage for work on public holidays. The LC does not specify with respect to which executive employees such procedure may be applied by the employer in the employment contract. Therefore, it applies with respect to all executive employees, irrespective of the vertical degree of management, who are charged, on individual levels of management, with determining and imposing work tasks on subordinate employees, organizing, directing and controlling their work and giving them binding instructions for that purpose (such an employee must have at least one subordinate employee).

§ 9 Wage surcharge for night work

For an hour of night work, the employee is entitled, besides the wage attained, to a wage surcharge for every hour of night work equal at least to 20 % of the minimum wage in euros per hour. Collective agreements, but also employment contracts may contain more favourable rules of remuneration for the performance of night work. The employer must provide the employee with a proportionate part of the wage surcharge also for periods of night work shorter than one hour.

Executive employees do not have the right to a wage surcharge for night work provided that, in the employment contract, the amount of their wage was agreed as to reflecting any night work. Executive employees are employees within the meaning of Section 9 of the LC (for example, those organizing and directing work and having at least one subordinate employee). Such employees are not entitled to a wage surcharge for night work.

§ 10 Wage compensation for work performed in difficult conditions

An employee is entitled to wage compensation for work performed in difficult conditions if he performs work indicated in Section 124(2) of the LC and is classified in categories 3 or 4 under special regulation. Moreover, the employee must, in order to eliminate the health risk when performing such work, use personal protective equipment. Work classified in categories 3 and 4 is risky work within the meaning of Act No. 355/2007 Coll. on the protection, support and development of public health and amending certain acts. The regional public health office determines the classification of such work.

In the case of work performed in difficult conditions, the law does not allow the employer to agree with the employee that the wage agreed will reflect work performed in difficult conditions.

The minimum limit of the surcharge agreed upon for work performed in difficult conditions that does not qualify as a threat to the employee's life and health or in the case of lower intensity of harmful effects is not determined. The assessment of the work environment for these purposes is carried out by the regional public health office as determined on the basis of the employer's registered office.

The LC establishes only a minimum amount of this surcharge at 20 % of the minimum wage in euros per hour according to special regulation. More favourable conditions of providing wage surcharge, as well as the extension of possibilities of providing it may be, under the LC, contained in collective agreements and employment contracts.

Under current legislation, it is primarily up to the employer whether and how the wage surcharge will be provided, also in the case of lower intensity of harmful work factors or working environment or in the case of other effects of working environment. If the employer decides to do so, he has, unlike under former legislation, several options. Apart from the collective agreement and the employment contract, he may provide a wage surcharge in accordance with his work rules or wage rules. The LC explicitly does not deal with the situation of the collision between such rules contained in the collective agreement and the employment contract. In this case, if the employment contract contained less favourable rules than the collective agreement, it would be, under Section 231 of the LC, void in this part, on the basis of the principle of favouring the employee.

Chapter 15

Obstacles to work

§ 1 General characteristics

Obstacles to work on the employee's or employer's part mean a temporary suspension of performance resulting from the employment relationship in the case of the occurrence of legal facts that are considered by the legislature as legally relevant, without the employment relationship being terminated. Obstacles to work impede the employee from performing his work duties with respect to the employer and they also impede the employer from performing his duties with respect to the employee, mainly with respect to assigning work in accordance with the employment contract. The burden of proof regarding the existence and the duration of the obstacle to work in question on the employee's part is borne by the employee himself. The existence of an obstacle to work establishes legal consequences foreseen by the law. The employee has the right not to perform the work agreed upon with the employer in the employment contract and he loses the right to wage for work performed.

The legal regulation of obstacles to work applies to all employers, whether they are legal or natural persons, businesses or employers in the public sector. If the employee has several employment relationships, obstacles to work are examined separately in each employment relationship (Section 50 of the LC). The LC imposes a duty on the employer to provide time-off due to the performance of a public function or the performance of civic duties or other acts in general interest, only if the employee cannot perform such activity outside his working time. The extent of time-off provided is limited to what is necessary.

In the case of a long-term time-off due to the performance of functions of a trade union organization with an employer, the employee's long-term time-off depends on the conditions agreed upon in the collective agreement and in the case of a long-term time-off of a member of a works council or of an employee representative, the employee's long-term time-off for the performance of these functions depends on the agreement with the works council or the employee representative.

§ 2 Obstacles to work on the employee's part

Obstacles to work are, under the LC in force, formulated generously with respect to the employee. In particular, important personal obstacles to work limited in the LC in specific terms mean, for many employees, often two more weeks of paid holiday. This applies specifically to obstacles to work caused by treatment and obstacles to work caused by accompanying a family member in a medical facility. In this generously formulated model of important personal obstacles to work, many employees strive to use in practice the maximum limits of tolerated time-off from work, for which the employer must provide wage compensation in the amount of their average earning.

Obstacles to work on the employee's part are classified by the LC in force as:

- obstacles to work in the case of performing civic duties and other acts in general interest,
- obstacles to work due to volunteering,
- obstacles to work in the case of discharge of compulsory military service and specialised training in the armed forces,
- obstacles to work associated with increasing qualification,
- important personal obstacles to work.

I. Obstacles to work in case of performing civic duties and other acts in general interest

Time-off from work of necessary duration with wage compensation must be provided, under the LC, by an employer only in case of remedial stays, mandatory medical examinations and in the case of the participation of employee representatives in training. The participation in remedial stays is defined by the Occupational Safety and Health Act as a legal duty of the employee. The content of such important reasons at the employer's workplace may be defined in his work rules.

More favourable rules concerning wage compensations may be agreed upon by the parties to employment relationships in the employment contract, but also in collective agreements.

II. Increasing qualification

Further education must be distinguished from obtaining or increasing qualification. The term increasing qualification is not defined by the LC. These terms are not defined by other labour-law regulations either. From the perspective of labour-law theory, obtaining or increasing qualification is such a qualitative change in the content of education that is reflected in the increase of the qualification degree. For instance, an employee obtains qualification if he had no qualification before or he increases his qualification degree by completing university education.

III. Important personal obstacles to work on the employee's part

The term 'important personal obstacles to work' means that these obstacles to work consist in the employee's person and are considered by the legislature as so legally relevant that, if they occur, it grants the employee a right to time-off from work and, in case of some of these obstacles to work, also a right to wage compensation or sickness insurance benefits.

In the case of obstacles to work establishing a right to sickness insurance benefits, the employee need not ask the employer for time-off from work, rather it is sufficient if he demonstrates the obstacle to work. The LC imposes a duty on the employee to inform his employer of an obstacle to work without undue delay. The employer must excuse the employee's absence at work.

In the case of important personal obstacles to work of mandatory character, the LC imposes a duty on the employer to provide the employee both with time-off from work and a wage compensation:

- beyond the statutory extent in the collective agreement or in the employer's internal regulation and
- for other than statutory reasons or
- to grant time-off from work for personal obstacle to work so that the employee may work more time.

A. Examination or treatment of employee in a medical facility

The examination or treatment of an employee in a medical facility is one of the most common important personal obstacles to work. The extent of time-off from work in case of this important personal obstacle to work is set by the LC at seven days in the calendar year. Apart from that, it must be an examination that could not have been performed outside of working time. However, the employer may provide the employee with more time-off from work beyond the statutory limit of seven days in a calendar year, not only without, but also with wage compensation. Should the employee need, during the year, more time-off from work for the purposes of his own examination, the employer must provide such time-off, but no wage compensation will be provided for that time if the examination or treatment could not have been performed outside of working time, unless more favourable rules are contained in the collective agreement. The period of one day means the period corresponding with the average length of the work shift resulting from stipulated or reduced weekly working time.

B. Accompanying a family member in a medical facility

Just like in the case of the employee's own treatment or examination in a medical facility, in the case of accompanying a family member in a medical facility, the LC limits the extent of time-off from work in the case of which the employer must provide wage compensation corresponding with the amount of average earning. The employer only has this duty with respect to seven days in a calendar year that the employee takes in order to accompany a sick family member in a medical facility. The accompanying of a sick family member must be necessary and the acts concerned could not have been performed outside of working time. Wage compensation will be provided only to one family member. The employer may provide the employee with time-off from work beyond the stipulated statutory extent with or without wage compensation.

1. Possibility of reducing time-off from work with wage compensation in case of examination in a medical facility and in case of accompanying a family member in a medical facility for examination or treatment

Under current legislation, the employer has the right to reduce the statutory length of time-off from work with wage compensation due to the employee's own or accompanying a family member in a medical facility for examination or treatment if the employee's employment relationship was established during the calendar year so that the employee has not worked with the employer during the entire calendar year. The extent of this reduction of time-off from work with wage compensation is, according to the LC, at least one third of the employee's right concerning a calendar year for every third of a calendar year that has begun. The employer may use this new right, but he does not have to do so. If the wants to use it, he should establish it with respect to all employees who have not worked with the employer during the entire calendar year in an internal regulation in order to avoid infringing the equal treatment principle.

C. Preventative medical examination during pregnancy

The employer must provide time-off from work with wage compensation not limited by the extent of seven working days in a calendar year only to a pregnant woman for the purposes of preventative medical examination connected with pregnancy if the examination or treatment could not be performed outside of working time. With respect to the extent of time-off from work for which the employer also provides wage compensation, this is defined by the extent of the necessary time for preventative medical examinations and, just like any other obstacle to work, the extent of this obstacle to work must be demonstrated by the entitled person. The LC does not establish any statutory minimum for this type of obstacle to work, and therefore allows the employer to provide the entitled person with such extent of time-off from work as the physician may deem necessary, who also gives the pregnant employee necessary documents for recognizing the length of her absence from work and, at the same time, for the purposes of providing wage compensation. The content of this obstacle to work has been influenced by the EU Pregnant Workers' Directive (92/85/EEC), which establishes requirements with respect to the employer concerning time-off from work to be provided to pregnant employees.

D. Employee's wedding

The duty of providing time-off from work with wage compensation is related, under the LC, not only to the employee's own wedding. Parents in case of their child's wedding and employees with respect to the wedding of their parents also have the right to time-off from work of one day with no wage compensation.

E. Birth of the employee's child

Time-off from work with wage compensation is provided for the time necessary for transporting the child's mother to a medical facility and back. Unlike under former legislation, time-off from work with wage compensation can be provided not only to the employee's husband, but also to another natural person. Nonetheless, it may not be any natural person, since time-off from work is provided in the case ofthe birth of the employee's child, the employee being the mother or the father of the child. It means that a woman after the birth of a child may be transported to a medical facility and back only by the child's father, who need not be her husband, but may also be her partner, who invokes this right from his employer. Time-off from work with wage compensation is, with respect to its purpose, intended for the person whose child was born and not for other natural persons.

F. Other obstacles to work on the employee's part

These obstacles are, in particular, the obstacle to work when the employee is not able to travel to work due to bad weather conditions, in case of unexpected breakdown of transport or the delay of public transport and when looking for a new job before termination of the employment relationship.

G. Impossibility of travelling to work

The reason for the impossibility of travelling to work is legally irrelevant. Time-off from work with wage compensation will only be provided if an individual form of transport is used; the LC does not specify what type of individual means of transport it may be. It is sufficient that such an individual means of transport is used by the employee, but he does not have to own it. In the case of an unexpected breakdown of transport, when the employee is entitled to time-off from work with no wage compensation, it is irrelevant whether the employee was using public transport or a different means of transport. In case of a delay, the LC explicitly provides that it must be a delay of regular public transport. However, in both cases, another condition must be met, that is,that the employee could not have reached the workplace in a different way.

H. Employee's moving

The employee's moving as one of important personal obstacles to work is legally relevant only if the employee has his own home equipment. The employer's interest in the employee's moving may be demonstrated by the employer by means of providing time-off from work with wage compensation for that purpose.

I. Looking for a new job

Time-off from work with no wage compensation for the purpose of looking for a new job is only possible in the case of the termination of the employment relationship by the employee's notice or the employer's notice, since only in the case of a notice, there is a period of notice during which the employee is entitled to time-off from work for that purpose. In the case of the termination of employment relationship under Section 63(1)(a) to (c) of the LC, the employee has a right, in addition to his right to time-off from work, also to wage compensation in the amount of his average earning. The agreement on the termination of the employment relationship in case of the above grounds also establishes a right to time-off from work with wage compensation. Since, in the case of an agreement on the termination of the employment relationship, there is no period of notice during which the employee should take time-off from work, time-off from work will, by analogy to a notice, be provided to an employee only if, between the legal act of dissolving the employment relationship by agreement and the termination of employment relationship, there is a time period of one or several weeks during which the employee may take time-off from work for the purpose of looking for a job. Even in the case of an agreement on the termination of the employment relationship due to the above reasons, the employee is entitled to take time-off from work in the maximum extent corresponding with the statutory two-month period of notice.

§ 3 Obstacles on the employer's part

On the employer's part, there may also be obstacles to work that do not allow him, on a temporary basis, to fulfil his fundamental duty with respect to the employee (to assign work to the employee according to the employment contract). In the case of certain obstacles to work on the employer's part, the employer must provide the employee with wage compensation in the amount of his average earning and certain obstacles to work establish his right to a lower financial benefit.

I. Stoppage

The basic legal characteristic of a stoppage is the temporary interruption of work, which consists of organizational or technical problems on the employer's part. A stoppage is not a general overall repair planned in advance. It is, in essence, an unforeseeable obstacle to work on the employer's part. Wage compensation for stoppage in the amount of the average earning will be provided to the employee only if he was not, after agreement, transferred to other work. The basic legal characteristic of a stoppage is the temporary interruption of work, which consists in organizational or technical problems on the employer's part. The case of stoppage on the employer's part consists exclusively in technological, technical and operational errors. A stoppage is not a general overall repair planned in advance. It is, in essence, an unforeseeable obstacle to work on the employer's part.

II. Bad weather conditions

Bad weather conditions, just like stoppage, make the performance of work by the employee impossible. Unlike in the case of stoppage, the reason of interruption of work is different. In does not consist in the work process, but it is outside such process and has objective character. Unlike stoppage, obstacles to work due to bad weather conditions affect only those employers whose work also depends on weather conditions.

The LC establishes financial coverage of obstacles to work with wage compensation provided by the employer's. It lays down only a minimum amount of wage compensation equal to at least 50 % of the employee's average monthly earning.

More favourable rules may be included in the collective agreement or employment contract. If bad weather conditions are the reason why the employee cannot get to work in time, it is an obstacle to work on the employee's part. Once the employee starts working, any bad weather conditions are always an obstacle to work on the employer's part.

III. Obstacle to work consisting in operational grounds on the employer's part

In the case of obstacles to work on the employer's part consisting in operational grounds, the employee will receive wage compensation only in the amount of at least 60 % of average earnings. More favourable rules may be contained, in particular, in collective agreements. Given the rather broad term 'operational grounds' as well as in order to avoid lower wage compensation being applied by the employer for any 'operational' ground to the detriment of the employee, a special written agreement with employee representatives is required in these cases. In the written agreement, the parties define serious operational grounds on the employer's part. This provision may not be applied in cases where the employer has no organization of representatives of employees at his workplace. In these cases, the employer provides wage compensation in the amount of the average monthly earning.

IV. Other obstacles to work

Other obstacles to work on the employer's part (for example, failure to assign work to the employee) establish the employer's legal duty to provide the employee with wage compensation in the amount of his average earning. Obstacles to work of this type are not defined in terms of duration in the LC. For the existence of these obstacles to work, it is irrelevant whether the impossibility of assigning work to the employee is caused by objective or subjective reasons and whether these circumstances can or cannot be influenced by the employer and/or whether this obstacle to work was or was not due to the fault of the employer or it occurred objectively. When assessing the nature of an obstacle to work of this type, it is irrelevant whether, with respect to the occurrence and the legal consequences, it affects only one employee, a group of employees or all employees. If the employee could not perform work for other obstacles on the employer's part, the employer will provide him with a wage compensation in the amount of his average earning.

Chapter 16

Working conditions of women and men caring for children and adolescent employees

The labour-law regulation of the working conditions of women and men caring for children and the working conditions of adolescent employees is at quite a high level. Partially, it is caused by a dynamic development of EU law (pregnant women, men and women on maternity leave) and partially it is caused by the overly protectionist model from previous decades (in particular with respect to the length of maternal and parental leave).

§ 1 Work prohibited to pregnant and breastfeeding women and mothers after childbirth

The employer must, in particular, make sure that he does not assign, during the employment relationship, such work to pregnant women, breastfeeding women and women after childbirth that is prohibited for them.

If a pregnant woman performs work that is prohibited of pregnant women or that, according to a medical report, jeopardizes her pregnancy, the employer must make a temporary adjustment of working conditions.

In many workplaces, only persons older than 18 years of age may work and pregnant women, mothers within 9 months of childbirth and breastfeeding mothers may not work there.

The LC regulates the situation where the adjustment of working conditions is impossible, in particular within the type of work agreed upon in the employment contract. Then, the employer must transfer a pregnant woman or a mother within 9 months of childbirth to a work of a different type, after agreement with her. If no such transfer is possible, the employer must, under Section 162(4) of the LC, provide her with time-off from work with wage compensation.

In the case of a transfer to different work, the employer must respect the provisions of the LC on appropriate work. If the employer has no appropriate work for the woman to which she may be transferred, she is entitled to a compensation benefit as a sickness insurance benefit.

Pregnant women, mothers within 9 months of childbirth and breastfeeding women may not be, under any circumstances, forced to perform work that is known to constitute a possible threat to her safety and health and produce possible effects on her pregnancy or breastfeeding.

I. Other prohibitions of work

Other prohibitions are concentrated on the prohibition of work associated with vibrations that may lead to the maximum limits being exceeded, and the prohibition of work requiring the use of respiratory protective equipment. In general, women may not perform any work in which they are exposed to harmful effects to such an extent that they are threatened by diseases with specific permanent consequences that are liable to jeopardise their maternity (for example, function of reproductive organs, decreased fertility, risk of miscarriage, risk of damage to fetus, etc.). The list of the types of work and the workplaces prohibited for pregnant women, mothers within 9 months of childbirth and breastfeeding women is included in Annex No. 1 of the LC and the list of the types of work and the workplaces associated with specific risks for pregnant women, mothers within 9 months of childbirth and breastfeeding women is included in Annex No. 2 of the Decree of the Government of the Slovak Republic No. 272/2004 Coll.

The employer fulfils the duties according to the Decree of the Government of the Slovak Republic No. 272/2004 Coll. by establishing a list of the types of work and the workplaces prohibited for pregnant women, mothers within 9 months of childbirth and breastfeeding women, a list of the types of work and the workplaces associated with specific risks for pregnant women, mothers within 9 months of childbirth and breastfeeding women and by establishing certain duties for employers in connection with employing these women, with respect to pregnant women, mothers within 9 months of childbirth and breastfeeding women also in the case of other types of work and workplaces other than those indicated in annexes 1 and 2.

The employer must, in all types of work and workplaces associated with specific risks for pregnant women, mothers within 9 months of childbirth and breastfeeding women (to be exposed to harmful factors, effects, processes and working conditions), evaluate the character, degree and duration of such exposure. The employer must evaluate all risks for their safety and health and, on the basis of a professional assessment of health capability with respect to the possible effects on the pregnancy or breastfeeding of such women by the competent physician, he takes necessary measures.

Pregnant women, mothers within 9 months of childbirth and breastfeeding women may not be, under any circumstances, forced to perform work that is known to constitute a possible threat to her safety and health and produce possible effects on her pregnancy or breastfeeding.

§ 2 Maternity leave and parental leave

Under Section 166 of the LC, in connection with the childbirth and care for a new born child, the woman is entitled to a maternity leave of 34 weeks. A lone woman is entitled to a maternity leave of 37 weeks and a woman who gave birth to two or more children simultaneously is entitled to a maternity leave of 43 weeks. In connection with the care for a new born child, the man is also entitled to parental leave from the birth of the child, in the same scope, provided that he cares for the new born child.

In order to deepen the care for the child, the employer must provide a woman or a man upon their request with parental leave until the day the child turns three years old. In the case of a child with a long-term bad health state requiring special care, the employer must provide the woman and the man, upon their request, with parental leave until the day the child turns six years old. This leave is provided for the length requested by the parent, as a rule for not less than one month.

An employer may agree with an employee that parental leave can be provided at most until the child's fifth birthday and, in the case of a child with a long-term bad health state requiring special care, until the child's eighth birthday, no longer than the corresponding extent. These cases do not involve a longer parental leave, but a possibility to take parental leave in the extent necessary given the real needs of the entitled persons as foreseen by the Parental Leave Directive (2010/18/EU). A woman or a man will arrange the taking of parental leave in particular according to the needs of their family. It goes without saying that the above model of parental leave imposes specific requirements on the employer and his operational needs. A woman or a man may take their parental leave in smaller parts, which can disrupt the employer's operating conditions.

§ 3 Working conditions of adolescent employees

In order to ensure the efficient control of observance of increased labour-law protection of adolescent employees, the employer must keep records of adolescent employees employed by him in an employment relationship, including their date of birth, which should help to ensure the efficient control of observance of special working conditions of adolescent employees by the employer. Adolescent employees, unlike the employees over 18 years of age, may not exceed the maximum weekly working time even if working for several employers. The extent of the employment relationships is cumulated for this purpose, as explicitly provided by the directive on the protection of adolescent people at work (1994/33/EC).

I. Prohibition of inappropriate types of work
The LC establishes a prohibition of the performance of such work by adolescent employees that is not appropriate to their physical and mental development and poses a risk to their morals.

This category also includes work that is risky because it is associated with an increased risk for health, posing a risk of occupational disease or other disease conditioned by the work.

Section 174 of the LC establish a total prohibition of employing adolescent employees younger than 16 years of age for overtime work, night work and on-call duty work. A total prohibition of on-call duty work for adolescent employees is established by the LC even for the case that on-call duty work is requested by the adolescent employee himself. The LC explicitly excludes an agreement on on-call duty work and on the ordering of on-call duty work.

II. Other types of work prohibited to adolescent employees
Section 175 of the LC lays down the types of work that are prohibited for adolescent employees. The first group includes work underground in the extraction of minerals or drilling of tunnels and passages. This type of work is explicitly determined by the LC.

The second category of work prohibited for adolescent employees consists of those types of work that are not exactly defined by the LC. It only characterizes them as such work that, given the anatomic, physiological and mental peculiarities at this age, is inappropriate for adolescent employees, dangerous for them or damaging to their health. These types of work are defined in special regulations. Such work includes work with carcinogenic or mutagenic factors.

It is, in particular, work that is risky, because it is associated with an increased risk for health, posing a risk of occupational disease or other disease conditioned by the work.

Several types of work, due to their risky character, must be performed by employees over 18 years of age (for example, work in workplaces with dangerous chemical factors).

The lists of types of the work and workplaces prohibited for adolescent employees are contained in the Decree of the Government of the Slovak Republic No. 286/2004 Coll. establishing a list of the types of work and workplaces prohibited for adolescent employees and establishing certain duties for employees in connection with employing adolescent employees. This list is contained in Annex No. 1.

Chapter 17

Liability for Damage in Labour Law

§ 1 General characteristics of liability in labour law

The provisions of the LC regulating liability in labour law has, in comparison to foreign legal regulations, several peculiarities. One of them is the legal model of labour-law liability of employees and employers, which is very favourable to the employee. The provisions of the LC regulating liability in labour law are peculiar in that, in the case of damage caused in an existing labour-law relationship, legal rules concerning liability in civil law according to the Civil Code cannot be applied. Part I of the Civil Code is only of subsidiary application with regard to the general part of the LC.

An advantage of the existing legal model of liability in labour law is that if an employee causes damage to the employer by negligence (unless intoxicated by alcohol, narcotics or psychotropic substances), the employer may claim damages from the employee only up to the statutory maximum, which is set at 4 times average monthly earnings of the employee. Special rules contained in the LC also apply to loss in the form of shortage and loss of entrusted assets based on a written confirmation, when fault is presumed and the employee compensates real loss. However, in most cases when damage is caused, the employer has no chance of obtaining compensation of real loss from the employee.

It can be said that it is also the existing legal model of employee liability in labour law that motivates many top managers or members of statutory bodies of business companies to regulate their relationship with the company by an employment relationship, which protects them, from the perspective of liability, much more than a relationship based on commercial law or civil law.

Labour law liability for damage has formed one of the most important parts of LC contents since the 1965 labour law codification. Liability relations in employment relationship are not subject to the Civil Code. In contrast to numerous foreign regulations the Civil Code cannot be applied even as a subsidiary law.

In legal theory the labour law liability for damage is defined as a sanction relation arising as a new derived statutory relation from the breach of obligations in existing labour law relation. The contents of the statutory liability relation in labour law is the obligation of the guilty party to compensate the damage caused and the right of the damaged party to obtain this compensation.

Legal literature contains also another legal concept of liability according to which the liability forms part of every legal relation from its very beginning as a threat of sanction for the breach of an obligation.

The function of liability is not defined uniformly in legal writings. According to the prevailing part of legal theory, the fundamental functions of the liability for damage include the preventative function, the reparation function and the sanction function. The function of liability in labour law, however, is the reparation function. In contrast to civil law and/ or commercial law, however, in labour law the reparation function is distinctly modified. If the employee causes damage by negligence, he does not compensate the employer for the whole amount of the damage, but only to the amount of three times his monthly earnings.

The number of important functions of liability in labour law includes the preventative function in the interest of which the very LC provides numerous concrete legal obligations for both parties to the employment relationship. Under Section 177 of the LC, for instance, the employer is bound to assure such working conditions for his employees as will enable them to fulfil properly their working tasks without any threat to health or property. If he ascertains any defects, he is bound to take the necessary steps for their remedy. At the same time he is bound to check, whether the employees fulfil their working tasks in such a way that would not give rise to damage. On the other hand, the employee is also bound under Section 178 of the LC, to behave so as not to cause damage to health or property. At the same time the LC imposes the duty of notification and intervention on the employees and sanctions the employee with the liability for the ensuing damage, should he fail to comply with this duty.

§ 2 Employee's liability for damage caused to employer

The LC construes the employee's liability for damage as a subjective liability with the presumption of guilt and the subjective liability with the presumption of innocence. The liability with the presumption of innocence is the employee's general liability in the case of which the employer must prove the employee's culpability. In case of liability with the presumption of guilt, the employee must prove his own innocence (exculpation).

The employee's liability for damage is subjective liability. Therefore, if the employee suffers from a mental illness, he is liable for the damage caused by himself only when he is capable of controlling his actions or assess their consequences (Section 180 of the LC). However, if the employee puts himself into such a state, he is liable for the damage caused by him (Section 180 of the LC).

In the case of the employee's liability with the presumption of guilt, the employee can exculpate himself. If he does not succeed in doing so, he is liable for the damage. In the case of the employee's liability with the presumption of guilt, the employee is bound to compensate the whole damage without limitation, like in the case of liability without the presumption of guilt.

The employee is not liable for the damage,which he has caused while averting the damage, threatening the employer or the danger directly threatening life or health, unless he has brought about such a state wilfully, and if he has acted in the way consistent with the circumstances, which arises from economic hazard (Section 181 of the LC).

I. Employee's general liability for damage

Under Section 179 of the LC the employee is liable to the employer for the damage caused by his culpable breach of his duties during the fulfilment of his working tasks or in direct relation thereof.

Also the employee who has caused the damage by a wilful act contrary to the rules of fairness and civic coexistence is liable for the damage.

The employer is bound to prove not only the origin of damage and the unlawful action of the employee, but also his culpability and the causal link between the origin of the damage and the unlawful action of the employee.

II. Liability for the failure to fulfil the obligation to avert damage

Under the provisions of Section 181 of the LC the employee is liable for the damage which has originated by his failure to fulfil his obligation to avert damage, even if such damage has originated for other reasons than those related to the employee's person. In the case of this type of the employee's liability, the employer must prove that the employee acted with wilful negligence and that he had the possibility to intervene. The employee's liability must be based also on the causal link between his failure to intervene and the origin of the damage. This liability can be applied only if the employee's intervention could have prevented the origin of the damage. The compensation of the damage is of subsidiary character (for example, the employer may require it) if the damage cannot be compensated in any other way.

III. Liability for the deficit in accountable entrusted assets

The liability for the deficit of entrusted assets for which the employee is accountable is the employee's liability with the presumption of guilt; therefore, the employer is not bound to prove the employee's culpability (Section 182 through 184 of the LC).

The employer shall prove only:

- the valid conclusion of an agreement on material liability,
- the existence of the deficit of assets for which the employee is accountable, and
- the absence of the assets entrusted to him by the employer.

The breach of the employee's legal obligation consists in that the employee has not fulfilled his accountability obligation. The damage consists in the deficit in entrusted assets not accounted for.

On principle, the liable subject is the employee in the employment relationship. However, material liability may concern only an employee who has attained 18 years of age. An agreement on material liability cannot be concluded with an employee who has been deprived of the legal capacity by a court, whose legal capacity has been restricted by a court or who has been punished by a prohibition of some activity.

An agreement on material liability is a condition of substantive law for the establishment of this type of liability.

The object of an agreement on material liability may consist only in the objects intended for circulation and turnover. Their number includes cash, valuables, goods, inventories and other assets intended for circulation and turnover.

The objects which form the object of the agreement on material liability must be properly handed over and taken over. On the other hand, it is not necessary for the employee to keep these objects continuously under his personal care. It is sufficient, if he keeps them secured against interference by others.

The deficit is the accounted difference between the actual state of entrusted assets for which the employee is accountable and the data of the accounts showing that the actual state is lower than the recorded state. The fundamental legal characteristic of the deficit is the absence of the goods. If the goods are not missing, it is impossible to establish this type of liability. It is possible to establish only the employee's general liability in which case the compensation of damage is limited, on principle, to four times the employee's monthly earnings.

IV. Liability for the loss of entrusted objects

The condition for the establishment of the employee's liability for the loss of entrusted objects is the valid employment relationship. The necessary prerequisite for the establishment of the employee's liability is, apart from other general liability conditions, the damage in the form of the loss of the entrusted object, written confirmation of the take-over of the object.

The liability under Section 185 of the LC may be established in the case of the loss of entrusted objects, but not in the case of their damage. The employer must prove that he has entrusted the object to the employee against a written receipt. The loss is deemed to mean that the entrusted object is missing and the employee cannot reliably prove how it was lost.

A written receipt can be used, if the employee is entrusted with tools, protection aids and other similar objects. The objects entrusted to him against signature may include only such objects that do not wear in their use and as may be returned. The absence of the prerequisite of take-over of the respective object against a written receipt cannot be replaced by any other proof.

The employee must have the objects entrusted against a written receipt at his personal disposal (for example, the employer must create adequate conditions preventing their loss during the employee's absence from his worksite).

V. Scope of compensation of damage by the employee

Decisive for the determination of the compensation of damage by the employee is the form of culpability, type of liability and the employee's personal characteristics. The LC prefers the compensation in terms of money, even though it enables the employee who has caused the damage to compensate it also by the restoration of it to its initial state.

The scope of the compensation depends particularly on whether the damage has been caused wilfully, by negligence or in a drunken state. The scope of the damage is solved specifically in the case of the employee's liability with the presumption of guilt, when the employee is bound to compensate the full actual damage. In the case of compensation of damage with the presumption of innocence, the amount of the compensation paid by the individual employee must not exceed the sum equal to four times his mean monthly earnings before the breach of his obligation which has caused the damage. This limitation of the amount of compensation does not apply in the case of damage caused in a drunken state to which the employee has brought himself and in the case of damage caused while under the influence of other intoxicants. In such cases, the employee is bound to compensate the whole actual damage, even if it is the case of the damage with the presumption of innocence.

When the employee has caused damage wilfully, regardless of whether it is the case of liability with the presumption of guilt or innocence, the employer may request him to compensate not only the whole damage, but also the lost profit. The labour law is based on the principle of the so-called divided liability which means that every employee is liable in accordance with the rate of his culpability. The division of liability between several employees may be used only in the case of liability of all of these employees. Consequently, it is divided and not joint liability. Every one of the liable employees is bound to compensate only such a quota of his liability that corresponds with the rate of his culpability. The jointly liable employees do not bear collective liability, either. The culpability and liability must be proved to everyone separately.

Under Section 186 of the LC, an employee is liable to compensate damage incurred to the employer if the employer so requests.

§ 3 Employer's liability for damage caused to his employees

The employer's liability is an objective liability (for example, a liability regardless of culpability). On the basis of its content, the LC divides it into the employer's general liability (Section 192 of the LC), and the special employer's liability, comprising liability for damage in the case of an accident at work and occupational diseases (Section 195 through 198 of the LC), liability for damage to things laid aside (Section 193 of the LC), and liability in averting damage (Section 194 of the LC).

I. Employer's general liability for damage

Under the provisions of Section 192 of the LC the employer is liable for the damage caused to the employee by unlawful action. It is an objective liability which is applied when all the required legal conditions for the establishment of the employer's special liability are not available.

The provisions of Section 192 contain the facts establishing the employer's general liability for damage.

The first involves the breach of his legal obligation, while the second involves the wilful action against the rules of fairness and civic co-existence. In either case, it is not decisive who has broken the legal obligation or who acted wilfully against the rules of fairness and civic coexistence. It may be the employer, fellow employees or other persons. The burden of proof lies with the damaged party. When establishing the employer's liability under Section 192 (1) of the LC; however, it is decisive whether the breach occurred during the fulfilment of working tasks or in direct connection therewith.

In contrast to Section 192 (2) of the LC, it is not decisive whether the damage has originated in the course of the fulfilment of working tasks or in the direct connection therewith.

However, decisive is who ever has caused the damage and who ever has broken the legal obligation. The scope of the legal obligations for the breach of which the employer is liable is considerably narrower than specified in Section 192 (1) of the LC. The employer is liable only for an unlawful act of his statutory bodies, heads of organizational units and all authorized employees (Section 9 and 10 of the LC). The employer is liable only for such an unlawful act as has been committed by his employees acting on his behalf in the framework of the fulfilment of his tasks.

II. Liability for damage to things laid aside

The employer's liability for the things laid aside is the employer's special and objective liability. The necessary prerequisite for the establishment of this liability is the fact that the employee has laid aside his personal belongings which he currently wears or carries to work at a place designated for this purpose or where such things are usually laid aside. It is not decisive who has caused the damage or how the damage occurred. The employer's unlawful act consists in the breach of his obligation imposed to him in Section 151 (3) of the LC to assure for his employees a safe keeping of personal belongings customarily worn or carried to work and customary means of transport. The means of transport for this purpose, however, do not include passenger cars used by the employees for their travel to work. They are expressly excluded from the framework of the customary means of transport by the provisions of Section 151 (3) of the LC.

The causal relation consists in the fact that the employee has laid aside the things which he usually wears or carries to work at the place designated for this purpose or where they are usually laid aside and the damage occurred to them during the time of their being laid aside. The damage may involve the damage, the destruction or the loss of the things laid aside. The usual character of the things the employee wears or carries to work must be assessed not on the basis of their financial value, but particularly on the basis of their functionality.

Decisive for the assessment of the employer's liability is the employee's proof that he has suffered damage on things laid aside during the performance of his work or in direct relation thereto and that these things have been laid aside at the place designated for this purpose or where they are usually laid aside and that they are things he usually wears or carries to work.

The employer is bound to reimburse the employee his whole damage. For the things the employees usually do not take to work and which he has not accepted for special safekeeping, the employer is liable only to the amount of 165,97 €.

III. Liability in averting damage

An employee who has suffered material damage when averting damage threatening the employer is entitled to its compensation by the employer, as well as the reimbursement of effectively expended costs. The condition for the establishment of such employer's liability is that the employee has not wilfully generated the danger himself and that he acted in a manner consistent with circumstances.

IV. Liability for damage in case of accident at work and occupational diseases

The social risk of an accident at work and an occupational disease is part of social insurance. The employer's liability for accidents at work and occupational diseases is construed in the LC as a specific liability. It enables the employers to get released from this liability in entirely exceptional cases only. This liability is an objective employer's liability. It is the employer with whom the employee is in an employment relationship with at the time of the accident who is liable for the origin of the accident at work.

The liability for the damage arising from an occupational disease is construed differently from the liability for an accident at work, even though the compensation is based on the same provisions as that for the accident at work. The difference consists in the fact that that the liability for an occupational disease rests with the last employer for whom the employee has worked, in the conditions under which this occupational disease originated before its ascertainment. Decisive for the ascertainment of the employer's liability for the damage caused to the employee by an occupational disease is the time of the ascertainment of this disease and not the time of its origin.

The LC defines the accident at work in Section 195 (2). An accident at work is damage to health sustained by an employee while performing his duties or in direct relation to the employee, independently of his will, by short-term, sudden and forceful effects of external influences. According to Section 195 (3) of the LC, an accident sustained by an employee on his way to and from work is not an accident at work.

The case law has defined the accident at work as an injury to health suffered by the employee in the course of the fulfilment of his working tasks or in direct connection therewith independent of his will, by a sudden, violent, short-term effect of external factors which have resulted in the impairment of his health. Also an accident due to the fulfilment of the employee's working obligations must be considered an accident at work.

The LC does not define the notion of occupational disease. It can be understood as an impairment of health caused by the mechanical influence of certain works or substances or mental factors. Occupational diseases usually involve a long-term influence of a hazardous worksite on the employee's health. In concrete terms, the occupational disease is determined by its inclusion in the List of Occupational Diseases annexed with the Act No. 461/2003 Coll. on Social Insurance, as amended. The List of Occupational Diseases is enumerative, but it can be supplemented continuously with further diseases.

Important for the conclusion as to whether the disease is an occupational disease, is the compliance with all the conditions for the origin of an occupational disease specified in the List of Occupational Disease.

Release from Liability
The employer may be released entirely from his liability, if he proves that:

a) the damage was caused by that of the affected employee's is culpability of the breach of legal or other regulations concerned with the assurance of occupational safety and health protection at work or the instructions for the assurance of occupational safety and health protection at work, although he has been dully acquainted with them and their knowledge and observance has been consistently required and controlled, or

b) the employee has caused the damage by his drunkenness or the abuse of other intoxicating substances, the employer could not prevent the damage and these facts were the sole cause of the origin of damage.

The employer may be released partly from his liability, if he proves that:

a) the affected employee is culpable of the breach of legal or other regulations or instructions concerned with the assurance of occupational safety and health protection at work although he has been duly acquainted with them and that this breach was one of the causes of the damage,
b) one of the causes of the damage was the drunkenness of the employee or the abuse of some other intoxicating substances by the employee concerned,
c) the employee has suffered the damage because he acted at variance with the usual way of behaviour so that it is obvious that although he has not broken the legal or other regulations or instructions intended to assure occupational safety and health protection at work, he acted recklessly and must have been aware, due to his qualification and experience, that he can cause injury to his health.

§ 4 Compensation of damage

The employee who has suffered an accident at work or whose occupational disease has been ascertained must be paid by the employer, within the scope of his liability for the damage, a compensation for the material loss. Material damage does not involve only the damage to material things, suffered by the employee during his accident (such as destruction of or damage to his clothing), but also the costs required for the performance of works by another person which the damaged employee cannot perform because of the accident and, therefore, has to assure their performance by a hired person. The compensation may cover any material damage not covered legally by any other partial compensation.

Chapter 18

Collective labour law

Besides the Constitution of the Slovak Republic, documents of essential legal significance for collective labour law are the LC and the Collective Bargaining Act No. 2/1991 Coll., as amended (hereinafter referred to as "the collective bargaining act").

The Slovak labour legislation is presently based on dualism in representing the rights and interests of employees. In addition to trade union organisations, employees may also be represented in their employers' undertakings by works councils.

§ 1 Trade union pluralism

According to Section 230(2) of the LC, employers are obliged to allow the operation of trade union organisations in their undertakings.

Where two or more trade union organisations operating within an employer's undertaking fail to reach a mutual agreement on matters affecting a larger number of employees within 15 days of the employer's request, the organisation that will act as the social partner for the employer will be the one with the largest membership. Regarding individual employment relationships, the partner for the employer will be the trade union organisation to which the employee belongs. The representativeness principle also applies to individual labour law relationships in the case of non-unionised employees. In that case, the social partner for the employer is the trade union organisation with the largest membership, unless otherwise decided upon by the employee concerned. Such individual determination by the employee takes precedence over the application of the representativeness principle in individual labour law relationships.

In the case of the absence of an agreement between several trade union organisations, employers have the right to conclude a collective agreement with that trade union organisation which has the largest membership. Such collective agreement has legal effects for all employees, (for example, employers act in conformity with the representativeness principle).

I. Powers of trade union bodies in employer's undertaking

The major part of the powers of trade union bodies is laid down in the LC. Key elements of the legislation governing the role of trade union bodies in labour law relationships are set out in Sections 229 to 232 of the LC. The LC defines the scope of competence of trade union

organisations depending on whether they are exclusive social partners of employers, or whether a works council operates in the employer's undertaking in parallel to a trade union organisation. In case there is only a trade union organisation in the employer's undertaking, Section 229(4) of the LC provides that this organisation has the right of
- co-decision,
- consultation,
- information,
- control, and
- collective bargaining.

In the case of a trade union organisation and a works council operating in parallel in an employer's undertaking, the works council has the right of consultation and the right of information.

If employees do not establish a works council in their employer's undertaking, the LC provides in Section 229(4) that the trade union organisation exercises the powers that would otherwise pertain to a works council.

If only a works council operates in the employer's undertaking, it exercises all the powers relating to the representation of the rights and interests of employees, except for collective bargaining, which falls under exclusive competence of trade union organisations.

A. Right of co-decision

In the area of co-decision, the competent trade union body grants, for example, a prior consent with a notice given by the employer or termination of the employment relationship with immediate effect of a representative of employees (member of a trade union body, member of a works council, member of a body of employee representatives in the area of labour protection). As a consequence of the absence of such prior consent, a notice given by the employer or the termination of the employment relationship by the employer with immediate effect is invalid.

Similarly, an employer is obliged to request a prior consent of the trade union body with the promulgation of work rules. The same applies to the introduction of labour consumption standards by the employer.

According to Section 149(1)(c) of the LC, the trade union body has the right to request that the employer removes operational shortcomings. According to Section 149(2) and (3) of the LC, the trade union body even has the right to suspend work for the employer if the work directly and seriously endangers life or health.

B. Control activities

According to Section 239 of the LC, the trade union body has the right, in particular:
a) to enter the employer's undertaking at the time agreed upon with the employer or, where such agreement is not reached, not later than within three working days from notifying the employer of the intention to enter the employer's undertaking,
b) to request, as necessary, information and background documents from managers,

c) to raise suggestions for improvement of working conditions,

d) to ask the employer to give instructions to remedy the identified shortcomings,

e) to propose the employer or a different body responsible for overseeing compliance with labour law provisions to take appropriate measures against managers who violate labour law provisions or duties arising for them from collective agreements,

f) to request information from employers concerning measures taken to remedy the shortcomings identified during the performance of control.

According to the LC, the performance of control activities is entrusted to trade union organisations. If there is no trade union organisation in the employer's undertaking, control is performed by the works council.

C. Right to collective bargaining

One of the most important powers of trade union organisations, is their exclusive competence to conduct collective bargaining with employers or with organisations of employers.

D. Right to consultation

Under the current legislation, the trade union organisation in its role of social partner of the employer, uses consultation very often as a form of employee participation in the management of the undertaking.

The employer is obliged to consult the trade union organisation, in particular:

– with regards to the economic situation of the employer,

– changes in the organisation of work,

– the employee remuneration and evaluation system,

– the issue of uniform allocation of work,

– introduction of flexible working time.

E. Right to information

According to Article 4 of the Fundamental Principles of the LC, employees or employee representatives have the right to be informed of the employer's activities and about basic issues related to the employer's economic position and development.

Substantive legal provisions regarding the activities of trade union bodies in labour law relationships are set out in the LC and in the collective bargaining act.

§ 2 Works councils

By introducing works councils in 2001, the LC of the Slovak Republic laid the foundations for legal dualism in the representation of employees' rights and interests. Works councils represent all employees and are established according to a voluntary principle. Unlike trade union bodies, works councils cannot create structures at supra-company level and, consequently, cannot take part in the social dialogue at the supra-company level. Works councils do not have legal personality.

Works councils may operate in undertakings employing no less than 50 employees. A works trustee may be appointed in undertakings with less than 50 and no less than five employees. The rights and responsibilities of works trustees are identical with those of the works council.

According to Section 234 of the LC, the employer is obliged to enable the election of members of the works council if such request is made in writing by at least 10 employees.

The number of members of works councils depends on the number of employees.

Every employee who has reached 15 years of age and has been employed in the employer's undertaking for no less than three months at the time of announcing the election has an active voting right. To acquire a passive voting right (for example, the right to stand for election as a member of the works council), employees must have reached the age of 18.

I. Powers of works councils

According to Section 229, paragraph 7 of the LC, if a trade union organisation and a works council operate in parallel in an undertaking, the works council has the right to be consulted and to be informed. If no trade union organisation has been created in the undertaking and the only social partner of the employer is the works council, the works council carries out all forms of employee participation which, in the dual form of representation, pertain to trade union organisations, except for the right to collective bargaining.

Employee representatives may not be disadvantaged by their employer or suffer any other prejudice in connection with the performance of their function. Employee representatives, during and one year after the expiry of their term of office, are protected against any measures that could harm them, including dismissal, motivated by their status or activities.

Chapter 19

Collective agreements

In the legislative practice and labour law theory, collective agreements are perceived as a bilateral normative legal act. The underlying assumption behind the collective bargaining act is the existence of social peace between social partners during the time of validity of a collective agreement. Under the current legal status quo, a strike can be used only as an extreme form of resolving collective labour disputes in the case of collective conflicts relating to the conclusion of collective agreements, but not to amendments to collective agreements.

§ 1 Types of collective agreements

Section 2 of the Collective Bargaining Act provides for two types of collective agreements and three types of higher-level collective agreements.

Collective agreements that are most frequently concluded in the application practice are company-level collective agreements.

One of the types of higher-level collective agreements is a collective agreement concluded for a larger number of employers between the pertinent higher-level trade union body and the employers' organisation.

The second type of higher-level collective agreements is a collective agreement concluded between the relevant higher-level trade union body and the state acting as employer.

The third type of higher-level collective agreements is a collective agreement concluded between the relevant higher-level trade union body, government-appointed representatives, and representatives representing employers. These are higher-level collective agreements in the area of civil service.

Although the general principle according to which collective agreements cannot lay down less favourable labour-law employee entitlements than relevant higher-level collective agreements remains applicable, an opposite principle applies to company-level collective agreements concluded in the civil service area. In company-level collective agreements concluded between a service office and the relevant trade union body, labour law entitlements of civil servants can be provided for only within the scope laid down by the relevant higher-level collective agreement. The scope of labour law entitlements of civil servants must not exceed the boundaries of the higher-level tariff agreement.

§ 2 Formal particulars of collective agreements

Subject to a sanction of invalidity, collective agreements must be concluded in writing. Contracting parties must attach their signatures to the same instrument. This legal requirement does not apply to collective agreements concluded in the framework of the proceeding before an arbitrator whose award replaces the conclusion of a collective agreement.

§ 3 Validity and effectiveness of collective agreements

According to Section 4 of the Collective Bargaining Act, a collective agreement or part thereof can be considered invalid:
- if it is in conflict with generally binding legal provisions,
- if it lays down more restricted employee entitlements than the relevant higher-level collective agreement, or
- if, in the civil service area, a company-level collective agreement provides for greater civil servants' entitlements than the relevant higher-level collective agreement.

A collective agreement enters into effect as of the date of its signature by the contracting parties. Binding effects of the normative part of collective agreements consist in the right of employees to pursue their entitlements arising from a collective agreement in court in the same way as other labour law entitlements set out in generally binding legal provisions.

The collective bargaining act does not specify the duration of time for which a collective agreement is to be concluded, leaving it at the discretion of contracting parties. If a collective agreement does not specify the period of its validity, the agreement is presumed to have been concluded for one year. Higher-level collective agreements in the area of the civil service and in the area of the public service are always concluded for a period of one year.

The period of validity of a collective agreement means the period of its effectiveness, which starts on the first day of its validity period and ends upon the expiry of that period. Moreover, the collective bargaining act allows for the setting out of different periods of effectiveness for individual commitments, especially with regards to commitments arising for the employer from the normative part of the collective agreement (such as wage claims or wage indexation).

The Act does not provide per se for the withdrawal from a collective agreement by one of its parties, but the parties may agree on this possibility and on other preconditions in a collective agreement.

I. Validity and effectiveness of collective agreements in relation to the transfer of rights and obligations

Section 27 and following of the LC provide that, in the event of the winding-up of the employer's undertaking or part thereof that entails legal succession, all the rights and obligations arising from labour law relationships (for example, including rights and obligations arising from normative provisions of collective agreements), pass on to the new employer. This legislation is in conformity with Council Directive 2001/23/EC on safeguarding of employees' rights in the event of transfers of undertakings, businesses or parts of undertakings or businesses. The rights and obligations arising from labour law relationships, laid down in the normative provisions of collective agreements, are transferred also in case of a lease of the employer's undertaking.

§ 4 Extension of applicability of collective agreements

The extension of applicability of collective agreements can only be considered in the case of higher-level collective agreements. The law stipulates that the main purpose of envisaging an extension of applicability of higher-level collective agreements is to enhance the protection of employees. Although, on the one hand, the extension of higher-level collective agreements constitutes significant interference with contractual freedom, it makes it possible to guarantee by law a uniform standard of labour law and wage entitlements of employees on the other hand, especially in the case of employers deliberately avoiding entering the employers' association in order to not have to fulfil obligations arising from the agreement.

According to Section 7 of Collective Bargaining Act No. 2/1991 Coll. as amended, applicability of higher-level collective agreements can be extended only to employers who do business in similar areas and under similar economic and social conditions, that are established in the territory of the Slovak Republic, and that are not bound by other higher-level collective agreements.

As a consequence of extension of its applicability, a higher-level collective agreement becomes legally binding also on those employers who did not join the association of employers.

The proposal to extend the applicability of a higher-level collective agreement can be filed with the Ministry of Labour, Social Affairs and Family of the Slovak Republic no later than six months before the expiry of a higher-level collective agreement.

Bibliography

BARANCOVÁ, H.: *Zákonník práce. Komentár*. Prague: C.H.Beck, 2010, pp. 553 – 562, ISBN 978-80-7400-172-7

BARANCOVÁ, H.: *Výnimky zo zákazu diskriminácie*, In: Justičná revue : časopis pre právnu prax. - ISSN 1335-6461. - Vol. 57, no. 2 (2005), pp. 165-172.

BARANCOVÁ, H.: *Zákonník práce. Komentár*, Prague : C. H. Beck, 2010, 693 p., ISBN 978 – 80 – 7400 – 172 – 7.

BARANCOVÁ, H. a kol: *Nadnárodný pohyb zamestnancov a služieb*. Bratislava: Sprint dva, 2011, 315 pp., ISBN 978-80-89393-61-9.

BARANCOVÁ, H.: *Európske pracovné právo. Flexibilita a bezpečnosť pre 21. storočie*. Bratislava: Sprint dva, 2010, pp. 546 – 560, ISBN 978 – 80 – 89393 – 42 – 8.

BARANCOVÁ, H.: *Ústavné právo združovať sa a súčasný stav kolektívneho pracovného práva v Slovenskej republike*. In: Právo a zaměstnání, 2002, no. 8, pp. 14 *et seq.*, ISSN 1211 – 1139.

BARANCOVÁ, H.: Analysis of the 2003 labour law reform in the Slovak Republic. In: Darbo teise suvienytoje Europoje = Labour law in United Europe: tarptautines mokslines konferencijos medžiaga 2003 m. spalio 16–18 d. Vilnius: Teisines informacijos centras, 2007, pp. 169–182.

BARANCOVÁ, H.: Budete mi svedkami. In: Univerzita v službe nového humanizmu: zborník z vedeckej konferencie [organizovanej Radou pre univerzity pri Konferencii biskupov Slovenska v Badíne, 11.–12.9. 2008]. Badín: Kňazský seminár sv. Františka Xaverského 2008, pp. 99–103.

BARANCOVÁ, H.: Budete mi svedkami: [abstrakt]. In: Univerzita v službe nového humanizmu: zborník abstraktov z vedeckej konferencie, 11.–12. september 2008. Badín: Kňazský seminár sv. Františka Xaverského 2008, pp. 10.

Dočasné vyslanie zamestnancov v rámci Európskej únie: vedecké sympózium s medzinárodnou účasťou: 19. máj 2008. 1st ed. Trnava: Typi Universitatis Tyrnaviensis, spoločné pracovisko TU a Vedy, vydavateľstva SAV 2008, pp. 145

BARANCOVÁ, H.: Flexicurity und ein Arbeitsrecht für das 21. Jahrhundert = Flexicurity and labour law for the 21st century In: Flexible and secure employment = Prožno in varno zaposlovanje: 3. International labour law dialogue: 13th in 14th November 2008, Maribor / [authors Etelka Korpič Horvat...[et al.]]. Ljubljana: GV Založba, 2009, pp. 76–92, 148.

BARANCOVÁ, H.: Pojem „závislá práca". In: Aktuálne zmeny v pracovnom práve v roku 2007: (6. dni pracovného práva): City hotel Bratislava 27.–28. september 2007. Košice: Calypso PM, pp.r.o. 2007, pp. 4–27.

BARANCOVÁ, H.: Pojem „závislá práca". In: Pracovné právo 2007: 4. apríl 2007, Radisson SAS Carlton Hotel. Bratislava: odborná konferencia: zborník referátov. Bratislava: EU Generation 2007, pp. 12–31.

BARANCOVÁ, H.: Zásada slobody a rovnosti v pracovnom práve = Der Grundsatz der Freiheit und Gleichheit im Arbeitsrecht. In: Základné zásady súkromného práva v zjednotenej Európe = Fundamentale Grundsätze des Privatrechts im vereinigten Europa: 9. Lubyho právnické dni: Medzinárodná vedecká konferencia. Smolenice, 20.–21. september 2007. Bratislava: Iura Edition 2007, pp. 169–202.

BARANCOVÁ, H.: Vybrané problémy pracovného práva. In: Pracovné právo 2008: 2. apríl 2008, Radisson SAS Carlton Hotel, Bratislava: odborná konferencia: zborník referátov. Bratislava: EU Generation, 2008, pp. 12–64.

BARANCOVÁ, H.: Vzťah Občianskeho zákonníka a Zákonníka práce. In: Návrh legislatívneho zámeru kodifikácie súkromného práva: materiály z odbornej konferencie: [odborná konferencia poriadaná Ministerstvom spravodlivosti Slovenskej republiky, Trenčianske Teplice 5. a 6. jún 2008]. Bratislava: Ministerstvo spravodlivosti Slovenskej republiky 2008, pp. 152–161.

BARANCOVÁ, H.: Dočasné vyslanie zamestnancov v rámci Európskej únie v judikatúre Súdneho dvora Európskeho spoločenstva. In: Dočasné vyslanie zamestnancov v rámci Európskej únie: vedecké sympózium s medzinárodnou účasťou: 19. máj 2008. Trnava: Typi Universitatis Tyrnaviensis, spoločné pracovisko TU a Vedy, vydavateľstva SAV 2008, pp. 15–50.

BARANCOVÁ, H.: Zásada rovnakého zaobchádzania v súčasnom vývoji pracovného práva. In: Pocta profesorovi Gašparovi: zborník príspevkov z medzinárodnej vedeckej konferencie: konanej dňa 7. decembra 2007 na Právnickej fakulte UPJŠ v Košiciach: vydaný pri príležitosti životného jubilea prof. JUDr. Michala Gašpara, CSc. Košice: Univerzita Pavla Jozefa Šafárika 2008, pp. 21–35.

Liberalizácia pracovného práva – možnosti a obmedzenia: zborník z [medzinárodného] vedeckého sympózia: Trnava 11.12.2006 / [editor: Helena Barancová]. – 1st ed. Trnava: Typi Universitatis Tyrnaviensis, vydavateľstvo Trnavskej univerzity, spoločné pracovisko TU a Vedy 2007, pp. 137.

BARANCOVÁ, H.: Predhovor. In: Dočasné vyslanie zamestnancov v rámci Európskej únie: vedecké sympózium s medzinárodnou účasťou: 19. máj 2008. Trnava: Typi Universitatis Tyrnaviensis, spoločné pracovisko Trnavskej univerzity a Vedy, vydavateľstva SAV 2008, pp. 7–8.

BĚLINA, M.: Vybrané problémy postavení zástupců zaměstnanců v pracovněprávních vztazích. In: Sborník z mezinárodní vědecké konference Třešť, 2007.

OLŠOVSKÁ, A.: Zmluvný systém pracovného práva. In: Zborník príspevkov z vedeckej konferencie doktorandov a školiteľov Právnickej fakulty Trnavskej univerzity v Trnave: [Trnava, 24. marec 2007]. Trnava: Trnavská univerzita 2007, pp. 267–279.

OLŠOVSKÁ, A.: Slovenské pracovné právo 21. storočia: (zmluvné typy pracovného práva de lege ferenda): [abstrakt]. In: "Aktuálne problémy práva a ekonómie a možnosti ich rozvoja v priestore Európskej únie": zborník z medzinárodnej vedeckej konferencie: [konanej 1.–2. júla 2008 v Bratislave] / [zostavil Jozef Králik, Jana Šimonová, Marian Suja]. Bratislava: Akadémia Policajného zboru, 2008, pp. 19.

OLŠOVSKÁ, A.: Postavenie a pôsobenie zástupcov zamestnancov. In: Debaty mladých právníků 2007: sborník příspěvků z konference Monseho Debaty mladých právníků, konané ve dnech 10.–12.9.2007 Právnickou fakultou Univerzity Palackého v Olomouci. Olomouc: Univerzita Palackého, 2007, pp. 76–79.

OLŠOVSKÁ, A.: Slovenské pracovné právo 21. storočia [elektronický dokument]: (zmluvné typy pracovného práva de lege ferenda). Iné vyd. na inom, alebo rovnakom médiu, Olšovská, A.: Slovenské pracovné právo 21. storočia: (zmluvné typy pracovného práva de lege ferenda): [abstrakt]. In: "Aktuálne problémy práva a ekonómie a možnosti ich rozvoja v priestore Európskej únie" [elektronický dokument]: zborník z medzinárodnej vedeckej konferencie: konanej 1.–2. júla 2008 v Bratislave. Bratislava: Akadémia Policajného zboru 2008, pp. 329–338.

OLŠOVSKÁ, A., HODÁLOVÁ, I.: Pracovnoprávne aspekty práva na štrajk v Slovenskej republike = Labour law aspects of the right to strike in the SR. In: Days of public law [elektronický dokument] = Dny veřejného práva: conference proceedings: sborník příspěvků z mezinárodní konference. Brno: Masarykova univerzita 2007, pp. 140–150.

PICHRT, J.: Některé aspekty postavení rad zaměstnanců a odborových organizací na pracovišti v minulosti a současnosti a související otázky (přednesený diskusní příspěvek na mezinárodní vědecké konferenci. Třešť 2007).

ŠKUBAL, J., VARGA, P., OLŠOVSKÁ, A.: Hiring the best qualified and most talented employees: handbook on global recruiting, screening, testing en interviewing criteria. Alphen aan den Rijn, Kluwer Law International 2008.

Teoretické úvahy o práve [elektronický dokument]: zborník z vedeckej konferencie doktorandov a školiteľov Právnickej fakulty Trnavskej univerzity v Trnave: 29.3.2008. Trnavská univerzita v Trnave, Právnická fakulta 2009. – 1 CD, [407] s. + 1 brož., 26 s. – elektronické dokumenty. – Zborník zo 4. vedeckej konferencie doktorandov PF TU.

ŠKUBAL, J., VARGA, P., OLŠOVSKÁ, A.: Littler editor: Marguerite S. Walsh. In: The Littler Mendelson guide to international employment and labour law / [Littler international employment and labour law practice group editors Jeffrey L. Adams...[et al.]]. – [S.l.]: LexisNexis 2008.

Aktuálne otázky pracovnej legislatívy v EÚ a SR, Zborník príspevkov z vedeckej konferencie s medzinárodnou účasťou konanej v Banskej Bystrici dňa 9. novembra 2006. Banská Bystrica: Eruditio Mores Futurum 2007.

BARDENHEWER, N.: *Der Firmentarifvertrag in Europa, Ein Vergleich der Rechtslage in Deutschland, Grossbritannien und Frankreich.* Baden Baden : Nomos Verlag, 1. Auflage, 2006, pp. 24 – 25, ISBN 3 – 8329 – 1717 – 9.

BĚLINA, M. a kol.: *Zákoník práce.* Prague: C. H. Beck, 2008, pp. 112, ISBN 978 – 80 – 7179 – 607 – 7.

BĚLINA, M.: *Vybrané problémy postavení zástupců zaměstnanců v pracovněprávních vztazích.* In: Pracovní právo 2007 : Aktuální problémy pracovního práva a práva sociálního zabezpečení: S b o r n í k p ř í s p ě v k ů z mezinárodní vědecké konference na téma Kolektivní pracovní právo. Brno : Masarykova univerzita, Právnická fakulta, 2007, pp. 10 – 25, ISBN 978-80-210-4513-2.

BĚLOHLÁVEK, A. – J.: Římská úmluva a Nařízení Řím I. Komentář. 1. vydání. Prague: C.H. Beck, 2009, pp. 1338 – 1341, ISBN 978-80-7400-176-5.

BERGER, V.: *Judikatura Evropského soudu pro lidská práva.* Prague : IFEC s.r.o., 2003, pp. 551 – 557, ISBN 80 – 86412 – 23 – 7.

BLANPAIN, R.: *European Labour Law*. 10th ed. Amsterdam: Kluwer Law International, 2006, pp. 393 – 394, 978-9041121837.

BRANDT, J.: *First Jot Agreement*. In: CEDEFOP no. 2/2000. Available online: http://www. cedefop.europa.eu/etv/upload/information_resources/bookshop/165/C20JAEN.html.

DEMARNE, V.: *Anwendung nationaler Tarifvertäge bei grenzüberschreitenden Arbeitsver-hältnissen. Ein deutsch-französischer Vergleich*, Frankfurt am Main: Peter Lang Verlag, 1999, pp. 74-75, ISBN 978-3-631-35164-2.

FUCHS, M. – MARHOLD, F.: *Europäisches Arbeitsrecht*, Wien : Springer Verlag, 2010, pp. 271 – 275, ISBN 978-3-211-99402-3.

HENSSLER, M. – BRAUN, A.: *Arbeitsrecht in Europa*, Köln: Verlag Otto Schmidt KG, 2007, pp. 362, ISBN 978-3-504-42665-1

JUNKER, A.: *Internationales Arbeitsrecht in Konzern*, Tübingen: Mohr Siebeck, 1992, pp. 459 – 465, ISBN 978-31-6145-985-6.

KOCHER, E.: *Kollektivverhandlungen und Tarifautonomie – welche Rolle spielt das europäis-che Recht?*, In: Arbeit und Recht no. 1-2/2008, pp. 13 – 18, ISSN 0003-7648.

KUČERA, Z.: *Mezinárodní právo soukromé. 7. opravené a doplněné vydání*. Brno – Plzeň : Doplněk a Aleš Čeněk, s.r.o., 2009, pp. 236, ISBN 978-80-7239-231-5.

LAZAR, J.: *Občianske právo hmotné. Tretie doplnené a prepracované vydanie*. Bratislava: IURA EDITION, pp. 12 – 30, ISBN 80 – 8078 – 084 – 6.

PEKKA, A.: *The unemployment situation of young people: statistical dimensions, The Inter-American Centre for Knowledge Development in Vocational Training*, ILO (available online: http://www.ilo.org/public/english/region/ampro/cinterfor/publ/bole-tin/151/pekkaaro.htm)

PRUSÁK, J.: *Teória práva*. Bratislava: Vydavateľské oddelenie Právnickej fakulty UK, 1999, pp. 252, ISBN 80 - 967169 – 9 – 9.

PFEIL, W. J.: *Grenzüberschreitender Einsatz von Arbeitnehmern*, Teil 1, Das Recht der Ar-beit, 2008, no. 1, pp. 9, *ISSN 0342-1945*.

PIIR, R.: *Eingreifen oder nicht eingreifen, das ist hier die Frage. Die Problematik der Bestim-mung und des Anwendungsbereichs der Eingriffsnormen im internationalen Privatrecht*, In: Juridicia International, XVII, 2010, pp. 199 – 206.

RADLINGMAYR, Ch.: *Customer Preferences und arbeitsrechtliche Diskriminierungsverbot*, In: Zeitschrift für Arbeits- und Sozialrecht (ZAS), no. 4/2010, pp. 192 – 198, ISSN 0044-2321

Tackling early school leaving: A key contribution to the Europe 2020 Agenda, COM(2011) 18 (available online: http://ec.europa.eu/education/school-education/doc/earlycom_en.pdf)

RUDKOWSKI, L.: *Tarifpluralitäten und ihre Auflösung im spanischen Arbeitsrecht – zugleich eine Einführung in das spanische Tarifrecht*. In: Recht der Arbeit, no. 5, 2010, ISSN 1028 – 4656.

SVÁK, J.: *Ochrana ľudských práv. Z pohľadu judikatúry a doktríny štrasburských orgánov ochrany práva*. Žilina : Poradca podnikateľa, 2006, pp. 836 – 864, ISBN 80 – 88931 – 51 –7.

ŠTEFKO, M.: K problému sledování vlastních zaměstnanců. In: *Právo a zaměstnání*, no. 1, 2005, pp. 7 – 11, ISSN 1211 – 1139.

SCHÖMANN, I. et al.: *Der Einfluss von Codes of Conduct und Internationalen Rahmenvere-inbarungenauf die soziale Regulierung in Unternehmen*. Brussels: Europäisches Gewerk-schaftsinstitut für Forschung, Bildung und Arbeits- und Gesundheitsschutz, 2008, pp. 1 – 128, ISBN 978-2-87452-132-4.

THÜSING, G.: *International Framework Agreements: Rechtliche Grenzen und praktischer Nutzen*. In: Recht der Arbeit, 2/2010, pp. 78 – 93, ISSN 0342- 1945.

VAN HOEK, A. – HENDRICKX, F.: *International private law aspects and dispute settlement related to transnational company agreements*. Brussels: European Commission, Employment Social Affairs and Equal Opportunities DG, Second meeting of the Expert Group on transnational company agreements of 27 November 2009, 2009.

European legislation

1. Council Directive 91/383/EEC of 25 June 1991 supplementing the measures to encourage improvements in the safety and health at work of workers with a fixed-duration employment relationship or a temporary employment relationship (OJ L 206, 29.7.1991).

2. Council Directive 91/533/EEC of 14 October 1991 on an employer's obligation to inform employees of the conditions applicable to the contract or employment relationship (OJ L 288, 18.10.1991)

3. Council Directive 92/85/EEC of 19 October 1992 on the introduction of measures to encourage improvements in the safety and health at work of pregnant workers and workers who have recently given birth or are breastfeeding (tenth individual Directive within the meaning of Article 16 (1) of Directive 89/391/EEC) (OJ L 348, 28.11.1992)

4. Council Directive 94/33/EC of 22 June 1994 on the protection of young people at work (OJ L 216, 20.8.1994)

5. Council Directive 94/45/EC of 22 September 1994 on the establishment of a European Works Council or a procedure in Community-scale undertakings and Community-scale groups undertakings for the purposes of informing and negotiating employees (OJ L 254, 30.9.1994) as amended by Council Directive 97/74/EC of 15 December 1997 (OJ L 10, 16.1.1998) and as amended by Council Directive 2006/109/EC of 20 November 2006 (OJ L 363, 20.12.2006).

6. Council Directive 96/34/EC on the framework agreement on parental leave concluded by UNICE, CEEP and the ETUC (OJ L 145, 19.6.1996) as amended by Council Directive 97/75/EC of 15 December 1997 (OJ L 10, 16.1.1998).

7. Directive 96/71/EC of the European Parliament and of the Council of 16 December 1996 concerning the posting of workers in the framework of the provision of services (OJ L 18, 21.1.1997)

8. Council Directive 97/81/EC of 15 December 1997 concerning the Framework Agreement on part-time work concluded by UNICE, CEEP and the ETUC (OJ L 14, 20.1.1998) as amended by Council Directive 98/23/EC of 7 April 1998 (OJ L 131, 5.5.1998).

9. Council Directive 98/59/EC of 20 July 1998 on the approximation of the laws of the Member States relating to collective redundancies (OJ L 225, 12.8.98).

10. Council Directive 99/70/EC of 28 June 1999 concerning the framework agreement on fixed-term work concluded by ETUC, UNICE and CEEP (OJ L 14, 20.01.1998)

11. Council Directive 2000/43/EC of 29 June 2000 implementing the principle of equal treatment between persons irrespective of racial or ethnic origin (OJ L 180, 19.07.2000).

12. Council Directive 2000/78/EC of 27 November 2000 establishing a general framework for equal treatment in employment and occupation (OJ L 303, 2.12.2000)

13. Council Directive 2001/23/EC of 12 March 2001 on the approximation of the laws of the Member States relating to the safeguarding of employees' rights in the event of transfers of undertakings, businesses or parts of undertakings or businesses. (OJ L 82, 22.3.2001).

14. Directive 2002/14/EC of the European Parliament and of the Council of 11 March 2002 establishing a general framework for informing and negotiating employees in the European Community (OJ L 80, 23.3.2002).

15. Directive 2003/88/EC of the European Parliament and of the Council of 4 November 2003 concerning certain aspects of the organisation of working time (OJ L 299, 18.11.2003)

16. Directive 2006/54/EC of the European Parliament and of the Council of 5 July 2006 on the implementation of the principle of equal opportunities and equal treatment of men and women in matters of employment and occupation (recast) (OJ L204, 26.7.2006, p. 23).

17. Directive 2008/94/EC of the European Parliament and of the Council of 22 October 2008 on the protection of employees in the event of the insolvency of their employer (codified version) (OJ L 283, 28. 10. 2008).

18. Directive 2008/104/EC of the European Parliament and of the Council of 19 November 2008 on temporary agency work (OJ L 327, 5. 12. 2008).

19. Directive 2009/38/EC of the European Parliament and of the Council of 6 May 2009 on the establishment of a European Works Council or a procedure in Community-scale undertakings and Community-scale groups of undertakings for the purposes of informing and negotiating employees (Recast) (OJ EU L 122, 16 May 2009).

20. Council Directive 2010/18/EU of 8 March 2010 implementing the revised Framework Agreement on parental leave concluded by BUSINESSEUROPE, UEAPME, CEEP and ETUC and repealing Directive 96/34/EC (OJ EU L 68, 18 March 2010).